*The Choices Program:
How to Stop Hurting
The People Who Love You*

*The Choices Program:
How to Stop Hurting
The People Who Love You*

William E. Adams, Ph.D.

Copyright © 2003, 2010, 2011, 2014, 2016 by William E. Adams, Ph.D.
All rights reserved.

No part of this publication may be reproduced or transmitted in any form or by any means, electronic or mechanical, including photocopying and recording, or any information or storage and retrieval system, without the expressed written permission of the author.

The "Power and Control" and the "Equality" wheels are taken from *Power & Control: Tactics of Men Who Batter*. Copyright © 1993 Domestic Abuse Intervention Project. Used by permission of the Domestic Abuse Intervention Project.

For information regarding the purchase of this book, please contact:

William E. Adams, Ph.D.
1945 Palo Verde Avenue, Suite 204
Long Beach, CA 90815
Phone: (562) 799-1226 Fax: (598) 799-7033
www.drwilliamadams.com

ISBN 10: 0-69272-232-7
ISBN 13: 978-069272-232-9

First Edition
December 2003

Last Revised
June 2016

Acknowledgements

This book is dedicated to the men and women, all perpetrators of domestic abuse, who shared their lives with me in the group room. They taught me everything I know about the concepts and skills in this book. Week by week, they showed courage and dedication to the goal of making meaningful changes in their lives. Through their effort and feedback they taught me what worked and what didn't, and I'm sure I learned more from them than they ever did from me. In the process, they taught me how to treat verbal abuse and domestic violence. Thank you.

I also wish to thank Mabel Gardner, my friend and colleague, for her contributions to this book. I've had the pleasure of working with Ms. Gardner for many years now, and her skill and knowledge as domestic violence facilitator is, in my opinion, unrivaled. I've always strived to be as good a counselor as she is. Mabel's contributions to the development of the concepts and skills in this book will always be appreciated. Thanks also to Jim McDaniel, veteran and drill master sergeant. He was tough, but no one "joined" with a group more completely than Jim did. An outstanding counselor, he is still a legend in our group rooms. Thanks, Jim, for your contributions to the ideas presented here.

I want to express my gratitude to Judge Deborah B. Andrews of the Long Beach Superior Court, who for many years brought acumen and dedication to the problem of family violence. Judge Andrews presided over one of the nation's first dedicated domestic violence courts. My clients appeared before Judge Andrews every three months to give her a report on their progress in counseling. Whether they were admonished or commended by the Judge during these appearances, my clients inevitably saw her as knowledgeable and fair. Over the years, I never heard a client talk about Judge Andrews in a way that conveyed anything but respect. I've often wished that all presiding judges were as professional and learned about domestic violence issues as she.

Thanks to my friend Kiran Ghumman and my daughter Rachel for their kind assistance in editing this book.

Last but not least, I want to thank my wife, Deborah S. Adams. Deborah is a paralegal, a group facilitator, and the Program Manager of the Choices Domestic Violence Counseling Program. We have worked together for many years, and she is a continual source of encouragement and inspiration. For countless hours, we have discussed the concepts presented here, and her insights and contributions, both to this work the success of our program, cannot be overestimated. Finally, I want to express my love and appreciation to Darby, Jason, Rachel and Emily for being such a large part of my Big Picture.

*I am today what my
choices were yesterday.*

*I will be tomorrow what my
choices are today.*

(Author unknown, but often quoted)

Table of Contents

Chapter 1:	Stay In "The Box"	1
Chapter 2:	Take Time Out	11
Chapter 3:	Take Inventory	21
Chapter 4:	Skill Building	31
Chapter 5:	Thoughts and Emotions: Take Responsibility for Your Anger	37
Chapter 6:	Thoughts and Behavior: Responsibility, Violence, and Control	49
Chapter 7:	Automatic Thoughts, Core Beliefs, and Self-Talk	63
Chapter 8:	Skill Building	77
Chapter 9:	Solve Your Problems (And Stop Fighting About Them)	81
Chapter 10:	The Problem Solving Steps	91
Chapter 11:	Letters That Get You Talking Again	103
Chapter 12:	Skill Building	113
Chapter 13:	See the Big Picture	117
Chapter 14:	Social Influences and Violence	127
Chapter 15:	Changing the House Rules	137
Chapter 16:	Skill Building	147
Chapter 17:	Personality, Acceptance, and Encouragement	151
Chapter 18:	Fear and Respect, Tyrants and Leaders	161
Chapter 19:	The Children	171
Chapter 20:	Skill Building	183
Chapter 21:	Drugs and Alcohol	187
Chapter 22:	Choices Chains	199
Chapter 23:	Character and Trust	209
Chapter 24:	Skill Building	217
Appendix		223

Chapter 1
Stay In "The Box"

Key Concepts: Domestic violence doesn't just happen. Violence occurs when people attack each other rather than their problems. Violence stops when couples choose to "stay in the box." The Box model will help you stop the abuse and make better choices for yourself and your family.

Skill Building: Use "The Box" as a roadmap the next time problems and anger arise. Lay the foundation for a violence-free relationship by choosing to "stay in the box" during times of conflict.

Evan slumped down on the sofa in my office, heartsick and dejected. He had plenty to feel bad about. A few weeks earlier, Evan had been arrested and convicted of spousal abuse after hitting his wife, Grace. The court ordered Evan to attend 52 weeks of domestic violence counseling and issued a protective order that barred him from any contact with Grace. Now, after twelve years of marriage, Grace wanted a divorce. Evan hadn't seen his children for weeks. On top of that, Evan lost his job while he was incarcerated. "I don't know what happened," he said. "Everything was great when Grace and I got married. Now all we do is argue and fight. Somehow, things just got out of hand."

Evan is typical of the men and women who find their way to my office. Like Evan, most people are unaware of the crucial choices they have made. Even fewer understand how the choices they make, day by day and year by year, slowly erode their relationship until nothing is left to save. How did Evan end up in jail? Who's to blame? Across town, Grace is struggling with questions of her own. She looks at photos taken on her honeymoon with Evan. It seems so long ago, like another lifetime. What happened to the two smiling people in the picture? They seem so happy and in love. But that was before all the hurt and pain, before attack and counterattack became the norm, before the abuse.

What happened to Evan and Grace, and to thousands more like them? How did a loving relationship turn abusive? How did twelve years of choices sweep Evan from a honeymoon in Hawaii to the back of a police car? This book will answer these questions. It was written over the years with the help of hundreds of people who wanted to stop their abusive behavior and enjoy violence-free relationships. There were also people in my groups who had no intention of changing; they also made their contribution to these chapters, albeit in a different way. The people in these pages came from all walks of life, and you'll meet them in the chapters that follow.

To understand what happened to Evan and Grace you need a map that shows the chain of events that led Evan from feeling "OK" to an act of physical abuse. You need a roadmap that shows you how verbal and physical abuse happens. Once you can recognize the road to family violence, you can choose to avoid that road in the future. The map in this chapter is called *The Box*. The Box will let you know where you are, what to expect next, and the choices you need to make to avoid violence and resolve conflict. Like a navigator's chart, it will help you make wise choices during times of crisis and avoid unseen dangers around the corner that can be disastrous for you and your family.

It's tempting to blame abusive behavior on the problems in your relationship. This is a grave mistake. It's like a ship's captain blaming the rock for the shipwreck, rather than his own poor seamanship and navigation. In all relationships, periods of calm are broken by periods of tension and conflict. Alternating episodes of calm and conflict are a normal part of trying to live together. If handled properly, conflict is not destructive. Quite the contrary; conflict can make a relationship stronger if it results in problem solving and a greater understanding of each other. But if handled improperly, conflict can result in the abuse of loved ones, the destruction of the family, and, as with Evan, incarceration. Why do problems lead to violence in some relationships but not others? The Box below shows how problems are handled in violence-free relationships.

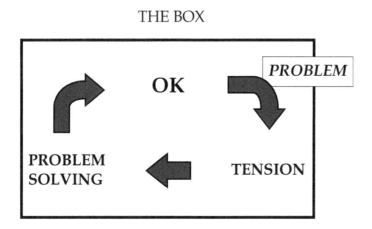

THE BOX

OK: Periods of Calm

Let's examine the parts of the box more closely. Everything starts at the top of the box in the area marked "OK." In the OK zone there are no serious problems to resolve. Everything may not be perfect, but you and your partner are generally satisfied with the way things are going. Like a table with four good legs, the relationship is balanced and stable. Enjoy this period of calm while it lasts. The calm OK zone never lasts for long. It ends as soon as a problem comes up between you and your partner.

The Problem

Following the arrows in the box, you see that things are OK until a problem comes up. Problems knock people out of the OK zone. As I stated earlier, problems are an inevitable part of living with another person, as no two people are exactly alike. You each have your own expectations and attitudes about things: how money should be spent, how much time to spend with friends, and how to use leisure time. You may disagree about the proper division of household chores, sex, work, children, the extended family, future goals, or anything under the sun. You may even disagree about the way problems should be handled and how anger should be expressed.

Falling in love will not protect you from the fact that there are differences between you and your partner. Differences are a challenge for every a couple. There will always be differences between the two of you because you were individuals before you were a couple. The struggle to cope with personal differences cannot be avoided; it's just the price two people pay to be in a relationship. They inevitably give rise to problems that knock you and your partner out of the comfortable OK zone. You will know you have been knocked out of the OK zone because *you will feel tension that was not there a moment ago.* A minute ago things were OK, and now they are not. Don't worry. When you get knocked out of the OK zone, it doesn't mean your relationship is in trouble. *It just means a problem has come up that needs to be solved.*

Tension: Things Are *Not* OK

Problems cause tension between you and your partner. Things were OK before the problem came up, but they are definitely *not* OK now. *You know things aren't OK because there's a feeling of "tension" between the two of you that wasn't there a moment ago.* The word *tension*, as used here, is a broad term that refers to feelings of anger, frustration, resentment, jealousy, or any other negative feelings.

Tension Can Take Many Different Forms

frustration	annoyance	defensiveness	insecurity
anger	resentment	indignation	irritation
jealousy	rage	bitterness	infuriation
contempt	rivalry	exasperation	aggravation

Problem Solving

What you do now is extremely important. How you choose to behave when problems and negative feelings arise will determine, by and large, the type of relationship you will have, and whether positive or negative feelings rule your home. The important thing to understand is that you cannot get rid of feelings like anger by venting, lashing out, or hurting your partner. Reckless venting only escalates tension and makes it harder to solve anything. Destructive outbursts of anger make your relationship more and more negative, and a deep feeling of dissatisfaction takes hold and defines it. Venting is not the answer. *The only way to get rid of tension and anger is to solve the problem that is causing it.* The tension that problems cause will not go away on its own. Tension builds over time, poisoning the relationship until the problem is solved in a way that you and your partner find acceptable. Even if you walk away and refuse to talk about it, the *tension* is still there because the *problem* is still there. Tension levels may go up and down, but the *tension never goes away until the problem is solved*.

What Happens When You Don't Solve Your Problems

Problems cause tension and knock you and your spouse out of the OK zone. You need to get back to OK zone, and the only road back is through problem solving. Solve the problem and the tension between the two of you will melt away. *But let me emphasize this point once again: tension will not go away by itself, and you can't drive it away by attacking your spouse.* Effective problem solving is the one and only way back to the calm and comfort of the OK zone. Tension (anger, frustration, jealousy) means you are out of the OK zone. Your goal is to get back to it. The only road home is to solve the problem that is causing tension between you.

In large measure, the quality of your relationship is defined by the way you choose to handle problems and tension. Successful couples understand that the feeling of tension is a signal telling them that they need to work together as a team to resolve a problem. It is *not* a signal to vent anger or abuse each other. An effective problem solving strategy does NOT include yelling, throwing tantrums, or acting like a spoiled child. Instead, successful couples work together as a team against the problem. **They are allies, not adversaries. They attack the problem, not each other.** They know that things will be *OK* again once the problem is solved. Actually, things will be better than they were before. They were there for each other. Confidence in their relationship and their trust in each other is affirmed when they work through a problem successfully. After all, they've demonstrated their ability to work together and successfully resolve a problem, and they know that they can do it again if they have to.

To sum it up, every couple has its share of problems. Whether your relationship flourishes or fails doesn't depend on whether there are problems. Rather, success depends on how you handle the problems that come up. Couples who have satisfying relationships have their share of problems to deal with, just like everyone else. Their relationships work because they use effective problem solving strategies that get them back to the OK zone. They know that *communication, respect, compromise, and negotiation will get good results, while venting, yelling, and controlling tactics do not.* Unfortunately, many people in relationships have yet to figure this out.

Problem solving isn't always easy. Maybe you don't agree that there is a problem, or you disagree how to solve it. Perhaps you get defensive and hostile when problems are brought up because you hate being criticized. Real problems require a real solution. That means you must be willing to examine your role in the problem, and be willing to make meaningful changes in your behavior that contribute to the solution. Who will do the changing? Maybe you don't want to change; instead, you're determined to make your partner change, but blaming and denying your role in the problem will never get you back to the OK zone.

When a problem is handled this way, you and your partner end up on opposite sides of the fence. *You become adversaries instead of teammates,* and the tension grows higher. When you deny your role in the problem and refuse to compromise or change, the problem drives a wedge between you and your spouse, making problem solving virtually impossible. This is why some couples never really solve their problems. They only argue and fight about them. They never get back to the OK zone. When this happens, the tension from unresolved problems builds up over months and years and bleeds over into new problems. The average tension level - the tension they feel when they wake up in the morning before anything is even said - rises. They blow up over relatively minor problems and fight constantly. Over time, the softer feelings of love, support, and caring are buried beneath a heavy blanket of anger, mistrust, and resentment. The relationship feels unsafe and insecure. Negative feelings come to define the way the whole relationship is perceived. Communication becomes increasingly hostile and abusive; each new abusive act and hostile word further erodes the relationship. The erosion continues until, like a beach washed away in a storm, there's nothing left. There is so much damage that the relationship can't be fixed. There's no relationship left to save. They can never again get back to OK. But we're getting ahead of ourselves.

Let's return to The Box. When the solution to a problem is not readily apparent to both partners an argument begins, as shown by the dark arrows in the illustration below.

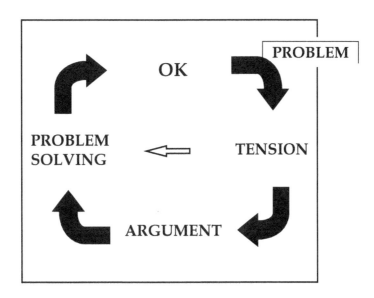

Argument

Notice that the word "Argument" lies inside the box. It's hard to image two people living together without arguing. Even happily married couples have arguments. However, it is important to know when an argument stops and a fight (or abuse) begins. *An argument, as discussed here, never involves verbal abuse or physical violence.* That may seem self-evident, but you'd be surprised what some people call an argument. Helen is a good example. One day Helen drove to the apartment of her boyfriend, Tom, where she saw him talking to a voluptuous young woman in the parking lot. Helen assumed the worst and flew into a jealous rage. Stomping on the gas she sped straight for Tom, who heard her coming. Seeing what was happening, Tom leapt onto one of the nearby cars. Helen slammed into the car Tom was perched on, threw her car into reverse, and raced at him again. Tom jumped nimbly from car to car as Helen repeatedly tried to turn him into road-kill. Finally, the police arrived and pulled Helen from the car. After her release from jail, the court ordered Helen to see me for counseling. When I asked her what happened on the day of her arrest, she whispered meekly, "I had an argument with my boyfriend."

Arguments and fights are different. In an argument there is no attempt to abuse (or in Helen's case to maim and kill) your partner. Anger may be expressed during an argument, but it is expressed without yelling, swearing, or physical violence. You can tell someone you're angry without telling them off, and that's the difference between an argument and a fight. During an argument you respect your partner. In a fight you disrespect you partner. If you engage in verbal abuse, contempt, or aggressive behavior you are *not* arguing. You are fighting. You are "out of The Box." The chart below shows the difference between behavior that we will refer to as "in the box" (arguing) or "out of the box" (fighting).

In The Box:
- Keep your tone of voice down
- Show respect in the words you choose
- See yourselves as teammates
- Constructive focus: Attack the problem, not your partner

Out of The Box:
- Yelling and shouting
- Swearing, insulting, and calling your partner names
- Treating your partner as an adversary
- Destructive anger: Attacking your partner rather than the problem

It's not realistic to expect that you and your partner will always avoid arguments. Nor should you always try. When you assume personal responsibility by expressing anger in a non-abusive way, positive changes can take place in the relationship. Couples that respect and care for each other understand that anger must be expressed in a respectful way. They tell their partner that they are angry without "telling them off." When people choose to express their anger constructively their partners do not feel personally attacked or threatened. They listen without getting defensive. They trust each other enough to express themselves and their feelings openly. Communication improves, resulting in a deeper understanding of each other's needs and expectations. This is important, because the better you understand each other the more effective you will be at finding solutions to problems. As problems are solved, tension is lessoned. The feelings most often experienced in the relationship are positive ones.

We will spend more time developing problem solving strategies in the chapters to come. For now, just remember the difference between an *argument* and a *fight*. Successful partners argue; abusive partners fight. Effective partners value solving their problems rather than winning battles. Healthy partners choose not to vent their anger in a destructive, blaming and hurtful manner. Rather, they are interested in solving problems and working as part of an intimate team. They are not motivated to control, hurt, blame, or intimidate, and when something goes wrong they attack their problems rather than each other. In times of trouble they are an ally to their partner, not an adversary.

Take time to study *The Box* carefully. It's the model that will guide you through times of anger and conflict with your partner. The Box will tell you where you are during an argument, and help you make wise choices for yourself and your family. Most importantly, it will tell you when you're "in The Box" (making constructive choices) and when you're "out of The Box" (making destructive choices).

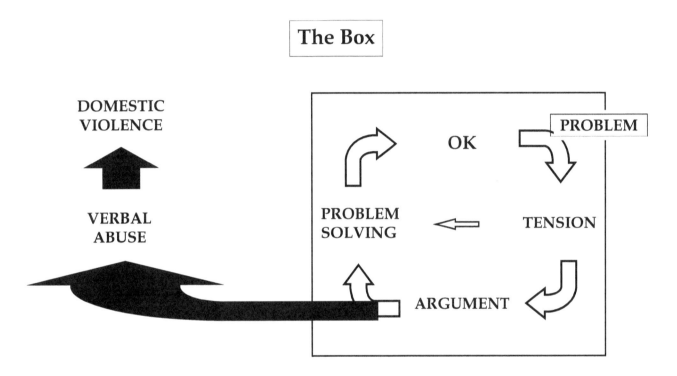

The dark arrows in The Box show the road that leads to abuse and violence. If you don't want to go down that road again, you need to remember this roadmap. *Memorize it and use it during times of conflict.* In time you will recognize the road you're on and tell yourself, "I've been down this road before. I know where I'm headed, and I don't want to go there." Once you are aware of what is happening you can make choices about what you want to do. The Box will help you make better choices in the future. Let's follow the arrows in The Box to see how problems lead to violence.

Tension starts to build when a problem comes up. An argument follows. When tension reaches a certain level of intensity the problem is forgotten, and the abuser gets "out of the box" and starts to attack the partner. In most instances the attack starts with verbal abuse, which is usually the first sign that you're out of the box. The verbal abuse greatly escalates the tension between the couple. Verbal abuse is like throwing a match into a pool of gasoline – it's just as explosive.

Verbal Abuse Has Many Forms

yell	harangue	chew out	humiliate	rip into
shout	sarcasm	denigrate	offend	lambaste
insult	curse	bully	nettle	put down
name call	berate	swear	rant	castigate
threaten	belittle	insult	scold	condescend

Getting Out Of The Box: Verbal Abuse

After listening to thousands of people relate the chain of events that led to violence against their partner, I am convinced that in the vast majority of cases verbal abuse "unlocked the door" for the violence that followed. ***One of the most beneficial and important resolutions that you can make is to stop your verbal abuse.*** The next time you become angry you have a choice to make. Do you take the road out of The Box by engaging in verbal abuse, or do you stay in The Box and take the road back to the OK zone by problem solving? Whichever road you take, the choice is yours alone and you must take full responsibility for it.

Stay In The Box

The goal of this book is to help you stop your abuse by staying in The Box when things aren't going your way. As long as you stay in The Box, you won't engage in abusive behavior. To accomplish this goal, you must become more aware of your own words and behaviors, especially words and behaviors that are abusive. *The first sign that you are outside of The Box will usually be your own verbally abusive language.*

Verbal abuse greatly escalates anger, and it's destructive to you and your partner. As we have discussed, verbal abuse is a sign that you are out of The Box and moving toward another incident of physical violence. Verbal abuse is also a sign that you are "emotionally flooded." According to Dr. John Gottman of the University of Washington, emotional flooding occurs when severe emotional distress activates the body's fight or flight response during an argument. When this happens, it is nearly impossible for you to have a productive conversation. Your ability to communicate or listen to what your partner is saying is impaired, and your capacity to find creative solutions to problems is drastically reduced. If you keep arguing when you are emotionally flooded, you just make things worse and get further outside The Box.

Nothing good *ever* happens outside of The Box. Heartbreak, ruined relationships, divorce, arrest, jail, a criminal record that lasts a lifetime, lost jobs and reputations, families destroyed; these are the costs of getting out of The Box. When you hear yourself getting out of

The Box, step back and cool off. *Use your head rather than your hands*, avoid abusive language, and take a time-out to calm down and get control of yourself. You will learn more about using the time-out procedure in the following chapter. For now, familiarize yourself with The Box. I suggest you memorize it. Develop an awareness of where you are on the chart during times of conflict so you can start making better choices for yourself and your family.

Verbal and physical abuse usually occurs after a lengthy period of tension-building and arguing, especially when relationships are young. But that is not always the case. Over time, a person may start to verbally and physically abuse their partner with little or no argument phase, and the partner is helpless to stop it. The road out of The Box is traveled so often that it becomes a superhighway, and minor problems elicit swift and immediate acts of abuse that were unthinkable in earlier stages of the relationship. Abuse becomes the norm, the customary response to tension. Can it be stopped? Yes, but only by taking responsibility for your behavior and choosing better for yourself and your family. Understand this: in any stage of a relationship, every person who abuses does so *because he or she wants to; because he or she chooses to*. No one forces you to abuse. ***In every case, without exception, the only person responsible for verbal abuse is the one doing the yelling. The only person responsible for physical abuse is the one doing the hitting. There are no exceptions.*** Until you accept this fact, nothing will change.

HOMEWORK ASSIGNMENT
CHAPTER 1

It's important that you become very familiar with "The Box" because it is the model that will guide you through future conflict. Study it until you can draw The Box on a piece of paper from memory. The following exercise will help you apply the model to your relationship. Think about the last time that you were out of The Box with your partner, and answer the following questions. Remember to stay focused on your own behavior rather than your partner's behavior.

1. *What was the problem that knocked you and your partner out of the "OK Zone?"*

2. *Describe the tension between you. What did you feel (e.g. angry, jealous, controlled, blamed, hurt, sad, anxious)?*

3. *Did the two of you argue? Describe her side and your side of the argument.*

4. *Did you try to solve the problem through negotiation and compromise?*

5. *What was the first thing you said or did that was out of the box (yelling, swearing, insulting)? Be specific about what you said that was verbally abusive.*

6. *What effect did the verbal abuse have on the tension level?*

7. *If there was an act of physical abuse, describe it in detail (throwing or breaking things, punching a wall, pushing or grabbing, slapping or punching your partner).*

8. *How did getting out of The Box affect you and your family?*

9. *How might things have turned out differently had you stayed in The Box, focused on problem solving, and avoided abusive behavior?*

Chapter 2
Take Time-Out

Key Concepts: Warning signs tell you when you're about to get out of The Box. If you watch for them and recognize them when they appear, you will know when you are emotionally flooded and need to call a time-out. By applying the time-out procedure correctly, you can avoid verbally or physically abusive behavior.

Skill Building: Identify your personal warning signs. Recognize them when they appear and call a time-out to avoid verbal or physical abuse. Apply the rules and steps of the time-out procedure appropriately.

Imagine that you are the coach of a professional basketball team. The score is tied and there is a minute left to play. Suddenly, the other team scores two quick goals. As the coach, what are you likely to do? If you're a sports fan, you know the answer: *call a time-out!* Professional sports teams call a time-out when they're not playing well. A time-out gives them a chance to get organized, calm down, and plan the next play. Hopefully, they start working together as a team again. We can use time-out in our relationships for the same reasons. In this lesson we'll be talking about calling a time-out to stay in control of feelings and behavior. A time-out can help you and your partner work together as a team and, more importantly, it can prevent future episodes of verbal or physical abuse.

Time-out seems like an easy tool to use. "When you think you're going to lose it, you just leave until you calm down. That's all there is to it, right?" Wrong. First of all, time-out is not a cure-all. It won't work for everyone, and it won't solve all your problems. Secondly, there's a lot to know about taking a time-out. If used incorrectly, a time-out can actually make things worse. Many people who come to me for counseling tell me that their domestic violence incident took place as they were trying to walk out the door. Lastly, a time-out is very different from just leaving or storming out. There are rules to the time-out procedure that you and your partner should know about.

Before going over the time-out procedure in detail, let's be very clear about what a time-out is not. It is *not* the purpose of a time-out to avoid talking about problems. The purpose of a time-out is to give you a chance to regain your composure and judgment so that you can discuss problems calmly and without verbal or physical abuse. Occasionally, I hear of clients who call a time-out whenever their partner brings up something that they don't want to talk about. The wife of a client once called me to ask, "What in the world are you teaching my husband in that group of yours?" I could tell she was upset. "What's wrong?" I asked. "I'll tell you what's wrong!" she shouted. "Every time I try to talk to him he calls a time-out and leaves the house!" I made the correct use of time-out clear to the client the following week. Don't use a time-out to dodge your problems.

It's also a mistake to call time-out to control your partner. One client tried to use time-out to control his wife by placing her on time-out whenever she was angry with him. Using a voice that a parent might use when sending a naughty child to her room, he would point and say in his most officious voice: "You're out of control. Go take a time-out!" I can't tell you how badly that worked. The time-out procedure is not meant to be a way of controlling or punishing your partner for expressing anger towards you. *Never call a time-out for anyone but yourself.* Time-out is the way you take responsibility for *your own* anger; it is not a strategy to control the anger of others.

Then there was Scott. Scott was a new client attending his first session. As it happened, we were talking about time-out that week. When he heard the words "time-out" Scott sat up and practically shouted to the group, "Listen to this, guys. This time-out stuff really works! Last time my ol' lady and I got into it, I left and went to Vegas. I didn't come home for three days! Man, was she sorry!" Scott's remarks drew many comments from the others in the group that day. He learned that a time-out does not mean storming angrily out of the house, deliberately causing your partner to worry about what you're doing and whether you're ever coming home. Nor is it used as an excuse to leave and have fun. It's certainly not a way to win a fight by making your partner feel "sorry."

Time-Out Is Not Storming Out

During a heated argument, people sometimes *storm out* of the house. You know what storming out is. When you yell in your loudest and most dramatic voice, *"I'm not listening to this s*** anymore!"* stomp through the door and slam it behind you, you have stormed out. Some people call this a time-out; I assure you it is not.

Storming out is unfair to your partner and it only makes the situation worse. When you think about it, storming out is nothing more than an attempt to punish your partner by causing him or her worry about where you are, what you're doing, who you're with, and when you'll come home. Your partner doesn't know whether you're leaving for a short time or for good. Storming out of the house is a form of "angry withdrawal" that provokes feelings of anger, anxiety, and abandonment in your partner. It suggests that you don't take your problems seriously enough to stay and work them out, and that you don't care about your spouse anymore. It escalates anger and increases the risk of violence, because when you storm out your partner may try to prevent you from leaving. As I noted earlier, many domestic violence incidents happen just this way.

Time-out is different. There are rules to follow during the time-out period, and it's important to follow them. In fact, you should discuss the rules calmly with your partner before you attempt to use time-out in the heat of conflict. If you discuss the purpose of a time-out and the guidelines that you promise to follow during the time-out period, your partner will be more likely to cooperate and let you leave when you call a time-out. Study the time-out rules that follow. Take time to memorize them and talk them over with your partner, so when you call a time-out it will go smoothly.

The Time-Out Rules

RULE 1: NEVER USE ALCOHOL OR DRUGS DURING THE TIME-OUT PERIOD

It's very important that you avoid alcohol or drugs during the time-out period. You call for a time-out when you are in a domestic crisis. Your anger is growing. Your warning signs are flashing (more about these later) and you're about to get "out of the box" and express your anger in an abusive and destructive way. You are emotionally flooded. Things could get a lot worse if you aren't careful. When you're in a crisis like this, the last thing you need is to drop twenty or thirty IQ points by getting hammered. Think about it. Have you ever seen a professional sports team pass around a bottle of booze during the time-out period?

When an argument deteriorates into a fight, you need to be at your best. You need all of your judgment, self-control, and skills intact. The whole purpose of a time-out is to recover your judgment and emotional stability. Your thinking needs to be unimpaired when you come back to discuss the problem, and you must be able to skillfully apply the concepts and tools that you learn in this course. You won't be able to perform to the best of your ability if you are under the influence of alcohol or drugs. When you impair yourself by getting intoxicated, you defeat the whole purpose of the time-out.

RULE 2: SPEND THE TIME-OUT PERIOD ALONE

It is also important that you spend the time-out period alone. Your friends and family usually take your side of the argument. Rather than calming you down, they can escalate your anger by reinforcing the notion that you are a victim, and that your partner is the sole problem. *Your* friends and *your* family generally take *your* side in a conflict. Expect them to be unfairly biased in your favor. Statements like, "I always knew she wasn't the woman for you," or "I wouldn't take that s*** from my girlfriend!" or "You've got to show her who's the boss!" are one-sided, and they don't help you see the bigger picture. It's better to spend the time alone. Calm down and think objectively about your role in the conflict. Try to understand your partner's point of view and look for solutions to your problems. It's not helpful to blame your partner or see yourself as a victim. As family and friends tend to promote these perceptions, it's best to avoid them for the time being. Another reason to spend the time-out period alone is to avoid provoking feelings of jealousy. Your partner needs to know that you're not headed for your ex-partner or the good-looking neighbor across the street to complain about your problems.

Spend your time-out period alone, and do things that calm you down. Listen to music, take a walk, shoot some baskets, or choose some other solitary activity. Relaxation techniques such as deep breathing and progressive muscle relaxation can help you to feel calmer. Most importantly, *you must talk to yourself rationally about what's going on*. In his classic book, *Feeling Good: The New Mood Therapy*, David Burns provides excellent strategies to reduce anger by thinking in a rational, common sense way. His book inspired some of the questions below.

Think your way through the time-out period by asking yourself:

> - *Is my partner being malicious and trying to hurt me, or do we just have an honest difference of opinion?*
> - *Will getting angry help us solve this problem?*
> - *How can I compromise and negotiate a solution that works for us both?*
> - *Am I blowing this problem out of proportion?*
> - *Am I managing my anger responsibly?*
> - *What would I say to a friend who was in my situation?*
> - *Would I feel better if I calmed down and stopped making myself mad?*
> - *Is there a better (calmer/more rational/more useful) way of thinking?*
> - *What are the consequences going to be if I get out of the box?*
> - *Can I say and do what I need to without getting angry?*
> - *Do I want to be angry?*
> - *Have I said or done anything that I need to apologize for?*
> - *Am I coming across as hurtful, blaming, or controlling?*
> - *Have I shown respect for my partner's point of view?*
> - *Am I acting like a friend or an adversary?*
> - *Have I been trying to solve a problem, or just trying to win an argument?*
> - *Have I been attacking the problem or my partner?*
> - *How can I use the skills I have learned and lead by example?*

RULE 3: IT'S NOT A TIME-OUT UNLESS YOU SAY THE WORDS: "TIME-OUT"

Don't expect your partner to read your mind. If you need a time-out, you have to say so. When you use the words *"time-out,"* you're telling your partner that you promise to abide by the rules during the time-out period. Unless you say: *"I need a time-out,"* you're just leaving or storming out. This is a common mistake made by people who don't really understand the time-out procedure. Remember, you have to say the words or it's not a real time-out.

RULE 4: TELL YOUR PARTNER WHEN YOU'LL BE BACK

How long should a time-out last? A time-out lasts between 15 minutes to an hour. This is in sharp contrast to those who advise: *"Don't come back until you calm down."* If you call a time out early, as soon as you see your warning signs, and do what you are supposed to do during the time-out period, one hour is plenty of time to lower your anger and start thinking rationally. Your partner will usually let you leave if he or she knows that you'll be back in a reasonable period of time. If it takes you longer than an hour to calm down, you probably are not using the time-out wisely, or you may have "run too many stop signs" and waited too long before calling a time-out. You don't have to be completely calm, just calm enough to stay in The Box.

RULE 5: RETURN ON TIME

Suppose you tell your partner that you'll be back in 30 minutes but come home three hours later. You've created a whole new conflict. Also, what happens the next time you want a time-out? Will your partner let you leave again? Probably not. The effectiveness of time-out depends upon your willingness to follow the rules. Breaking the rules reduces the chances that time-out will be successful in the future. To summarize, time-out works better than leaving or storming out because your partner knows that:

- *You are not trying to avoid talking about a problem, but taking responsibility for your own anger.*
- *You will not be drinking alcohol or using drugs.*
- *You will be spending the time alone to calm yourself down.*
- *You will come back at a reasonable and specified time to continue the conversation.*

Monitor Your Warning Signs

When do you call a time-out? You should call a time-out when you see your own warning signs. Warning signs tell you that you are "emotionally flooded," and that you are about to express your anger in an abusive and destructive way. You're acting out of anger rather than good judgment. Anger is running the show and you aren't thinking rationally. Most likely, you aren't doing much thinking at all, and you've lost sight of the original problem. Problem solving has stopped because you're getting out of the box. You're about to attack your partner rather than the problem. When you see your warning signs, *stop and call a time-out!*

The moment that tension starts to rise, monitor yourself and watch for your warning signs. It's *vital* that you have a keen awareness of your personal warning signs. People who fail to monitor themselves or recognize their warning signs have difficulty using the time-out procedure, and they are much more likely to engage in new incidents of abuse because they won't call a time-out when needed. Now is the time to pinpoint your personal warning signs. There are at least three distinct types that you need to think about:

1. **Behavioral Warning Signs**: This refers to what you start to do when you are really angry. Behavioral warning signs are aggressive words and hostile behaviors that you use when you get really angry. They are things you say and do that are hurtful and abusive. Some examples of the three types of warning signs are in the boxes below. This is not a complete list. You may have other warning signs of your own to add.

YELL	INVADE OTHER'S PERSONAL SPACE
CURSE	SLAM A DOOR
THREATEN	PUNCH A WALL
INSULT	THROW OR BREAK SOMETHING

DEGRADE	GLARE IN A THREATENING MANNER
HUMILIATE	RAISE A FIST
RIDICULE	SAY THINGS INTENDED TO HURT

2. **Cognitive Warning Signs:** Cognitive warning signs refer to the thoughts that run through your mind as your anger level rises. When you get angry, there are changes in the way you think. Examples of these warning signs are:

> MENTAL IMAGES OF VIOLENCE TOWARD YOUR PARTNER
> YOU'RE SUCH A .... (NAME-CALLING)
> I OUGHT TO TEACH YOU A LESSON YOU'LL NEVER FORGET
> I'LL SHOW YOU WHO'S BOSS
> I CAN'T STAND IT ANYMORE (AWFULIZING)
> ONE MORE WORD FROM YOU AND I'LL ....
> I'M GONNA TEACH YOU TO RESPECT ME
> YOU'VE GOT THIS COMING, YOU ASKED FOR IT

3. **Physiological Warning Signs:** Physiological warning signs refer to the changes that take place in your body when you get mad.

CLINCHED FISTS	TIGHT STOMACH	TUNNEL VISION
FAST HEART RATE	SWEATING PALMS	UNMINDFUL PACING
TREMBLING HANDS	FLUSHED FACE	RAPID BREATHING
CLINCHED TEETH	MUSCLE TIGHTNESS	TENSION HEADACHE

Warning signs vary from person to person. With thought and practice, you'll start to understand the warning signs that are meaningful to you. After giving it some thought, some of my clients have identified warning signs that are unique and distinctive to them alone:

- *John:* "When I'm really mad I start to smile. This means I'm ready to hit someone."
- *Kareem:* "I get really quiet. I mean, I just stop talking. It's like I'm trying to hold the lid on and not explode."
- *Lisa:* "I start to bite my cheek and pinch myself."
- *Andrea:* "I think about the way I was abused by my ex, and now I'm going to hit first."
- *Patricia:* "I start to clean everything around me as hard and as loud as I can."
- *Pedro:* "I start to feel sorry for her, really sorry for her, because I know what I'm going to do to her."

If you're having trouble identifying your warning signs, find people who know you well and ask them, *"How do you know when I'm getting really angry?"* They will be able to tell you. When they say, *"You start to . . . ."* take note of what they say. They're describing your warning signs. Be sure and write them down so you will remember them. Put vigorous effort into acquiring a clear awareness of your warning signs; it's one of the most vital skills in *The Choices Program*.

Sea-going skippers keep a vigilant watch for reefs or rocks that may lie ahead. Once seen, they take decisive action to avoid them. To do otherwise would mean shipwreck and disaster. Warning signs are like reefs and rocks that are directly ahead. Failure to recognize them and avert them is reckless and foolish. Like the skipper of a sailing ship, *you have to watch for your own personal "warning signs" that signal the need for a time-out*. Warning signs are like huge stop signs that say: "STOP HERE! DANGER AHEAD! CHANGE COURSE NOW! *Do not proceed any further down the road you're on. It will only end in abuse and trauma.*

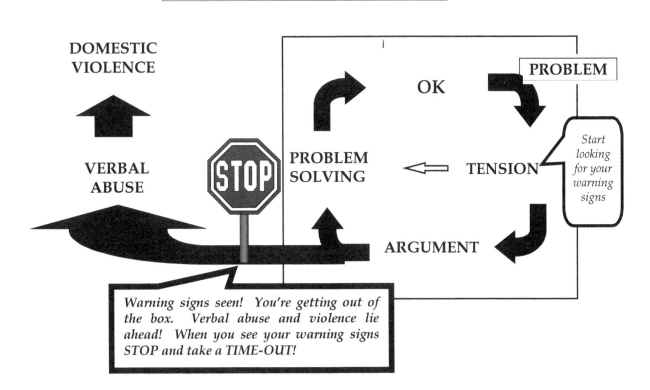

Whatever your warning signs are, you need to be aware of them. You need to know them as well as you know your own name. They are personal warnings that you're about to act in an abusive and destructive manner. Get into the habit of looking for them during every argument. Search for them when you start to feel tension or anger. At the first appearance of one of your warning signs, call a time-out and get control of yourself *before* you become verbally or physically abusive.

Be Your Own Coach

At the beginning of this lesson, we discussed the way coaches of professional sports teams call a time-out to help their players calm down, regroup, and work together as a team. Unfortunately, there will be no coach on the sidelines when you need a time-out. You have to be your own coach. You'll have to call the time-out for yourself when you need it. Success demands that you learn to monitor yourself closely during an argument. You also have to develop the self-discipline to call a time-out in the heat of anger, when part of you wants to fight. These are vital skills that are acquired through practice and perseverance. Make a personal commitment to master the skills needed to call a time-out successfully.

Timing Is Important

From time to time, I have the unfortunate experience of talking to clients who have committed a second domestic violence offense. I say unfortunate because these clients are usually facing dismissal from our program and a period of incarceration. When I ask them why they didn't call a time-out before the abuse started, they often tell me that they tried to call a time-out, but it was not successful. Their attempt to call a time-out usually failed because they waited too long before calling it.

Rather than calling a time-out at the *first* sign that their anger was becoming destructive, they "ran the stop sign." They saw their warning signs, but ignored them. As anger escalated they plowed on, swearing and yelling, running stop sign after stop sign. They knew they were out of the box, but they didn't care. Anger escalated to a point that common sense was ignored. They no longer thought or cared about the consequences of their behavior. *As anger mounted, they crossed the* **"I don't care what I say"** *line. Then they crossed the* **"I don't care what I do"** *line.*

Let me tell you about the *"I don't care what I say"* and *"I don't care what I do"* lines. Many people avoid responsibility for their behavior by saying, "I lost control of myself." That's nonsense. We all know when we're saying and doing abusive things. We know exactly what we're saying and doing. We also know it's wrong. It's just that we allow our anger to grow to the point that WE DON'T CARE ANYMORE! That's very different from "losing control." We don't lose control; rather, we get so mad that we "don't give a shit." When we stop caring about our partner or the consequences of our behavior we allow ourselves to get abusive.

The first sign that you no longer care is when you choose to get verbally abusive. We call this behavior *flipping our lid, going off, blowing our stack, and losing it*. These terms mean that we have reached the *"I don't care what I say line."* We're out of The Box at this point. Problem solving has stopped, and verbal abuse causes anger to build like the tornado illustrated below.

Crossing the *"I don't care what I say line"* is like throwing a match into a pool of gasoline. Anger intensifies swiftly. As the verbal battle rages, you move toward the dangerous *"I don't care what I do line."* When you reach that line, the hitting starts. Like our sea captain, you've sailed your ship onto the rocks with disastrous results.

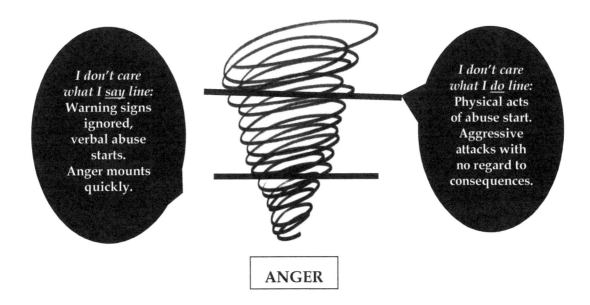

Warning signs and time-out will keep you in the box during times of conflict, but only if you make use of them. Ignore them at your peril. Ignoring warning signs is like running stop signs on a busy street. You may run one or two without incident, but eventually you will find yourself in a wreck. *The more verbal abuse that transpires before a time-out is called, the less likely it is that the time-out will be successful.* Once the "*I don't care*" lines are crossed, you probably won't call a time-out. Time-out should be called at the first appearance of your warning signs. Don't wait until you cross the "*I don't care what I say*" and the "*I don't care what I do*" lines. Don't wait until you become verbally abusive or physically violent. Call for a time-out while you still have the judgment and emotional stability you need to make wise choices.

When Time Out Is Over

Taking a time-out will not solve the problems between you and your partner. It only stops you from saying and doing things that make your problems worse. In Chapter One you learned that problems cause tension between you and your partner, and that the tension lingers until you solve the problem. Problem-solving is the only passageway back to the "OK" zone. When the time-out is over, resume your efforts to problem-solve as a team and in the spirit of friendship. Compromise, negotiate, and listen like a sponge. If you need more time to think things over, say so, but offer to set aside time in the near future to talk. Stick to it until you and your partner are truly "OK." To summarize, the steps in the time-out procedure are:

1. *Monitor your behavior by watching for your warning signs. Call a time-out as soon as you see them.*

2. *Acknowledge your anger to your partner and say you need a time-out. Use the words "time out" to let your partner know the rules are in effect.*

3. *Tell your partner how long the time-out will last (15 minutes to an hour).*

4. *Agree to pursue the problem further when you return.*

5. *Spend the time-out period working to reduce your anger. Tools like relaxation exercises and physical exercise can help. Most importantly, use self-talk and ask yourself the questions on page 14 in this chapter.*

6. *Come back on time and offer to continue problem solving.*

7. *Call another time-out if you need to, but keep at it until you solve the problem and get back to the OK zone of The Box.*

HOMEWORK ASSIGNMENT
CHAPTER 2

1. Explain the time-out procedure to your spouse.

2. It's important to know your personal warning signs. List three of your warning signs in each of the categories below:

    A. My Behavioral Warning Signs:
        1.
        2.
        3.

    B. My Physiological Warning Signs:
        1.
        2.
        3.

    C. My Cognitive Warning Signs:
        1.
        2.
        3.

Chapter 3
Take Inventory

Key Concepts: Anger Inventories reveal the effects of abuse, both in your life and in the lives of your family members. Once aware of destructive patterns and behaviors, you can choose to avoid them in the future. However, denial, blame, and minimizing must be avoided. They hinder your ability to make meaningful changes in your life.

Skill Building: Develop greater self-awareness and promote change by writing a searching and fearless Anger Inventory. Recognize denial, blame, and minimizing as your adversaries and choose to avoid them.

Jesse had been working on his Anger Inventory for several weeks. He was surprised by what he found. "I would never have believed it," he told me. "The more I write about my life, the more I see that I've become just like my father. When I was a kid I hated the way he used to treat my mom, and I swore that I'd never, ever be like him. But now I see that I've done everything to my wife that my dad did to my mom. The put-downs, the yelling, the hitting, it's the same shit, and I've become just like him. I had no idea."

Martha also learned a lot from her Anger Inventory. She wrote, "I can't believe how abusive I've been. I can see how I used to go off on others to get my way. I deliberately tried to intimidate people and make them afraid of me. You know, don't get *her* mad cause you don't know what she might do! I knew exactly what I was doing. It was all about getting my way."

What's An Anger Inventory?

Twelve-step programs such as Alcoholics Anonymous have helped countless people maintain their sobriety and regain their self-respect. Step four of twelve-step programs, ***making a searching and fearless moral inventory***, is an important part of recovery. A personal inventory provides an understanding of how alcohol affected a person's life. It's a detailed account of a person's history with alcohol, from childhood to the present day. Writing a personal inventory is no small undertaking. As the inventory is written, the writer gets an honest look at himself or herself, and acknowledges problems and personal weaknesses openly. A person sees, perhaps for the first time, the way he or she really is. Starting a personal inventory is a major undertaking.

People in our domestic violence program also write a personal inventory, with the focus on destructive anger and abuse rather than alcohol. We call it the Anger Inventory. Anger Inventories help people understand the way destructive behavior affected them as children and in their adult relationships.

Clients come to see long-standing patterns in their lives that they were not aware of, and gain insight into how the same mistakes, when repeated over and over, work havoc upon their relationships. We've found this exercise to be so beneficial that every person in *The Choices Program* is required to write an acceptable anger inventory before completing the program. An honest, searching, and fearless Anger Inventory can be a remarkable journey of self-discovery. This chapter will get you started on your own journey. Begin writing your Anger Inventory now, and keep adding to it as you work through the chapters in this book.

The questions below provide a starting point for your Anger Inventory, but don't feel like you have to stick to just these questions. Add questions of your own. As you write about the people and experiences that are unique to *your* life, be sure to include any important people and events that are not on this list. Most importantly, resist the temptation to write a superficial paper. Superficiality profits you nothing. Find the courage to delve into your life honestly, courageously, and thoroughly.

Sometimes it's hard to remember the past accurately. This is especially true of painful childhood memories. Indeed, you may have worked hard to *forget* some negative events from your past. If you have trouble remembering parts of your past, look at old family photos and talk to relatives. If possible, visit places you have lived before. Take long walks and give yourself time to reflect. This may help you recover your past. Remember, it takes time to write a thoughtful Anger Inventory, so allow yourself several weeks to work on it. The insights and self-knowledge you gain will be worth the time and effort. Here are some questions to start with. Remember, these questions are only a starting point.

Anger Inventory Questions:

1. How did your parents express anger towards each other?
2. How did they express anger toward you?
3. How did you know when your mother and father were getting angry? What were their warning signs?
4. Do you have memories of them getting out of the box?
5. Did you ever see your parents hit or verbally abuse each other?
6. If so, how did it make you feel?
7. Were you abused by anyone as a child? If so, how did you cope with the abuse? Did you tell anyone?
8. As a child, how did you show anger to other members of your family?
9. Do you remember getting out of the box during your teenage years?
10. Did getting out of the box have anything to do with controlling others?
11. How did you express anger to your peers as a teenager?

12. In junior high school and high school, what did you learn from your peers about expressing anger? How did they act when they got mad?

13. By the time you were in high school, how did you think you were supposed to act when you were angry with someone? What did you believe was OK to say and do?

14. How did you handle anger towards people you were dating?

15. How did you handle anger in the beginning of your first long-term relationship?

16. Did your behavior change over time, after the honeymoon period ended?

17. Towards the end of the relationship, how often were you verbally hostile? How often did physical abuse occur? How did the rules about anger and hostility change over the course of your relationship (Chapter 15)?

18. Have drugs or alcohol negatively affected your relationships?

19. What acts of verbal and physical abuse have *you* engaged in? *(Be specific and give a full account of past abusive behaviors! Do not deny or minimize.)*

20. Has your anger ever frightened your children?

21. Has the way you express anger caused relational, occupational, legal, financial, or health problems for you or your family?

22. What hardships has your behavior caused for your partner and children?

23. Have you engaged in acts of verbal or physical abuse to get control of the relationship and dominate your partner? Did you 1) make your partner do something he/she did not want to do, or 2) punish him/her for doing something you did not like?

24. Do you blame others or take full responsibility for your past acts of abuse?

25. Do you owe anyone apologies? If so, have you tried to make amends?

26. Has your behavior meaningfully changed for the better? If so, how has it changed?

27. What concepts and skills from this book are most important and useful to you?

28. Give some specific examples of your ability to apply the concepts and skills you've learned.

29. What have you done to ensure that your relationships stay abuse-free?

30. Is your Anger Inventory free of denial, blame, and minimizing?

Denial, Blaming, and Minimizing

I should warn you about three opponents to change that you will come upon as you write your Anger Inventory. These are *denial*, *blaming* and *minimizing*. If allowed, they will defeat your efforts to be truthful and honest with yourself. They are your enemies. They're opponents to growth, and they prevent you from making positive changes in your life. Because they keep you from seeing the truth of things, denial, blame, and minimizing undermine your ability to learn from the past.

If you do not learn from the past, you will keep making the same mistakes. This is how they block growth and meaningful change. They keep you from acknowledging the problem of abuse, and prevent you from doing what you need to do to stop abuse and violence in the future. To the degree that you avoid seeing things as they are, and shirk full responsibility for your actions, no important changes will take place. You'll probably behave abusively again, and the devastating consequences of domestic violence – destroyed relationships, damaged lives, and incarceration – are likely to follow.

For these reasons, it is important that you confront denial, blaming, and minimizing whenever you meet them. With a little practice they're easy to recognize. If you listen to yourself or others, you'll hear them in various forms almost every day. If you recognize them for what they are – impediments to growth and meaningful change – you won't be blinded by them, and you will have a much better chance of maintaining a violence-free relationship. So how do you learn to recognize denial, blaming, and minimizing? Let's look at denial first.

Denial

Clients attending their first session of domestic violence counseling often use denial to avoid talking about their hurtful behavior. Consider Robert. The court ordered him to get counseling following his arrest for spousal abuse. In his first court-ordered counseling session, he looked his fellow group members in the eye and declared with heart-felt sincerity, *"I don't need counseling! I didn't do anything wrong, and I never put my hands on anybody! This is all bull!"*

If you are new to domestic violence counseling, you may be inclined to believe Robert. After all, he *sounds* like he's telling the truth. But the more experienced clients in the group have heard it all before. They did not believe Robert and they let him know it. Consider everything that happened before Robert joined their group:

- *His behavior was so bad that someone - his children, his spouse, the neighbors, or the physician who examined his wife's injuries - called the police for help. Someone was very frightened and concerned. Otherwise, the police would never have gone to Robert's home.*
- *When the police arrived on the scene, they found sufficient evidence of domestic violence to arrest Robert for spousal abuse.*
- *The District Attorney's Office, after reviewing the evidence, found enough evidence charge Robert with criminal spouse abuse.*
- *Robert either plead guilty to the charge of domestic violence or, after hearing the evidence, a jury convicted him of spousal abuse.*

Now, a couple of weeks after his arrest, Robert was trying to convince the group that nothing happened, that it was all a big mistake. But in all likelihood, there was no mistake. The group understand that. The challenge is to help *Robert* understand it.

Unless he can overcome his denial of the problem, it is doubtful that he will be able to make meaningful changes in his behavior. That is why I and the other group members confronted his denial. Confronting denial is the responsibility of every counselor and every member of a counseling group. In turn, Robert's responsibility is to acknowledge past abusive behaviors. It's his first step towards making meaningful changes in his behavior. *Until he takes this first step, nothing meaningful is going to happen.*

You may ask, "Isn't it possible that Robert really is telling the truth?" In my experience, it's not likely. When a person comes for domestic violence counseling, whether voluntarily or by order of the court, I assume that something is very amiss in his or her relationship. In addition, many people - Robert's family, the police, attorneys, the jury, and the Judge who presided over the case, and perhaps others - played a role in getting Robert into counseling. Everyone involved saw a problem; well, everyone but Robert. Now it's up to him to muster the courage to acknowledge the problem and deal with it honestly. At this point, it's the responsibility of the counselor and the group members to let Robert know that his old way of dealing with the problem (just deny it) won't work anymore. The job of the counselor and the group is to: (1) confront Robert's denial, (2) help him summon the courage within himself to face his problem, (3) provide the tools he needs to change, and (4) support his efforts towards positive change.

Do not let denial mislead you. You must overcome it before any meaningful growth can take place. Change starts when you c*onvict yourself* of imperfections and *make a conscious choice to change*. When it comes to making meaningful progress in any area of life, denial is the enemy of growth.

Blame

Let's get back to Robert, who was attending his first session of court-ordered counseling. Seeing that his old way of dealing with this problem (just deny it) was not working, he changed gears: *"I'm here because of my wife. She is to blame. She's always pushing my buttons and she knows just what buttons to push. She's the one who needs counseling, not me."* Robert wanted to convince us that *he* was the real victim, so he tried to blame his wife for his legal and relational problems. He pointed out her every flaw. He related in detail every bad thing she ever said or did to him in the hope of justifying his abuse. He tried to convince us that he had NO CHOICE other than violence. The group tired of this before long. They told Robert that they understood why he was angry with his wife, but pointed out that righteous anger does not justify abusive behavior. Every couple has legitimate problems, they told him, but the only person responsible for domestic violence is the one doing the hitting. They told him that while he does not get to choose the situation he must deal with, he *always* chooses how he responds to it. If he responds with verbal and physical abuse, he has to take responsibility for it. They told him that regardless of how angry he was, HE STILL HAD A CHOICE. Robert chose violence.

This is not what Robert expected to hear. His usually handled his problems by denying them or blaming his behavior on his wife, but that approach was just making things worse, and the other men in the group were losing patience with him.

We'll get back to Robert in a moment, but first let's take a closer look at the subject of "blame." Why is blame such a big problem? How can you recognize it, and why do people often blame others for their own choices? Whether you are attending a formal counseling group like Robert, seeking couple's counseling, or working on your problems individually, you must *stop* blaming and *take responsibility* for your choices if you want a better life. Blame is an irrational attempt to hold others responsible for your bad choices. Like denial, it will prevent you from reaching your goal of an abuse-free relationship. Blame is easy to recognize if you know what to listen for. People who blame start sentences with words like "*you*" and "*he*" and "*she*" and "*they*." They say things like:

• *She wouldn't leave me alone.*	• *She kept nagging me until I blew up.*
• *He had a message from his ex on his cell phone.*	• *He pushed my buttons.*
• *All I did was defend myself.*	• *It's her fault I have to take this counseling.*
• *He should be in counseling, not me.*	• *She disrespected me.*

The easiest way to recognize a blaming statement is to listen to the first words in a sentence. Usually, the first words in a blaming statement will be "*He*" or "*She*." When you hear those words, you can be sure that the speaker is trying to take the spotlight off oneself, and place it on their partner. The blamer wants to talk about their partner's shortcomings to avoid talking about their own. The blamer hopes to show that they were justifiably angry on the chance that it may excuse their own abusive behavior. Let us put that issue to rest now. Anger, however justified, is *never* an excuse for abuse.

As stated earlier, you do not get to choose how your partner behaves towards you, but you *always* choose your reaction. **You are 100% responsible for how you respond to every situation and person in your life. Everyone else is 0% responsible.** If you choose to respond with abuse and violence, you must take full responsibility for that choice. You are the problem, and you are the solution. Blaming others does not make abusive behavior more acceptable, nor does it make violence against a family member any less destructive. Don't blame others for your mistakes. Rather, acknowledge them and learn from them. You alone are responsible for your actions, including the actions you take when you are provoked. Your spouse cannot force you to behave in a way that you are unwilling to behave. If you express your anger in a destructive and harmful way, you alone are to blame. Righteous anger is never an excuse for abuse.

Like denial, blaming is your adversary. It prevents you from seeing things as they are, and from accepting responsibility for your choices. Focusing on your spouse keeps you from learning about yourself. Blaming others does not help you understand what to do the next time you are in a similar situation.

You won't learn new behaviors when your attention is on your spouse's choices, rather than on your own choices. If you spend a lot of time using the words *"she"* or *"he,"* rather than *"I"*, there is blaming going on. Keep the focus on yourself, on your own choices. After all, that's really all you have control over.

You may be telling yourself, *"If you only knew my wife (or husband), you would understand why I blew up!"* I'm not suggesting that your partner is perfect. At times, your spouse may behave in ways that provoke or hurt you. All the same, you are solely responsible for how you choose to respond. Let's face it; people are not always going to be nice to you. Sometimes people behave in ways that are childish and selfish. Still, if you respond to their irresponsible behavior with verbal abuse and violence, you are in the wrong. Period. No excuses. Remember, explaining why you were angry *does not* explain why you chose to express your anger through violence. The reason you got angry is one issue. Your choice to express your anger through abuse and violence is a very different issue.

So what's the bottom line? One of the best things you can do for yourself and your family is to stop blaming others. Fearlessly take responsibility for everything you ever say and everything you ever do. Do this, and you're well on your way to changing your life.

Minimizing

When we left Robert, he was having a hard time in his first counseling session. Robert was trying to avoid responsibility for his violence by engaging in denial and blaming his wife, but the other group members were not buying it. Frustrated, he changed tactics once again. He said, *"OK, maybe I was wrong! But I didn't hit her, I only bitch slapped her!"* Robert has just entered the magical world of minimizing. Words like "only" and "just," make things appear smaller than they really are. Unfortunately for Robert, the men in his group knew all about minimizing. I confronted his language first. "Robert, don't use the word *"bitch"* here. First of all, it's sexist and demeaning. Secondly, if you don't learn to express yourself in this group without using abusive language, how do you expect to avoid it at home? Words like *"bitch"* and *"bastard"* escalate anger between two people. They're out of the box, and they're unacceptable."

Next, the group confronted Robert's minimizing. Jorge, an experienced member of the group, stepped up. "Robert, you just said: 'I didn't hit her, I just bitch slapped her.' Say that again, but this time leave out the words *"only"* and *"bitch."* Robert hung his head and said quietly, *"I slapped her."* It sounds different without the minimizing words, doesn't it? With the group's help, Robert was learning to avoid the seductive but dangerous magic of minimizing.

As you have read earlier, minimizing is an attempt to make abuse magically appear insignificant. This is done by using words like those in the box below. Like denial and blaming, minimizing keeps you from evaluating your behavior honestly. *If you want to grow, minimizing has to go.* With a little practice, you will recognize minimizing words easily. Familiarize yourself with the minimizing words in the box below, then read the statements that follow to see how they are used. I didn't make the statements up; they were made by actual clients.

Magic Minimizing Words:

only	a little	merely	maybe	they said I	I might have
sort of	at most	barely	all I did was	kind of	not more than
once	just	only	no big deal	hardly	argument

Describing the incident that led to his arrest, one man wrote the following:

"I moved her on the bed in a little mean manner and then she tried to run outside. I grabbed her by the throat real lightly then let her go up against the wall, then she had her back to a big couch and I tried to keep her on the couch by laying her down in in a push, very lightly."

<u>More Minimizing Statements</u>:

- *It was only an argument.* (This client was charged with assault with a deadly weapon.)
- *I never really hurt her -- she just bruises easily.* (Client punched spouse repeatedly in the breasts and in her groin, where she would be too embarrassed to reveal her injuries.)
- *I never hit her, I just bitch slapped her.* (You already met Robert.)
- *I only pushed her away. I don't know how she hurt her head. Maybe she tripped.* (Client pushed his girlfriend so hard that her head slammed against the wall, causing severe bleeding.)
- *Maybe I had my hands around her throat, but I wasn't squeezing, so I never really choked her.* (What can I add? This is a classic as it is.)

When you use minimizing words like these while describing acts of abuse, you are minimizing. Like denial and blame, minimization keeps you from looking at your behavior honestly, learning about yourself, and making meaningful changes. To summarize, denial, blame, and minimizing sound like this:

Denial: "I didn't do anything wrong."
Blame: "I did something wrong, but it's his/her fault."
Minimizing: "I did something wrong, but only a little bit."

Martin, another group member, recognized his use of denial, blame, and minimizing (he called these behaviors "B.S.") to avoid looking at himself honestly. He knew that these ways of thinking would keep him from making positive changes in his life and reaching his goal of a violence-free relationship. He wrote the following note to himself:

As I was leaving group, I realized that I can B.S. (deny, blame and minimize) my way through my homework and my group and never change a thing. I can beat my next mate, go to jail, and return to this group, then repeat it all over again. It's up to me and me alone to take change to heart. I want to be different. I've got to take a more positive and active role in this group. I need to take responsibility for my life (no woman to blame everything on). As I see it, the stronger I am the better my chances are to learn how to make the right choices now and in the future.

Aaron, another member of the group, worked courageously to keep denial, minimizing, and blame out of his Anger Inventory even though he had to deal with painful memories and unpleasant truths about himself. Aaron struggled in the beginning of his counseling, as most people do, but he was ultimately successful in his personal mission to remove violence from his relationship. Here are some excerpts from his Anger Inventory:

If a person was to look at me he would see evidence of intelligence and high achievement. He would see undergraduate and graduate degrees, and one year of law school. He would also see a number of academic and professional honors. What he would not see is the profile of an abuser: a physically violent and verbally abusive and assaultive man. Until a year ago, I never considered the possibility that I was abusive or physically violent, but now I know that I am and that I have been for a long, long time. I am aware of the violent and abusive potential within me.

As I agonized in jail for four days I began my metamorphosis. My thinking evolved from "How could she!" to "What have I done?" Even so, a lot of my concern about what I had done was over the social ramifications and personal embarrassment of my awful behavior rather than on the horrible things I had said and done to my wife. My focus now is on my behavior and how to stay in "the box" and how I can make amends to my family. I never want to lose my vivid mental picture of the forgiving face of my wife through the glass of the visitor's section of the jail. I thank her for filing her complaint against me.

In the process of exerting my "male privilege" I physically and emotionally damaged my wife and caused my children inestimable pain and distress. I have seen fear in their eyes as they recognize my rage. I have noticed their avoidance of me at times and their timid demeanor with me. I will forever try to rectify the damage I have done to all my loved ones. I can now empathize with them from the perspective of the scared, bewildered and angry child that I was.

As I attended my weekly meetings that were mandated by Judge Andrews I recognized myself in every element that the course covered. I recognized profound denial, blame, and minimizing in my behaviors that eventually necessitated my arrest. I recognized my exercise of male privilege, verbal abuse, and hurtful statements. Ultimately, I recognized that I was a violent man. I also realized that I had considered myself the "victim" while I was victimizing others.

My experiences this past year as a result of my arrest for domestic violence have been the most profound of my life. I have learned more about myself than at any other time in my life. I sincerely appreciate the system that is in place to stop domestic violence and to compel me to take a long look at myself. I would not "reform" a single aspect of the unpleasantness that I experienced in jail. It should NOT be a pleasant experience!

Furthermore, the 52 weeks of domestic violence classes have helped me recognize the awful potential within me and honestly begin to make real changes in my life. I now have tools and lessons to rely on to help me avoid abusive encounters of any kind in the future. Should I fail to heed them, I will have no one but myself to blame.

But what happened to Robert? In time, he became a leader in his group. He was ultimately successful in his counseling, as were all the people whose work appears in this chapter. Their success was largely due to their willingness to look at themselves honestly and objectively. Follow their example as you write your own Anger Inventory, and as you read the chapters to come. By evaluating your behavior and your choices without fear or deception, you open the door for great things to happen.

HOMEWORK ASSIGNMENT
CHAPTER 3

Start writing your own Anger Inventory by answering the 30 Anger Inventory Questions in this chapter. After answering them, set them aside and read them again after a day or two. Are your answers complete? Did you eliminate all denial, blame, and minimizing from your answers? Did you accept full responsibility for your past choices and behaviors? What did you learn from the exercise?

If you are in a counseling group, share your answers with other group members, especially those who have been in the group longer than you have. Ask them to give you feedback about your answers. If you are reading this book on your own, ask your partner, your counselor, or a family member to read your Anger Inventory, and solicit their suggestions and advice. Keep adding to your Anger Inventory as you progress through this book, making it as thorough and thoughtful as you can. Don't cheat yourself! You have to keep denial, blame, and minimizing out of your Anger Inventory if you are going to benefit from it.

Chapter 4
Skill Building

Key Concepts: There will come a time when your ability to avoid abusive behavior will be tested. To prepare for that time, search for opportunities to practice the concepts and skills that you are learning and apply them in your daily life. It is not what you know, but what you can do that will make a difference.

Skill Building: Take the quiz below to review your knowledge of the first three chapters. Look for any gaps in your understanding of key concepts, then go back and review the material until you can answer all of the questions. Lastly, provide an example of your ability to apply one of the skills you have learned.

The previous three chapters have given you a lot to think about. Now it's time to review your mastery of the concepts and skills that you were taught. First, take the short quiz below. If you have a hard time answering the questions or if there are gaps in your knowledge, go back and review the questions that gave you trouble. Don't go any further in the book until you have the first three chapters down cold. Future chapters build upon the concepts taught in the first three chapters, so take time to master the basics before moving on. Use every fourth "Skill Building" chapter to review and consolidate the material from earlier chapters, and to practice applying the lessons in your relationships.

Next, provide a detailed example of how you used the lessons from the book in a real-life situation. This is how you develop your ability to apply what you have learned. To assist you in this exercise, you will find a *Skill Building Log* to use as a guide. I can't overstate the importance of daily practice. While knowledge of key concepts and skills is crucial, knowledge alone won't change anything. Knowledge has to be skillfully applied. It is one thing to know what to do, and quite another to be able to successfully act upon your knowledge in the heat of conflict. Skill building takes work and practice, but there is no way around it. It is not what you know, but what you do, that will make a difference in your life.

This book provides you with a toolbox full of the finest tools available for resolving conflict without verbal abuse or violence, tools that have proven themselves effective for thousands of clients who now enjoy abuse-free relationships. Their attempts to use tools such as time-out or recognizing warning signs were clumsy at first, but with practice their skills improved and they reached their goal of a violence-free relationship.

When it comes to practicing skills, I often use the analogy of an athlete training for the big game. When my son was active in organized baseball, he wanted to learn how to throw a pitch called a slider. I couldn't tell a slider from a screwball, but I wanted to help. We found books and video tapes that demonstrated the proper technique, but books and tapes can only take you so far. Reading about something is not the same as doing it. This is where the practice comes in.

Every day after school, my son tried to throw a slider. He pitched, I caught, but the slider was hard to pin down.

Then it happened. The wind up, the pitch, the ball on its way just like all the others, but in the last few feet the ball snapped sharply down and away. A slider! He threw it again . . . another slider! Beaming, he said he could "feel it" when he threw it right. In the next game he threw his slider a lot and pitched a shut-out (allowing me to strut around the other fathers and accept credit for the whole thing. Dads will be dads).

This book is getting you ready for the big game, a time when your skills will be put to the test. The contest will be waged within yourself. Will you resort to old habits when anger and hostilities commence, or will your training carry you to victory: successful problem solving without getting out of the box? Athletes may read a book that describes the plays, but that won't help much when the big game starts. Successful athletes refine their skills by rehearsing the plays over and over on the field. Like the athlete, this chapter puts you on the field to practice your plays. Now is the time to practice, to get ready for the game.

Take the following quiz. Check your answers to make sure they are correct. You can find the answers in the appendix at the end of the book. If any of the questions give you trouble, take time to read through those chapters again. Stick with it until you have the concepts in Chapters 1-3 down cold.

Quiz
Chapters 1-3

1. Fill in the missing parts in "The Box" below. (Chapter 1)

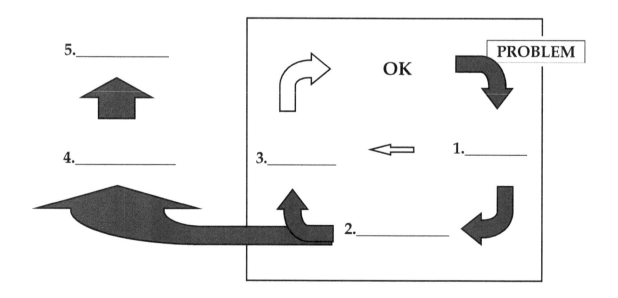

2. What is the purpose of "warning signs"? (Chapter 2)
3. What is the difference between verbal abuse and an argument? (Chapter 1)
4. List the Time-Out rules. (Chapter 2)
5. Define the following terms: (Chapter 3)
    i. Denial:
    ii. Minimizing:
    iii. Blaming:
6. Give an examples of your own Cognitive, Behavioral, and Physiological warning signs. (Chapter 2)
    i. Cognitive:
    ii. Behavioral:
    iii. Physiological:
7. What should you do when your Warning Signs appear? (Chapter 2)
8. What effect does Verbal Abuse have on anger? (Chapters 1 and 2)
9. What effect does Verbal Abuse have on Problem Solving? (Chapter 1)
10. What is the "I Don't Care What I Say Line?" (Chapter 2)
11. What is the "I Don't Care What I Do Line?" (Chapter 2)
12. What should you do when the Time-Out is over? (Chapter 2)
13. Can Denial, Blame, and Minimization prevent a person from growing? (Chapter 3)
14. Give examples of minimizing words. (Chapter 3)
15. What types of words do people use when blaming? (Chapter 3)

After you've completed the quiz and checked your answers, move on to the following Skill Building Log.

Skill Building Log

Step 1: Select one or more skills from the "Toolbox" below to practice for the month to come. Selecting the right skills to practice is easy. Just answer this sentence: *"It would help me and my family the most if I would _____."*

Step 2: On a separate sheet of paper, write a detailed example of how you put the skills to use. Describe (1) who you were with, (2) the problem you struggled with, (3) any of your warning signs that came up, (4) the skills you used to handle the problem, (5) how things turned out.

TOOLBOX FOR CHAPTER FOUR

- Memorize The Box
- Use The Box to guide my decision making
- Stay focused on problem solving during an argument
- Learn my own Warning Signs
- Watch for my Warning Signs when I start to feel angry
- Take a Time Out when I see my warning signs
- Memorize the rules to Time Out and follow them
- Explain the time out procedure to my partner
- Never cross the "I don't care what I say line"
- Never cross the "I don't care what I do line"
- Stop using any form of Verbal Abuse (stay in The Box)
- Recognize and avoid using Denial, Blame, and Minimizing

Below are two excerpts from the Skill Building Logs of Paulita and Darryl, two people in my counseling program. They will help you see what Skill Building Logs should look like. The following is from Paulita's Skill Building Log:

Skills I Select: Warning Signs and Time Out

My daughter Michelle and I got into an argument. I had placed her on restrictions. I said to her that she is grounded for failed grades. I went off to work and she decided to step out of the house. She disobeyed the rules. When I came home she was not in the house. I waited for her arrival. She walked in and said hello. I asked her of her whereabouts and she replied, "I'm not staying home - I don't care what you say. I'm not staying home - I'm on vacation."

My blood is boiling. I feel hot. My hands are perspiring, my voice cracking. I was <u>MAD</u>. Michelle was hostile. I recognized my warning signs. I decided to take a time out until I cooled off. I then asked her to come into the bedroom so we may have a discussion.

I could have behaved erratically and as hostile as she did. Because of the time out I was able to gather my thoughts and calm myself down for problem solving. I reminded myself of this quote I read in class: "I am today what my choices were yesterday, I will be tomorrow what my choices are today."

The following is taken from Darryl's Skill Building Log:

Skills I Select: Practice Using Time-Out

On Wednesday night, after getting out of class, my girlfriend picked me up from the classes. So right then when everything was fresh on my mind I explained to her every little detail I was taught in class and explained to her if she could help me with my homework. Anyway, the topic was about taking time out and setting up an agreement about taking time out. So we did (talked about the time outs) and agreed to get out of each other's face when tensions flare up, and take a 20 minute time out. About a few days ago we both got into an argument. (Hey, who would of knew that an argument would of come up!) A perfect time to practice my time outs. She noticed it first that me and her were going at it at each other. It started to build up (the argument). So right then she tells me, "I need a time out." (Why, I ask myself, didn't I notice it first?) But anyways, she tells me to leave the house and my first reaction was, "NO, I WANT TO FINISH THIS ARGUMENT." (As I said in my mind, and not out loud. Well really, thanks to Wednesday's classes for that practice.)

Anyhow, as I left out of the house and took off with anger inside me I finally snapped and told myself, "F***!!!! I need a time out." So as I left the house I took a ride to McDonalds, all mad and aggressive, but at the same time calming down. So I was gone for about . . . hmmmmmm, let's see, for about 15 to 20 minutes and she gave me a call on my cell phone and she asked me to come back home and talk about our argument.

Right there and then I realized something. I'm the type of person (like my father) who has to finish the arguments right then and now!!! But I say thanks to those time outs, cause if this was, let's say 2 weeks ago, I'd probably be in more trouble than what I'm already in!

As you read Paulita and Darryl's Skill Building Logs, you might notice that there are areas that still need improvement. Darryl, for example, is still having trouble seeing his own warning signs. Don't worry, he's on the right path and he will get more skillful over time. The important thing is that he's putting his skills to work in real situations. When the big game comes, Darryl and Paulita will be prepared.

More skill building exercises:

1. Sign a *Verbal Respect Contract* (see appendix) with your partner. Mark each day that you keep your part of the contract.

2. Make a commitment to avoid denial, minimizing, or blaming behavior. Mark each day that you successfully avoid these behaviors.

3. Make a list of the forms of verbal abuse that you use when angry with your partner, such as name-calling, yelling, making threats, or put-downs. Make a commitment to avoid them, and mark each day that you are successful.

Chapter 5
Thoughts and Emotions:
Take Responsibility for Your Anger

Key Concepts: Thoughts cause anger. My anger is not caused by what others say and do. My anger is caused by the way I think about what others say and do. In any situation, I can choose to think in ways that produce and escalate feelings of anger, or I can choose to think in ways that reduce it. I can take responsibility for my own emotional life. I can choose to stop creating my anger.

Skill Building: Study this chapter and complete the exercises until you obtain a complete understanding of how you cause your anger with your thoughts and beliefs. Practice thinking in ways that reduce anger.

"Anger reaches abusive levels when people think like an abuser."
"Think like an abuser and you'll feel like one."

In the first four chapters of this book, you learned basic concepts and skills that can forever change the way you handle conflict in your relationships. You learned how to use *The Box* as a guide in your decision-making. You identified your *warning signs*, and you know what to do when you see them. You've learned how to call a *time out*, and you know all about the three deadly sins of *denial, blame, and minimization*. Now it's time to move on to more advanced concepts and skills. In the next few pages, I'm going to try to change the way you think about anger and other emotions. It won't be easy, but once you've mastered these concepts you'll be in position to take charge of your emotional life.

Let me start by asking you a question. What makes you angry? If you are like most people, you will say things like: "I get mad when my husband yells at me;" or, "My girlfriend makes me angry when she flirts with other guys;" or, "It pisses me off when my wife bosses me around." When I ask people what makes them angry they describe *situations*. In other words, they describe things that *other people* say or do to "piss them off," or "push their buttons." If I ask you, "Has your partner ever made you angry?" you would probably answer with a resounding, "YES!" But you'd be wrong.

The things others say and do don't make you angry. Your partner doesn't make you angry, and neither does your boss. The guy who cut you off on the freeway didn't make you angry either. The things other people say and do don't have the power to make you feel anything. I know it *seems* like they do, but they don't. You piss yourself off and push your own buttons, and you do it all by yourself. I know this is a hard idea to get your mind around, but stick with me. It's important.

Anger is not caused by what other people say and do, but by *the way you think about* what other people say and do. Let me say it again: anger is not caused by others. The way you think determines what you feel. As the ancient Greek philosopher Epictetus taught, "People are not disturbed by things, but by the view they take of them." While your partner has never made you angry, you have angered yourself. You're probably saying to yourself, *"My partner never made me angry? Are you kidding? My partner says and does things that drive me absolutely nuts!"* Read on. I want to change your mind. Over the years, I've found that the best way to do that is by relating experiences from real life. Let me start by telling you about my "shark" encounter off the coast of California. As you read the story, ask yourself whether the feelings I experienced were caused by the *situation* or by the way I *thought about* the situation.

The Shark and the Psychologist

I love to scuba dive. Some years ago I was diving at my favorite beach in Southern California. The water there is usually clear and calm, but this day the water was dark and murky. I could only see about 8 feet in any direction. Still, I was enjoying myself and swam further from the beach. My feelings were about to change dramatically. About fifty yards from the beach something enormous (it seemed enormous at the time) flashed by at the very edge of my visibility. I could not see what it was, but I knew it was there with me, something big was swimming nearby in the murky water. Can you guess my first thought? (*Shark!*) Being a relatively inexperienced diver at the time, I believed there was a shark in the water nearby. What emotion do you think I experienced? (*Fear!*) In fact, I remember wishing that the fancy new diver's fins I had just bought would let me run on top of the water all the way to the beach.

Wide eyed, I swam in tight circles trying to see the shark that I believed was only yards away. Was it a Great White shark? Would it attack? Very soon, I saw movement at the edge of my visibility. The creature was only a few feet away and moving slowly toward me. My heart was pounding. I was very afraid. It came closer, and then I realized it wasn't a shark at all. It was a harbor seal! My "shark" was just a gentle, playful harbor seal! What do you think I said to myself? (*It's a seal! Seals don't eat psychologists . . . at least, I've never heard of a psychologist-eating seal.*) As my thoughts changed, so did my feelings. Believing that I was no longer in danger of becoming fish food, my fear vanished and I felt relief.

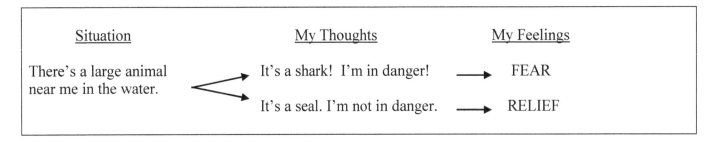

Notice the quick and dramatic change in my feelings. Nothing in the underwater environment had changed. While I did learn more about the situation, it was the same animal in the water throughout the experience. The swift change from anxiety to relief was due to the change in the way I thought about my environment. As long as I thought the situation was threatening and dangerous, I felt afraid. When I believed the situation was harmless, I felt relief. And what would I have felt if I believed seals were dangerous? In that case, I would have continued to be afraid. I know some divers don't think sharks are particularly dangerous, and they wouldn't have been afraid in the first place. The point is, when I *thought* I was in danger, I felt fear. When I *thought* I was safe, I felt relief. In both cases, my thoughts caused my feelings.

My fear and relief were caused by the thoughts in my head, not by the seal in the water. Suppose I did not see the seal when it swam by. What would I have felt? The answer is that I wouldn't have felt anything. Before I feel anything about a situation I had to perceive it, evaluate it, or think about it in some way. My feelings mirrored my thoughts, and as my thoughts about the situation changed, so did my feelings.

"Jaws" and the Little Boy

Here is a similar story that illustrates the relationship between thoughts and feelings. One day I was trudging back to my car after a beach dive at Shaw's Cove, one of my favorite Southern California beaches. As I started up the stairs leading to the street, I saw a young boy and his mother starting down the stairs to the beach. The boy seemed happy and carefree until he saw the beach at the end of the stairs. His eyes filled with terror and he screamed at the top of his lungs, "MOMMY, NO! THERE'S SHARKS IN THE WATER! I DON'T WANT TO GO TO THE BEACH!"

He started crying and tried with all his strength to pull his mother back up the stairs. She tried to calm her son by telling him the beach was safe and fun, but he didn't believe it. Through his tears he screamed again and again that there *were* sharks in the water. He pulled his mother up the stairs as though "Jaws" was waiting to eat him up the minute he set one toe in the sand. To the boy, the beach meant carnage and an awful death; safety lay in the other direction, UP THE STAIRS! Meanwhile, over the boy's panicked screams, I could hear the voices of other children laughing and playing happily on the beach below.

Why was the boy on the stairs afraid? Did the beach scare him, or was his fear caused by the way he thought about the beach? What about the other children? Why weren't they afraid? How can children who are in exactly the same situation (the same day, ocean, and beach) experience such different emotional responses (fear vs. joy)? The answer, of course, is that the children thought differently about the beach.

The Son-of-a-Bitch Guy

Thoughts also produce feelings of anger. I once had a client who flew into a violent rage whenever someone called him a "son-of-a-bitch." You could safely call him any other name under the sun, but as soon as the words S-O-B were spoken, look out! He told our group that, as he figured it, other curse words targeted him personally, and he could handle that. But when a person called him an S-O-B, well, they were talking about his mom, and he just wouldn't tolerate that. In his mind, a good son had to punch out anyone who insulted his mother. Unfortunately, his girlfriend did not know about this rule, and you can guess the rest of the story. Where did my client's anger come from?

When I teach this concept in my groups, I often stop and ask the group, "Does everyone understand that people and external events do not make you angry? You create your own anger. Your own thoughts create your anger. Understand?" Most often, everyone nods, "yes." Then, just to be sure, I say, "OK, raise your hand if you think your partner makes you angry." Half the hands go up. If you, the reader, still believe that your spouse makes you angry, we have more work to do. Keep reading. Other people can't make you angry, but you *can* anger yourself. Take Ed, for example. Ed was a client of mine several years ago. His story is an excellent example of how we anger ourselves.

Ed's Long Wait

Ed came home from work one day to find that his wife Sophie was not home. He wondered where she could be. Going to the kitchen for a beer, Ed found a note that Sophie had left on the kitchen table. Sophie's note said:

> *Hi Honey,*
>
> *I've gone shopping with my sister. I'll be home in about an hour.*
>
> *Love, Sophie*

Ed was annoyed. "I'm hungry and tired," he told himself. "I've been working all day and she can't even be here to make dinner when I get home."

An hour went by. When Sophie did not come home on time, Ed started a *negative feedback loop* - negative thoughts caused negative mood, and his negative mood led to more negative thoughts. Negative feedback loops grow into a true emotional storm if given enough time, and Ed was brewing an emotional hurricane.

His annoyance changed to genuine anger when his thoughts turned darker. "Where is she? What if she's cheating on me? You can't trust anyone. She could be out with some guy right now!" Ed's anger escalated rapidly as he pondered this new line of thinking. He got another beer and went outside. Sitting on the porch steps, he thought more about Sophie and the possibility that she was cheating. He spent another hour in the negative feedback loop, had a few more beers, and still Sophie still had not returned.

In the third hour, there was another change in Ed's thinking. He told himself that he knew Sophie was cheating. He was sure of it. Otherwise, he told himself, she would be home now. Ed's emotions mirrored his new line of thinking. He was not just angry anymore; he was enraged. He called her names in his head and tried to guess who she was cheating with. His thoughts fueled feelings of jealousy, rage, and indignation. His imagination ran wild, and the intensity of his feelings soared higher and higher as the minutes ticked by. By the time Sophie arrived home (two hours later than she said she would) Ed was shaking with rage. He flew at

Sophie's car, waving his arms and screaming obscenities and accusations at her. In his state of mind, Ed didn't even notice the shopping bags in her hand as he assaulted her. The police were called, Ed went to jail, and the rest is history. The chart below shows how Ed's feelings mirrored his thoughts.

SITUATION	ED'S THOUGHTS	ED'S FEELINGS
Sophie is gone longer than she said she would be.	Sophie should be here to make me dinner when I get home from work. She's selfish!	ANNOYED
	Maybe Sophie is cheating on me!	ANGER
	I'm sure she's cheating on me!	RAGE

Ed shook his head as he told his story to the other men in his counseling group. "I can't believe how stupid I acted!" he told us. He learned after the incident that Sophie was shopping with her sister, just like she said in her note. Enjoying herself, she shopped longer than planned. There was no cheating. Ed admitted that Sophie had never cheated on him. She was a happily married loving mother and wife. There was no reason to think she would ever cheat on him. "I just made it all up in my head," Ed told us. "I got myself spinning over nothing at all." Ed needlessly created his own upset.

Some of the group members had a hard time understanding why Ed had gotten angry in the first place. "Didn't you think she might have car trouble or need help?" asked one group member. Ed hadn't. "I wouldn't have been mad, I would have been worried," said another. "I'd have been afraid that she was in a car accident or something. Didn't that even occur to you?" Nope. Another said he would not have been upset at all. "Didn't you think that she was just out shopping and having a good time with her sister, and it was no big deal?" another asked. No, not that either. If any of these thoughts *had* crossed Ed's mind, he would not have made himself mad and things would have turned out differently. He would have had a very different emotional response (concern and anxiety rather than jealousy and rage, for example). Ed learned a lot about anger from his experience. What made Ed angry? Did Sophie make him angry, or did Ed anger himself? Was his rage caused by the situation (Sophie is not home), or was it caused by the way Ed *thought about* the situation (Sophie is not home, so she must be cheating)?

Given the same situation, some group members said they would have been unconcerned, while others said they would have been worried about her. Some said they would have felt mildly annoyed that Sophie didn't call to say she would be late, but they wouldn't have felt the intense rage that Ed felt. The emotional responses varied widely from group member to group member, depending on the way each person thought about the situation. The crucial point to understand is this: anger is not caused by what other people say and do, but by *the way we think about* what others say and do. Ed angered himself. We all do. The sooner we accept this, the sooner we can stop blaming others for the way we feel.

Sometimes Anger Is Justified

I'm not saying that you should never get angry. Anger is neither good nor bad; it is just a feeling. It can be healthy if handled responsibly. There will be times when you really are treated cruelly, disrespectfully, unfairly, or unjustly. Sometimes your anger is understandable, and perhaps there are times when you *should* be mad. People sometimes say and do things that you believe are irresponsible, offensive, and hurtful. But even "righteous" or "justified" anger has its source your own beliefs, values, and perceptions of the situation. You create the feeling. Right or wrong, your thoughts cause what you feel.

No one ever gets angry until they think about the situation they are faced with and form an opinion about it. To illustrate this point, imagine a person is walking down a path in the woods on a beautiful summer day, when a big bear jumps out. What will the person feel? This is a trick question. The truth is, you don't know what they will feel until you know what they think about the situation." If I have a big gun and I am looking for a bear rug to put in front of my fireplace, I might be happy to see the bear. Or, let's say I'm walking down a path in the woods on a beautiful summer day, when a big bear jumps out - but I don't see it. What will I feel? The answer, of course, is I will not feel anything at all. I cannot feel anything about an event unless I have a chance to perceive it and think about it. "Is this a good or bad situation?" "Am I in danger?" Events do not cause feelings. Feelings are formed by the way we think about events. The sooner we understand the relationship between thoughts and feelings, the sooner we can start taking control of our emotional lives.

While we're on the subject, how do you know whether your anger is "justified" or not? I can give you two guidelines to follow. First, anytime you are so angry that you think you should verbally abuse a family member (get out of The Box and cross the "*I don't care what I say*" line), or physically hurt your partner (cross the "*I don't care what I do*" line), you need to stop and check yourself. Your thinking is not rational. It is not rational *anytime* you think you should handle a problem by abusing a family member.

The second guideline is this: whenever you feel angry toward your partner, ask yourself, "Is my partner's behavior malicious? Is my spouse really trying to hurt me, or do we just have an honest difference of opinion? Will getting mad help me solve the problem? Am I blowing things out of proportion?" If Ed had followed this advice, he would have realized that his suspicions of Sophie were not rational. After all, the evidence indicated that Sophie was a caring and loving wife and mother. Ed would not have enraged himself if he had seen how irrational his thoughts were. There will be a lot more on this subject in later chapters, but for now just remember to give yourself a chance to evaluate your thinking when you start to get mad. Ask yourself, "Is my thinking rational and logical right now, or am I making a big deal out of a small problem?"

When teaching this lesson, I usually stop again at this point and ask the group, "Now, does everyone understand where anger comes from?" Most often, everyone nods, "Yes." I continue. "Do you see how Ed caused his own anger by the way he thought about Sophie being late?" Again, everyone nods - so far, so good. "Do you see that anger isn't caused by what others say and do, but by the way you *think about* what others say and do?" Everyone nods. "Ok," I say, "then raise your hands if you think your partner ever made you mad." Two or three hands go up! Now *I'm* using the anger management tools on myself, because I'm feeling pretty frustrated (I'm frustrating myself, that is). The concept that thoughts cause feelings is hard to grasp. "Let's try a different approach," I say. "I will make up a situation and tell you what the person in the story thinks about it. Then, you try to guess what the person would feel. Let's start with a story about two former clients of mine, Sharon and Charlie.

Sharon and Charlie

Sharon had been a homemaker for eleven years. One day she told her husband, Charlie, that she wanted to go back to school to finish her college education. What did Charlie feel? The answer, of course, depends upon the way Charlie thought about the situation. What would he feel if he had the following thoughts?

- *A woman's place is in the home.*
- *Sharon is bored and wants to have fun without me.*
- *My mother never went to college, and that was good enough for her.*
- *I work hard enough as it is – now I'll have to take care of the house too.*
- *Sharon doesn't think I can support her.*
- *If she goes to college, she will meet someone else and leave me.*
- *If she gets a degree, she will get a good job and make more money than I do. She won't need me anymore.*

These sorts of thoughts would cause Charlie to feel threatened and angry that Sharon wants to go back to college. On the other hand, what if Charlie had these thoughts:

- *We could sure use the extra income.*
- *She should choose for herself whether she goes to school. It's her life.*
- *With the extra money she makes, I could cut back on some of the hours I'm working.*
- *This is important to her; I should support her in reaching her goals.*
- *She's been there for me all these years. This is my chance to be there for her.*
- *I know she loves me. There's no need to feel insecure.*
- *I love her and I want her to be happy.*

With thoughts like these, Charlie would not feel angry or threatened by Sharon's decision to return to college. In fact, he would be happy for her and support her. The story shows how Charlie can experience very different emotional reactions, depending upon the way he *thinks about* the situation.

Sam and Rhonika

One day, Rhonika worked much later than usual. She forgot that Sam, her husband, made reservations earlier in the week to have a romantic dinner and celebrate their anniversary. On her way home, Rhonika realized that she had forgotten their anniversary plans. Upon entering the house, Sam confronted her angrily. He shouted and criticized her for forgetting their anniversary, and accused her of taking him for granted. What do you think Rhonika felt? Remember, Sam cannot make Rhonika angry. Whether she gets angry or not depends on how she chooses to think about the situation.

How would Rhonika feel if she had the following thoughts?

- *This is terrible! I can't stand him telling me off. I ought to go off on him too!*
- *Sam isn't perfect himself! He screws up all the time.*
- *How dare he talk to me this way! He's such a jerk!*
- *A woman should never let a man disrespect her. I should put him in his place.*
- *He is pushing my buttons!*
- *He's pissing me off! I'm not taking this crap!*

On the other hand, how would Rhonika feel if her thoughts were like those below?

- *I understand why Sam is angry. He was looking forward to this and I let him down.*
- *Stay calm. Look for my warning signs. Stay in The Box.*
- *If I start to yell or see any of my warning signs, I will take a time out.*
- *I need to acknowledge my mistake and try to make it up to him.*
- *Is there anything truth to what Sam is saying?*
- *Be strong and assertive, but do not get defensive and make things worse.*
- *I won't tolerate verbal abuse, but I am willing to listen and take responsibility for my mistakes.*
- *Sam is angry, but he is also someone that I love. Keep the Big Picture in mind.*
- *Put myself in Sam's place. How would I feel?*

Do you see how Rhonika's thoughts caused her feelings? Sam could not make her angry, but Rhonika could anger herself. If you understand this concept, you understand the key to getting control over your emotional life. There will be more about this in the chapters to come. For now, just understand that in any situation *you can choose to think in ways that produce and escalate feelings of anger, or you can choose to think in ways that reduce it.* You have the freedom to choose because you are the only person who can decide what you say to yourself. Sometimes, thoughts will jump into your mind and cause immediate anger, but you do not have to offer those negative thoughts a chair and invite them to sit down. You do not have to dwell on them, or engage in unending negative feedback loops. You have the power to choose what thoughts stay, and what thoughts go. You choose the way you feel.

To test your understanding of the relationship between thoughts and anger, try the following exercise. I have listed some thoughts expressed by people in my counseling groups.

Some thoughts (the thoughts in bold type) led to increased anger and greater risk of abusive behavior. The thoughts in italics are counter-thoughts. Counter-thoughts reduce or eliminate anger and help you feel balanced. As you read the thoughts, ask yourself if you have had similar thoughts and counter-thoughts.

HOMEWORK ASSIGNMENTS
CHAPTER 5

Exercise 1: Thoughts and Counter-Thoughts. *Read the thoughts in bold type and circle them if you have ever had similar angry thoughts. For each negative thought, develop counter-thoughts to help you feel less angry. Over the next week, repeat your counter-thought to yourself whenever you have thoughts similar to those in bold.*

It's my partner's fault that I have to get domestic violence counseling.
I am getting counseling because I need to change the way I behave towards my spouse.

It is OK to get violent if my partner hits me first.
There is no justification for domestic violence. As the saying goes, "two wrongs don't make a right." Violence won't stop as long as I'm a willing participant in it.

I should always be in control of a situation.
I should always be in control of myself.

No real harm is done by a little push or slap.
Physical hostility always harms a relationship. It destroys trust, creates fear, anger and resentment, ends open and free communication, and can even result in loss of employment and incarceration.

When domestic violence occurs, both partners are equally to blame.
The only person to blame for domestic violence is the one doing the hitting.

There is no harm in swearing name-calling like bitch, whore, bastard, and son-of-a-bitch during an argument.
Name-calling is verbal abuse, and verbal abuse is always harmful. It humiliates and degrades, escalates anger, and often leads to physical abuse. It turns your partner from a friend to an adversary and blocks problem solving.

If I hit my partner, it's as much her (or his) fault as mine.
I am the only person responsible for how I act. There are no exceptions.

When I get pushed too far, I can't be held responsible for what I say and do.
I am 100% responsible for everything I ever say and do, even when I am angry.

It is wrong for my spouse to say things that make me mad.
Others have the right to say what they think. It is my responsibility to handle my anger appropriately, even when I disagree with what my partner is saying.

People usually bring violence on themselves by the way they treat me.
The things my partner says or does can never justify my abusive behavior. I don't control the situations I have to deal with, but I am 100% responsible for how I choose to respond to every situation and person in my life. Everyone else is 0% responsible.

Exercise 2: Practical Applications. *Here are some hypothetical situations to practice with. For each situation, provide (1) thoughts that would produce and escalate anger, (2) thoughts that would prevent or reduce anger, and (3) the likely outcome for both ways of types of thoughts.*

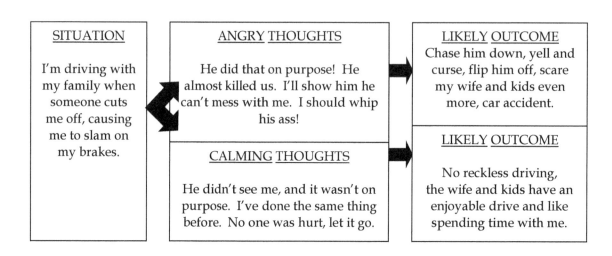

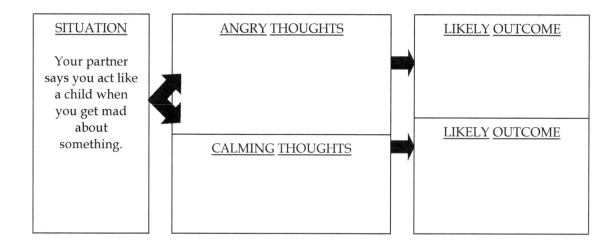

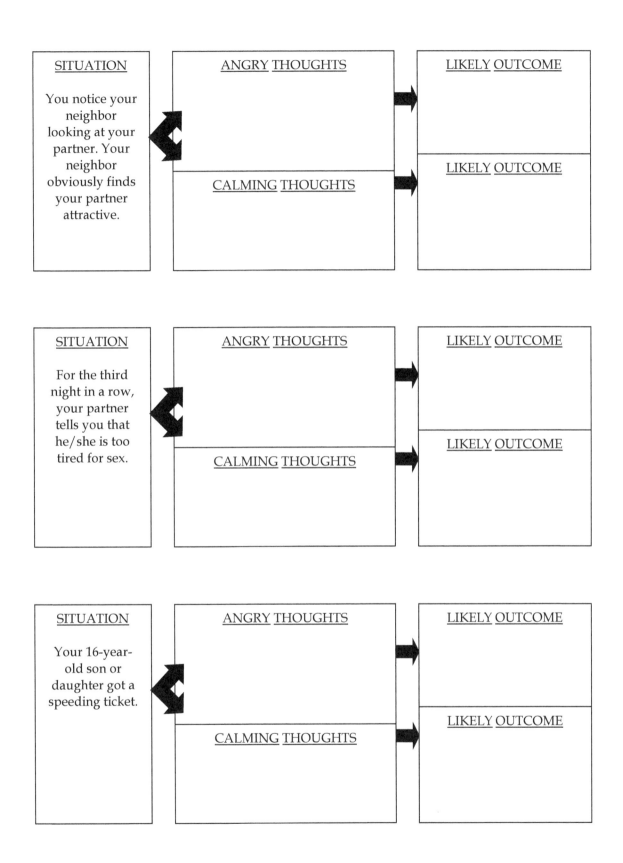

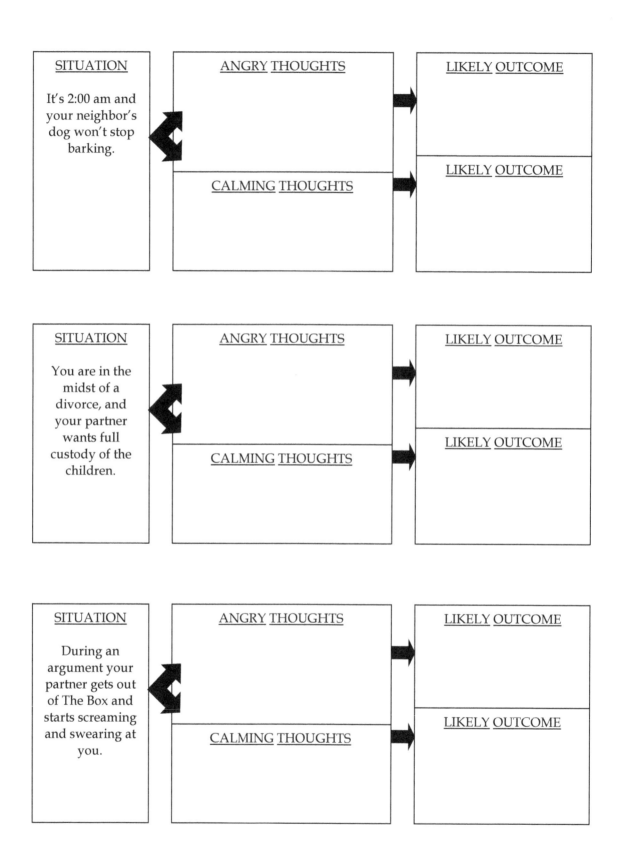

Chapter 6
Thoughts and Behavior:
Responsibility, Violence, and Control

Key Concepts: Anger doesn't make you behave abusively. Your thoughts and beliefs determine how you behave when you're angry. To make meaningful changes in your behavior, you must change the way you think about responsibility, violence, and control.

Skill Building: Work on accepting personal responsibility for your behavior, lowering your comfort level with verbal and physical abuse, and accepting your partner as your equal.

"Spousal abuse happens when people think like an abuser."
"If you think like an abuser you'll act like one."

Several years ago, a newspaper published statements that people made when filling out auto accident reports. Describing the reason for the accident, one motorist wrote, *"A pedestrian hit me and went under my car."* Another motorist described his accident this way: *"The telephone pole was approaching fast, I was attempting to swerve out of its path when it struck my front end."* I could not help thinking of these statements as I listened to Hank, a new client, talk about his abusive behavior toward his wife. When I asked Hank why he hit her, he answered, *"Because I was mad!"* When I asked him why he was mad he said, *"Because of what she did!"* According to Hank's line of reasoning, his own choices had nothing to do with his act of abuse; it's like Hank wasn't even there. Hank thinks like an abuser, and that's why he acts like one.

HANK'S WAY OF THINKING:

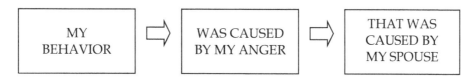

The problem with Hank's way of thinking is that he blames his behavior on his anger, and he blames his anger on his spouse. What is Hank leaving out? He's leaving himself out. The goal of counseling is to put Hank into the equation so he can understand the role his thoughts played in (1) the anger he felt, and (2) his choice to express his anger abusively.

In the last chapter, we examined the link between thoughts and feelings. You learned that situations alone (the things others do and say), cannot make you angry. The way you think about a situation determines whether you get angry. In this chapter, we'll look at the relationship between your thoughts and behavior. Anger alone cannot make you behave abusively. Don't blame your behavior on your feelings. Anger is just a feeling; it cannot *make* you hurt your spouse. Abusive behavior is a choice - you make the choice to behave abusively, or to behave responsibly. Either way, the choice you make depends on the way you think. Just as your thoughts determine how you feel about a situation, your thoughts also determine how you behave in a situation, as shown below.

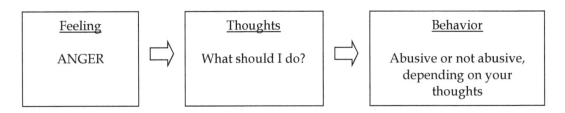

To maintain an abuse-free lifestyle, you need to understand the types of thoughts that are associated with abuse. My work with the men and women in my program suggests that, at the moment they abused their partner, their thinking was remarkably similar. They all thought in the same, predictable way while they were abusing their spouse. Psychologists refer to these thought patterns as *cognitive schemas*, or *sets*. You don't need to know the technical term, but you do need to understand the role that these thoughts play in abusive behavior. The thoughts I am about to describe "unlock the door" to abuse and violence, and they were present, with very few exceptions, in every act of abuse that I'm familiar with.

Let's start by looking at some actual incident reports of partner abuse. The statements below are from past clients, although their names and other identifying information have been changed. While the statements come from men and women in various kinds of relationships and from different backgrounds, their thinking at the time of the abuse was remarkably similar. They blamed the victim, were comfortable with violence, and wanted to control others. Here is how they described their actions:

- *She told me her friends invited her to a birthday party. Using power and control I told her no, and that I didn't trust her friends. She and the children went [anyway]. I became violent. I remember grabbing her around the throat and saying I could kill her.*

- *As I got older I found that sometimes hitting or beating up was a way to get what I wanted.*

- *I remember when I didn't get my way I ran my truck into her fence. I was trying to scare her so I could get my way! I told her I would kill myself if I didn't get my way. I got my way. I remember slapping her for the first time, then forcing her to sleep with me. She slept with me out of fear for her life.*

- *When my dad was finally told [that my sister was pregnant] he beat up her boyfriend while me and my brothers helped him. Then he beat up my sister bad, calling her whore, bitch, slut, and finished by kicking her really hard in the stomach three times.*

- *Then Ellen pulled out the butcher knife and chased me with my son in my arms. Then I put my son down and ran for the door realizing she wouldn't hurt my son. When I got to the door, WHAM! It pierced my leg, cutting it bad.*

- *My wife started telling me that I was not paying no attention to her. So at this time I reached over and slapped her in her face. So she ran in the house, and the kids woke up. My wife ran in the bathroom with me following her. All the kids were crying. By this time the police arrived. There I was, booked for a felony charge of domestic violence. The next day, my wife was at the jail trying to get me out, saying it was her fault. You know this is how much power and control I had over someone else's life. It's just sick.*

In each of these incidents, and in thousands more like them, the people committing the violence had similar thoughts about: *(1) their personal responsibility for their abusive behavior, (2) their comfort level with the use of violence to get their way, and (3) their desire to have power and control over the victim.* Just before the abusive act, they were thinking:

1. *I am not responsible for what I am about to say and do to you - it is your fault.*
2. *My behavior is justified and acceptable to me. I am comfortable with my behavior. I think it is "OK" to act this way; it is not abuse.*
3. *I am "the boss," and I have the right to control you. I have the right to control you by forcing you to do something you don't want to do, or by punishing you for doing something I don't like.*

The way people think about these three subjects can either cause or prevent abusive behavior. If you have ever abused your partner, I'm willing to bet that *at the moment of the abuse* you were thinking the same way they were about responsibility, violence, and control. Let's take a closer look at the mindset of an abuser.

Responsibility

This part of the book could be called: *How to Abuse Your Partner in Three Easy Steps*, because it describes the three steps that people take to transform themselves from a responsible partner into an abuser. The first step toward becoming an abuser is to deny personal responsibility for your behavior. Convince yourself that you're not responsible for what you're about to do. This is similar to the blaming that we talked about in chapter three, but here you avoid responsibility *before* the act is done. Tell yourself that he or she is to blame for what you are about to do, and get yourself to believe that your partner is responsible for *your* hostile behavior. Tell yourself things like:

- *He's driven me to this!* - *She's pushing my buttons!* - *He's gone too far!* - *She's asking for it and I can't control myself any longer!* - *I warned him, now he deserves what he gets!*	- *He provoked me, so it's his fault if I lose it!* - *She brought this on herself!* - *He's as much to blame as I am! (for what I say and do)* - *She isn't giving me any other choice!*

Once you convince yourself that you're not responsible for your own behavior, almost anything is possible. You can say and do things that you never thought yourself capable of, regrettable things that inflict real pain and trauma to your partner. All the while, you're thinking you're not responsible for your choice of words and actions. Now that step one is accomplished, it's on to step two.

Comfort with Violence: What I'm Doing is OK

The second step toward partner abuse is to convince yourself that what you're about to do to your partner isn't abusive. Tell yourself that it isn't *real* abuse. Abuse is something *other* people do to their partners, not you. One way to convince yourself that your behavior isn't abusive is to use magic minimizing words, like those in Chapter 3. You can also call the abuse something else. For example, tell yourself that you are not abusing your partner, you are . . .

- *just having an argument*
- *only acting in self defense*
- *just standing up for myself*
- *only demanding proper respect*
- *problem solving*
- *defending myself*
- *trying to get control of the situation*
- *refusing to be pushed around*
- *helping my "out of control" partner regain self-control*
- *stopping my partner's abuse*

This is irrational thinking. A thing is what it is, and not something else. But then, it is never rational to hurt the people we love. If our thoughts were always rational, we would never do it. One common way people try to turn abuse into something else is to call it "self-defense."

Self-Defense?

Clients who want to explain away their abusive behavior often claim they were acting in self-defense. Calling abuse self-defense is a common strategy among new clients. Men claim self-defense as often as women do. If you are tempted to call abuse self-defense, ask yourself, *"What is the main feeling of a person who is acting in self-defense?"* The answer, of course, is fear. Next, ask yourself, *"What was the main thing I was feeling when I got out of the box?"* If your answer is anger, and it almost always is, you weren't acting in self-defense. You were motivated by anger, not fear. You were mad about something and wanted to lash out. That is not self-defense.

With each new incident of verbal or physical abuse, the more "normal" it seems. Eventually, abusive behavior is the first thing that comes to mind whenever you're angry. Over time, the comfort level with violence can grow to deadly proportions. A client of mine, let's call him Dan, is an example of how high one's comfort level can grow.

Dan had a problem. His girlfriend, Alicia, had left him. That did not bother Dan – he didn't like her much anyway. It did bother Dan that Alicia took their two-year-old son with her when she left. His problem grew worse when the family court granted Alicia full custody, largely because of Dan's extensive history of criminal behavior. On top of all this, Dan learned that his son was starting to call Alicia's new boyfriend "Daddy." Dan was determined to get his son back, so he turned to his customary problem-solving strategy – violence.

Dan devised a solution he thought was foolproof. He planned to burst into Alicia's home and kill her boyfriend in front of her. She would be too terrified to fight him, and he would take their son. Dan thought it was an excellent plan, and he put it into action the following night. He drove to Alicia's apartment and kicked in the door, taking her boyfriend by complete surprise. Dan jabbed a gun against the boyfriend's head and called out for Alicia. But Alicia didn't answer – by sheer luck, she and her son were not home. Her boyfriend was home, but Dan wanted Alicia to see the killing in person. That was the point – to shock her, to terrify her so badly that she would surrender their son forever. His plan spoiled, Dan pistol-whipped Alicia's boyfriend and stormed off, frustrated that his plan failed. Dan was surprised that he was arrested a few hours after the incident. "I didn't even shoot anyone!" he said. "What's the big deal? I didn't think he'd even call the police over a thing like that! If I knew he would call the police, I would have killed him."

Dan's mindset at the time of the incident is typical of a person engaged in an act of abuse. He told himself that he was not responsible for the trauma he was about to inflict, convinced himself that his actions were justifiable, and believed he had a right to control Alicia. *(Step one: deny responsibility):* "Alicia forced me to do this. It's her fault. She brought this on herself by taking my son from me. She left me no other choice, and she has it coming. The court let me down, so I have to take things into my own hands. They all forced me into this." *(Step two: tell yourself it's not abuse):* "I'm not a killer – I'm a good father. This is an act of love to give my son a better life. Sometimes a dad has to do what he has to do for his son." *(Step three: tell yourself that you are the boss and have the right to control your spouse):* "I don't care what Alicia or the courts say. I won't let my son be raised by that "slut" of a mother. I have the right to take my son." Dan's actions were extreme, but his mindset was typical of all abusers.

Power and Control

The issue of power and control deserves special attention. It is the third and final step towards abuse and violence. You convince yourself that you are the boss, that you have the right to "control" others by punishing or forcing your will on your partner. Power and control issues have always been linked to domestic violence. I often ask new clients, "Who's the boss in your relationship?" The most common answer is, "I am!" Power struggles and the need to be the boss in the home have led to more acts of abuse than I can count. The need to control others, together with beliefs about responsibility and violence, make abuse possible. It usually works this way:

I'm the boss, so I have the right to make you do what I want. (power & control)

and . . .

If I have to get rough with you I will (comfort with violence)

and . . .

If I do it's your fault for not doing what I said in the first place (responsibility)

Making Meaningful Changes

If you want to stop hurting your family, you must change in the way you think about responsibility, violence, and control. The abuse and violence won't stop until you change the way you think. The way a person thinks about these three issues is the most important factor when evaluating the progress any client has made in his or her counseling. Learning skills like "time-out" and "staying in the box" are important, but they won't stop abusive behavior by themselves. Growth starts by changing the way you think about responsibility, violence, and control. Let me give you an example of the typical changes clients make in their belief system as they progress through counseling. New clients usually hold the following set of beliefs:

Belief System of New Clients

Responsibility: *New clients deny personal responsibility for their behavior. They believe their partner and everyone else is responsible for their behavior. When asked who is responsible for their abuse they will usually say, "He is!" or "She is!"*

Comfort with Violence: *New clients believe abusive behaviors are legitimate problem solving tools and minimize their hurtful nature. They tell themselves they weren't really abusive at all, and show a high comfort level with verbal abuse and violence. When asked whether their behavior was abusive, they will usually reply, "No way!"*

Power and Control: *New clients see themselves as the boss in their relationship, and want to control and dominate their partner. When asked, "Who is the boss in your relationship?" they usually reply, "I am!"*

Now jump ahead three months. Most clients have made some changes in the way they think. Their belief system looks like this:

Belief System of Clients Making Progress

Responsibility: *Clients who are starting to make progress accept some personal responsibility for their behavior, but not all. They still believe their partner is partly responsible for the abusive things they do and say. When asked who is responsible for their abuse, they will usually say, "We BOTH were!"*

Comfort with Violence: *Clients in the middle stages of counseling see their abusive behavior as wrong, but still want to focus on their partner's behavior. They still minimize their abusive behavior, but their minimizing is now more subtle and less obvious (Ex: These groups are great, but I think she (or he) should be here too.). Their comfort level with abusive behavior is reduced, and they are experimenting with the new skills and concepts they are learning. Asked whether their abusive behavior is acceptable, they reply, "No, it was wrong, BUT my partner was also wrong to . . . ."*

Power and Control: *Progressing clients are willing to share some of the power, but not all. When asked, "Who is the boss in their relationship?" they usually say, "We BOTH are!"*

Jump ahead a few more months. By now, most clients are making serious changes in their belief system, as described below.

Belief System: Seasoned Client

Responsibility: *Seasoned clients accept full responsibility for their behavior without blaming others for their own choices. When asked who is responsible for the abuse or their arrest, the reply is, "I am." They quickly recognize blaming comments made by others, and they confront less experienced clients when they hear them blame others. This issue is taken very seriously, and no pity is shown to the newcomer who tries to avoid responsibility for their actions.*

Comfort with Violence: *Seasoned clients see abusive behavior as wrong, period. They focus on their own behavior. There is far less minimizing, and they confront others who engage in it. Their comfort level with abusive behaviors is very low. They demonstrate a high level of proficiency in their use of the skills they've learned, and are very critical of themselves when they fail to use them. If asked whether their past behavior was acceptable, they reply "No" in a tone of voice that makes you feel stupid for having asked such a dumb question. They take a leadership role counseling groups. Their comments are so "on target" that the counselor often feels useless and unneeded.*

Power and Control: *Seasoned clients share power in their relationship, and they are very aware of controlling behaviors in themselves and others. They see their partner as an equal. If asked, "Who is the boss in their relationship?" they reply, "There are no bosses in our relationship."*

Compared to new clients, seasoned clients have greater confidence in their ability to resolve interpersonal problems without resorting to verbal abuse or violence. Their growth is seen in their comments, body language, and attitude, and a visitor to the group could quickly distinguish them from the less experienced clients. They have become leaders in the group, and others follow their example. They no longer see themselves as a victim, and they do not victimize others. They have made meaningful changes in their behavior and beliefs. They have taken charge of their lives.

More about Power and Control

Power in relationships refers to the ability to get your way and make the important decisions. In some relationships, power is equally divided between the spouses. Decisions such as where to live, money, time spent with friends, and the division of household chores are made by both partners through negotiation and compromise. Both partners are able to express their thoughts and feelings openly and without intimidation. They solve problems as equals through communication, negotiation, compromise, and mutual respect for each other's opinions. Couples who share power do not try to control each other. They don't bully or force their partner to do something against their will. They know that attempting to control others turns an ally into an adversary, and creates an atmosphere of anger, resentment, and intimidation where problems are never really solved, and they never get back to the "OK Zone" of the box. Couples that value equality in their relationships know that solutions that are forced on their partner probably won't solve anything, no matter how "right" the solutions seem to be. On the other hand, solutions reached through mutual compromise and negotiation usually work.

Tom and Chris

Unfortunately, not all relationships are based on mutual respect and equality. Sometimes one partner believes that he or she is the boss, the king of the castle and head of the household. These people don't share power. They demand to be treated as "the master." When one spouse has more power than the other, there is the potential to abuse that power. Tom was such a man. Like a king in his realm, Tom held total power over his partner, Chris. She and the children lived in abject fear of him, because Tom was capable of terrible acts of abuse when he didn't get his way. In order to maintain power over Chris, he socially isolated her and sought to control every detail of her life. He objected to her leaving the house without him. He became enraged whenever he checked the telephone bill, as he did every month, and found that Chris had talked to her mother or friends (trouble makers) on the telephone. She drifted away from her family and friends until she was totally isolated.

Chris did not give up any of her rights when she married Tom, but he didn't see it that way. He acted like her lord and master. Tom refused to let Chris work. In fact, she had to ask Tom for money whenever she had to buy groceries. After going to the store, Chris would surrender the receipt and the change, which Tom pocketed. Tom made sure that Chris' name was not on any of the checks, credit cards, or bank accounts. He often accused Chris of cheating, and used that as an excuse to beat her, although he was the only one who ever cheated in the marriage. Chris eventually got away from Tom. She left barefoot, without a cent, with the kids in tow, and ran all the way to a women's shelter. She was sure he would kill her if he found her leaving.

You may think, *"I'm not as bad as that! I've never gone that far!"* I assure you, *at the moment you laid your hands on your partner*, you had issues with control. You saw yourself as the boss. In order to hit your partner you have to convince yourself that have the right to 1) make your spouse do something he or she does not want to do, or 2) to punish your spouse for doing something you do not like. In your own mind, at the instant of abuse, you saw yourself as the boss.

Trisha and Christian

I used Tom in the last example, but there are also women who see themselves as the boss of the home. I have worked with women who were as controlling and as abusive as Tom. Any person, regardless of gender, race, or sexual orientation, can have issues with power and control. Anyone who abuses their partner fails to see them as their equal during the incident. It is a human issue, not limited to gender, race, or sexual orientation. Trisha is a good example. Trisha was a strong, athletic woman. She was in a gang during her adolescence, and by the time I met her Trisha had a long criminal record that included multiple convictions for battery and assault.

During her last stretch in jail, Trisha decided that it was time for her to stop the violence and start a new life. For one thing, she found religion. After her release from jail she started dating a slightly built, easy-going Christian man, and soon they were boyfriend and girlfriend. Things went well at first. They read the bible, prayed, and went to church every Sunday. Trisha seemed to have put her old ways behind her.

Unfortunately, the day came when Trisha and her boyfriend had their first serious fight. Trisha always saw herself as the "strong one" in the relationship. She usually made the important decisions, but this time her boyfriend was not going along. At first they argued. Then they yelled. Trisha decided to teach him a lesson. Grabbing her boyfriend around the shoulders, she tried to throw him to the floor. He pushed back, and as they wrestled Trisha saw his ear. Enraged, she bit the ear – hard, *very hard.* To her shock (and to the sound of her boyfriend's yelps), the ear came off in her mouth and fell to the floor. She told us sadly, *"The worst part was that we couldn't even sew his ear back on - because the dog ate it! I tried to catch him, but he ran off!"*

While both genders engage in controlling behavior, men have a cultural predisposition to see themselves as the boss. As Eve and Carl Buzawa describe in their book on domestic violence, men have held power over women since ancient times. Roman law, for example, granted the husband the right to sell a wife into slavery or, in some circumstances, to put her to death. A 15th century medieval scholar encouraged husbands to *". . . scold her sharply, bully and terrify her. And if this doesn't work . . . Then readily beat her, not in rage, but out of charity and concern for her soul."* English common law held that the wife lost rights to their property when she married. Even property she inherited from her family became the property of the husband, who could legally dominate her using violence "with restraint." In agreement with England's "rule of thumb" law, the Supreme Court of Mississippi ruled in 1824 that a husband could beat his wife with a stick if it was no thicker than his thumb. Not until 1871 did the first U.S. court, the Supreme Court of Alabama, explicitly rescind the right of husbands to beat their wives:

The privilege, ancient though it may be, to beat [one's wife] with a stick, to pull her hair, choke her, spit in her face or kick her about the floor . . . is not now acknowledged by our law. . . . In person, the wife is entitled to the same protection of the law that the husband can invoke for himself. *Buzawa, E. & Buzawa, C. (2003). Domestic Violence: The Criminal Justice Response. (3rd Ed.) Thousand Oaks, CA: Sage.*

Not long ago, women were denied the right to vote. In some cultures, they still are. Men have traditionally held a privileged position in which they were the "head of the household," and the home was their "castle." Women were relegated to a lower social status and expected to yield to the husband's decisions on matters of importance, as though his needs, wants, and opinions were more important than hers.

In the eyes of some men, this is as things should remain. After all, men are the traditional "breadwinners" for the family. Shouldn't the fact that his wife depends upon him for her financially well-being earn him some extra privileges around the home? Doesn't he "pay to have the say?" Hasn't he earned the right to have the final say about important family matters? The answer is no, he has not. Power in an adult relationship should not be based upon who earns a larger paycheck. How many husbands would be willing to assume a traditional "female role" the moment the wife earns a bigger paycheck? Not many. I have known men who lost their jobs and were forced to depend upon their wives for support. To a man, they complained (loudly) that the woman was abusing her new financial power, and using it to control and manipulate them. They didn't like it a bit. I don't think women like it either.

Other men argue that they should be the head of the household (have their way all the time) because "*that is the way things have always been.*" I point out that there are lots of traditions in our society, but not all of them were good. Slavery was once a "tradition" in this country, but today no reasonable person looks at slavery with anything but regret and outrage. Bleeding the sick, debtor's prison, and child labor were once common. The old ways were not necessarily better ways. Just because something was once a tradition does not mean that it was right - only that it used to be that way.

When you force someone to do something against their will, they resent you for it. Your partner may obey and fear you, but will not love or respect you. No one likes to be bullied. The harder you try to control people, the more they resist. To see how people react to being pushed, ask someone to raise their hand. Put your hand against theirs and slowly push. They'll push back. It's our nature to push back. No one likes to be pushed, *even if you think you are pushing them in the right direction.* The three stories that follow illustrate this point. The stories do not involve physical violence, but they are included as examples of how problems can be handled when partners treat each other as equals, and neither tries to force their will on the other.

Samantha and Laura

Samantha and Laura had been together for years, but they were on the verge of breaking up when I met them for couple's counseling. The problem was that Laura had a friend whom Samantha disliked intensely. Samantha firmly believed that Laura's friend was a bad influence on Laura, and wanted to undermine their relationship. When Laura visited her friend she usually drank a lot, and Laura would come home late at night intoxicated. Every time this happened, Samantha and Laura got into a shouting match. Samantha blamed Laura's friend for their fights, and believed she deliberately tried to cause problems between Samantha and Laura.

For example, if Laura promised Samantha that she would be home by midnight, Laura's friend would try to get Laura to stay later, knowing that it would provoke an argument between the couple.

Samantha tried everything she could think of to get Laura to stop seeing her friend. She reasoned, shouted, pleaded, and finally threatened to break up. Nevertheless, Laura was determined to keep seeing her friend. Laura admitted that her friend was a bad influence, but she wouldn't let Samantha say who she could and couldn't go out with. Unable to resolve the issue, Samantha and Laura seriously considered ending their relationship.

Through counseling, Samantha stopped pushing Laura on the issue, and she stopped trying to control Laura. She told Laura, "It hurts me that you continue to go out with your friend. I think she likes to cause problems between us. When you go out with her, I feel like you're choosing her over us. But I'm not going to ask you to stop seeing your friend. You have the right to see anyone you want. I don't like her, but you have the right to decide whether to continue your friendship with her. I just wanted you to know how I feel." After Samantha told Laura that she would respect her decision about her friend, the power struggle stopped. Laura no longer felt controlled, and both were free to focus on the things that they valued in their own relationship. About two weeks later, Laura surprised us all by announcing that she had stopped seeing her friend because she was a negative influence on her. Samantha was as surprised as anyone.

Gamblin' Joe

Joe loved to gamble. In fact, Joe gambled on anything and everything, no matter what the odds. Problem was, Joe was the worst gambler ever, and he was always broke. Though he was penniless, Joe fell in love a beautiful young woman named Naomi and asked her to marry him. Naomi loved Joe as much as he loved her, but being a sensible woman she was worried about his gambling. Joe promised to stop gambling once they were married, and after that Naomi agreed to marry him. I met Joe some thirty years later, and he told me the following story:

"I broke my promise twice in all the years we've been married. The first time, I lost most of my money, but Naomi didn't say a word about it. A few months later, I got the urge again. This time, I drove to Las Vegas after work without even telling Naomi. I gambled all night until I lost every dollar of my paycheck. There was nothing to do after that but go home and face Naomi. When I got home the next morning I expected the worst. I'd broken my promise, stayed out all night, and lost my whole paycheck. I walked in the house expecting her to be mad. Who wouldn't be, after what I did? But she just smiled at me and said, "You must be hungry, sit down and I'll fix you some breakfast." I couldn't believe it! I sat at the kitchen table while she made bacon and eggs, coffee, the biggest breakfast ever. She didn't say one word about me being gone all night, the money, or anything. I sure didn't bring it up! After all these years, she's still never said a word about it. Joe smiled as he thought back over the years and said, "I've never gambled since."

| The Lonely Sailor |

In his book *Thunder Below*, Admiral Eugene Fluckey tells a story about his life as a young naval officer in Panama during World War II. One of his duties in 1942 was to censor the mail of sailors stationed at the Coco Solo Submarine base. This was a dull and time-consuming job, but one day an interesting letter caught his eye. A sailor wrote to his wife that he had not left the base on liberty since the war began. He was so desperate for a woman that he could not trust himself to be faithful off the base, but abstinence was driving him crazy. He just *had* to have a woman, but he could not do such a terrible thing without her permission. Would she think it over - and give him her answer quickly?

Two weeks later her answer arrived. She told her husband that she loved him, and the letter had brought tears to her eyes. She wished they could be together, but she never wanted him to change. Permission was granted to be with another woman, provided that he didn't 1) fall in love with her, 2) bring home something that he didn't go away with, or 3) pay too much for it. Admiral Fluckey noted that the sailor never left the base.

In sharing the stories of Samantha, Joe, and the lonely sailor I am not suggesting that you should become passive in your relationships. To the contrary, you must be free to state how you feel, and free to bring up problems with your partner. Nor am I condoning alcohol abuse, reckless gambling, or infidelity - there are some behaviors that no partner should be expected to tolerate in a relationship. I *am* suggesting that forcing your will on your partner thwarts problem solving and creates resentment, while accepting your partner as your equal, as a person whom you have no right to control, makes problem solving easier and brings you closer. Mutual respect aids problem solving. Controlling behavior builds a wall between you and your partner that blocks problem solving and prevents you from getting back to the "OK" zone, as diagramed below.

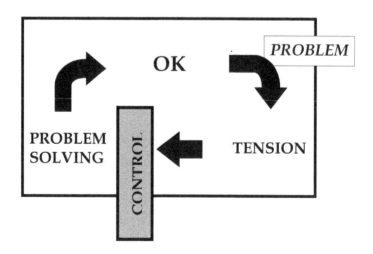

Change Your Belief System

If you want to stop future acts of verbal or physical abuse, you must make changes in the way you think, particularly about responsibility, violence, and control. The chart below shows a new belief system to activate when you are in your next argument:

- *Responsibility:* *I am responsible for everything I say and do.*
- *Comfort with Violence (It's NOT OK):* *Verbal and physical abuse is wrong. It is never OK, and never justified.*
- *Power and Control:* *My partner is my equal. I choose to stay or to leave the relationship, but I never have the right to force my will on my partner.*

HOMEWORK ASSIGNMENT
CHAPTER 6

To complete this homework assignment, think about an act of verbal or physical abuse you committed toward your partner. Answer the following questions about your frame of mind *at the moment of abuse*. Next, answer the same questions according to the way you see things now.

At the moment of abuse:

1. Who did you blame for what you were about to say or do?

2. How did you convince yourself that the verbal or physical abuse was OK? Did you minimize it, or call the abuse something else?

3. What power and control issues were you experiencing at the time? Did you convince yourself that you had a right to force your will on your partner, or to punish him or her for doing something you did not like?

The way you think now:

1. Who do you think was responsible for what you said and did? Why is that person responsible?

2. Do you still think your behavior was OK? Why or why not?

3. Do you treat your partner as your equal, or are there still power and control issues to work on?

Chapter 7
Automatic Thoughts, Core Beliefs, and Self-Talk

Key Concepts: Whenever you find yourself instantly angry and aggressive, core beliefs and automatic thoughts are at work. By recognizing your warning signs, giving yourself time to think before reacting, and using self-talk you can gain control over your emotional life.

Skill Building: Think clearly and rationally when you feel angry. Make it a habit to think before you act, and use self-talk to keep your emotional balance. Become aware of your core beliefs about anger and violence, and make sure they are rational.

Dave was a rocket. Some people are volcanoes – their anger builds slowly over time until they explode – but Dave was a classic rocket. His anger could soar to explosive levels in a heartbeat. Right now he had a puzzled expression on his face. "Dr. Adams," he said, "I understand everything you're saying. You're saying that anger isn't caused by the situation I am in, but by the way I think about it. That makes sense to me. But sometimes I get mad really fast, before I've had time to think anything at all. Like, someone says something and BOOM! . . . I'm mad! How can I get mad before I have time to think anything?" The other guys in the group looked at me and nodded. They were thinking the same thing as Dave. Sometimes anger comes up so quickly that it seems like there is no time to think. Anger materializes so fast it seems like an unthinking reaction, the way a person's foot jerks when a doctor taps his knee with a hammer. Can anger come before the thought? How can thoughts cause anger in situations like these? How can we get angry before we have time to think?

To answer this question, let me tell you a story about Brenda, a former client of mine. Like Dave, Brenda was an emotional rocket. One day, as she was leaving a department store, she heard her sister shout an insult to a man walking behind them. Brenda didn't see what the dispute was about, but the man must have thought Brenda had insulted him because he grabbed her by the arm. Enraged, Brenda reacted instantly and without thinking. She turned and punched the man in the face several times. Brenda told us it was self-defense. I might have believed her if she hadn't stopped "defending herself" long enough to hand her daughter to her sister so she could use both hands punch the guy. A security guard tried to pull Brenda away from the man, but she went after him too! If Brenda was really defending herself, as she claimed, she would have welcomed the security guard rather than beating the crap out of him. The police arrived, and Brenda gave them all they could handle before they were able to restrain and arrest her.

Brenda told me that she did not remember thinking *anything* when the man grabbed her arm. She got mad immediately – she didn't have time to think. She just reacted. The guy grabbed her arm and BOOM! . . . She was fighting mad. Did Brenda's thoughts play a role in this situation?

To answer this question, it helps to understand the concepts of *core beliefs* and *automatic thoughts*. Core beliefs are the basic attitudes, beliefs, and values that we develop throughout our lives. Core beliefs are formed early in life and continue to evolve over the years. They are shaped by our life experiences, the beliefs of others, and the way we see other people act in certain types of situations. They influence the way we think about everything, from our Big Picture of Life to the daily situations we have to deal with. *Am I good or bad? Can I trust people? Will they hurt me if given the chance? Is my world a safe or a dangerous place? Is anger good or bad? What types of things should I get angry about? Is it OK to get verbally abusive when I'm mad? Is violence OK? If I do get abusive, who is to blame? Can I make people do what I want? Should I?* Core beliefs determine how you answer these questions and countless more like them.

Let's return to Brenda. Remember, she became angry and aggressive very quickly when a man grabbed her arm. To understand her emotional and behavioral reaction, we need to understand her core beliefs. There was a time, as a little girl, when Brenda would not have known how to act if a stranger grabbed her arm. As a young girl she would have wondered, *should I be scared and cry and call for help? Should I ask the man what he wants? Should I tell him to let go? Run away? Fight?* She would not have known what to do without core beliefs to draw on. She would have had to think about it first. As Brenda grew older, she built a set of core beliefs, or rules to live by. She watched the way others handled similar situations, and listened to the advice of people who seemed to know more than she did. She experimented with different behaviors in a variety of life experiences to see what worked best for her, and developed beliefs about life based on her experiences. As the years passed Brenda's core beliefs took shape:

- *The world is dangerous.*
- *People are treacherous - you can't trust anyone.*
- *Strangers will hurt me if they get a chance.*
- *Anger makes me strong - fear makes me weak.*
- *I want to be angry and strong.*
- *When in doubt about a person's intent, assume they mean to harm.*
- *The best policy is to "do unto others" first, before they do it to me.*

Core Beliefs Create Automatic Thoughts

Brenda did not have to think when the man grabbed her arm - she had already done her thinking. She did her thinking years ago when she formed her core beliefs, before she ever met the man who now held her by the arm. Now her core beliefs told her what to feel and do, and they gave rise to her *automatic thoughts* - thoughts based upon the core beliefs she formed long ago, rather than upon a time-consuming analysis of the situation that was now happening to her. Automatic thoughts come instantly, and can generate instant anger and aggression. In contrast, thoughts based on our analysis of a situation *(analytic thoughts)* take much longer. Analytic thoughts require us to gather the facts about a situation and make some conclusions, and that takes time. Whenever you find yourself *instantly* angry and aggressive, core beliefs and automatic thoughts are at work. Before going further, make sure you understand the concepts of core beliefs and automatic thoughts, and become familiar with the definitions below.

Core Beliefs
: *Core beliefs are fundamental beliefs about ourselves, other people, and the world we live in. Everyone has them. They evolve during our childhood as we strive to understand the world, and continue to evolve throughout our lives. Core beliefs stem from our own life experiences, trial and error, and the things we see others say and do. They strongly affect the way we perceive and think about our experiences. Because core beliefs are formed early in life, they are often steeped in child-like thinking, and they may or may not be true. Harmful and irrational core beliefs are the source of a lot of misery in the world, and it is important to question our beliefs to make sure they are healthy, rational, and balanced.*

Adolescent Thinking
: *Adolescent thinking lacks the insight, understanding, and maturity that comes with greater life experience. For example, adolescent thinking usually ignores long-term consequences, favors immediate gratification over long-term goals, and overvalues anger and aggression as a way to solve problems. Decisions based on adolescent thinking put personal wants and needs above the best interests of the family.*

Automatic Thoughts
: *When an event activates a core belief, automatic thoughts flow spontaneously, as though by reflex. Core beliefs underlie all automatic thoughts. Sometimes we experience automatic thoughts as broken phrases, images, or vague impressions rather than complete sentences. In many cases, the automatic thoughts come from beliefs developed years earlier. For example, suppose Bob developed a core belief in his childhood that spiders are extremely dangerous. Years later as an adult, he sees a large spider on his arm. Bob immediately becomes a blur of activity! He experiences anxiety, jumps around and shouts, and frantically brushes the spider off. Core beliefs and automatic thoughts were at work. Bob did not have to analyze the situation - he did his thinking about spiders as a child, and he decided they were bad. Seeing the spider activated his core belief (spiders bite), and automatic thoughts told him what to feel (be afraid), and what to do (get it off fast).*

Analytic Thoughts
: *Unlike automatic thoughts, analytic thoughts emerge when we take time to consider all the facts about a situation, and think about the best way to handle it. When we pay attention to the long-term consequences of our choices, consider what is best for ourselves and those we love, and keep important relationship goals in mind, we are engaged in analytic thinking. It is thinking grounded in logic and good sense rather than emotional impulse. Analytic thinking is the opposite of adolescent thinking.*

In the case of anger, core beliefs are like beehives – beehives that are peaceful until stirred up by an activating event. When a negative event activates a core belief automatic negative thoughts (ANTS) stream from it like angry bees, instantly causing a storm of negative emotion, as in the following sequence of events:

CORE BELIEFS →	ACTIVATING EVENT →	AUTOMATIC NEGATIVE THOUGHTS (ANTS) →	NEGATIVE EMOTIONS
A real man never gets pushed around. →	Someone carelessly cuts me off on the freeway. →	That SOB is trying to push me around! He doesn't respect me – this is awful! →	Anger Fury Outrage

When ANTS swarm unchecked for a long time, a negative feedback loop develops. In negative feedback loops, negative thoughts cause negative mood, and negative mood leads to more dark thoughts and an even blacker mood. Over time, an emotional storm grows into an emotional hurricane.

Core beliefs that make sense at one time in our life may not make sense later on. Remember Brenda? Her core beliefs got her into trouble as an adult, but there was a time in her life when these same core beliefs kept her safe. Brenda grew up in a gang-infested neighborhood where violence was commonplace, and domestic violence was a frequent occurrence in her home. In the world of her youth, her tendency to mistrust and assume the worst of others was based in reality. Painful experience taught her that it was foolish to be trusting, and danger was everywhere. Yet the same core beliefs that made sense to Brenda as a child got her into serious trouble as an adult. Her life circumstances changed, but her core beliefs did not. The core beliefs that kept Brenda safe as a child led her to jail as an adult.

Do the beliefs you formed in childhood still make sense? Are you driving the people you love away from you? If so, this is a good time to examine your core beliefs. Beliefs developed with juvenile minds and limited life experience can continue to influence our feelings and behavior after we become adults. Childlike beliefs formed early in life, before we had the capacity to think and reason like an adult, can still affect us. This is especially true of beliefs about responsibility for your behavior, use of violence to solve problems, and the need to control of others. These beliefs are formed in childhood, and beliefs based on childish thinking lead to childish behavior. That's why you often see a grown man acting like a bad-tempered child when he's cut off on the freeway, or a grown woman throw a juvenile temper tantrum over some perceived insult. Think like a child and you'll act like one. That's how Brenda got in trouble.

Changing Your Core Beliefs

If you want to live an abuse-free lifestyle, you will have to understand your core beliefs and make your irrational beliefs more sensible. Core beliefs about anger and violence will change over time as you re-think these beliefs. Reading this book is a step in the right direction. By applying analytical thinking, your beliefs will become less childlike and more mature, and as your beliefs evolve so will the automatic thoughts that flow from them. In time, clients find themselves staying surprisingly calm in situations where they used to get angry. "Wow," their friends say, "you've changed!" They find it easier to stay in the box, and to keep anger levels below the *"I don't care what I say"* line. This is confirmation that core beliefs are changing:

MY CORE BELIEF	→	THE ACTIVATING EVENT	→	AUTOMATIC RATIONAL THOUGHTS	→	MY POSITIVE EMOTIONS
I'm a strong person, and I don't have to prove it.	→	Someone carelessly cuts me off on the freeway.	→	It was probably an accident. I'm not hurt – it's not worth upsetting myself about.	→	Calm Relaxed Self-confident

Making meaningful changes in your core beliefs take time. You can start the change process by: *1) watching your warning signs, and 2) stopping to think before reacting*. Warning signs tell you that your childish core beliefs are activated - you are starting to think and act like a kid. Warning signs are a signal to call time-out. During the time-out period, think about what you are thinking. Are irrational core beliefs active? What automatic thoughts are you experiencing? It is helpful to write them down and keep a log of these thoughts. Challenge irrational beliefs and thoughts while they are fresh in your mind and you are aware of them. Confront your childish core beliefs with adult reasoning, something you were unable to do when you formed them in your childhood or teenage years.

Whenever you feel yourself getting angry, *stop and think* before you say or do anything. By taking the time to think before you react, you minimize the influence of core beliefs and automatic thoughts, and increase your chances of staying in the box. Put your hands in your pockets and think. After all, relational problems are solved with your head, not with your hands. *Think your way through the situation.* By taking time to think rationally, you put the brake on automatic thoughts and give analytic thinking a chance. Marcus, a professional athlete who was in our groups several years ago, said learning to stop and think before reacting was the most important thing he learned in counseling. Marcus was a veteran defensive back in the NFL, and he told the following story:

"All my life I have been trained not to think before I act. Throughout football in high school, college, and the pro's I've been told not to think. You do your thinking during practice, but when the game starts, you have to react without thinking. If you have to think about what to do after the ball is hiked, you've already lost. Do that too many times, and you will be sitting on the bench watching someone else play. I learned that the better I could react to a situation on the field without thinking, the more years I had to play ball."

(That worked great for Marcus on the football field, but not so well at home.)

"One day my wife and I had a fight. She said something I didn't like and I hit her without thinking. I felt awful and ashamed. If I had just taken a few seconds to think I never would have done it. I have talked to other guys who've played in the pros, and they say they've experienced the same thing. The most important thing I have learned in this class is to STOP AND THINK BEFORE I REACT. It has made a big difference in my life."

The diagram below illustrates the important point that Marcus made. Let's say that "S" stands for the situation (usually, something that someone says or does) and "R" represents your response to it. As a professional athlete, Marcus had to get "R" (his response) as close as possible to "S" (the situation unfolding on the field) as shown in Figure 1. That worked fine on the football field, but his goals as a husband and father were different. At home, he wanted to *increase* the time between the situation he faced and his reaction to it, as shown in Figure 2.

Figure 1
(Less time between the situation and your response)

Figure 2
(More time between the situation and your response)

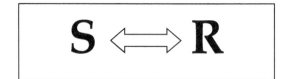

By giving himself time to think before he reacted, Marcus was actually taking time to reduce reliance on his automatic thoughts and increase the role of analytic thoughts in his decision-making.

Self-Talk

Self-talk is an indispensable tool that our clients use to stay in the box. Our clients consistently rate self-talk as one of the most important skills they take from their counseling experience. Self-talk thoughts more rational and keeps anger below "I don't care what I say" and "I don't care what I do" lines. It reduces anger during time-out periods, and increases analytic thinking when deciding how to handle a bad situation. Self-talk helps you take charge of your thoughts. Rather than allowing automatic thoughts to run through your mind unchecked and unchallenged, you use self-talk to think sensibly and rationally about the situation you're in, and to thoughtfully consider the best way to react. The better you become at self-talk, the more control you will have over your own emotional life.

Some people argue that they can't help the way they feel. They point to the selfish, unfair, or provoking behavior of others and say they cannot help getting angry and aggressive. They believe that their anger and abuse is beyond their control. If you believe that, you're fooling yourself. While it is true that many things influence your emotions, they are never totally beyond your control. As long as you have the power to think in a sensible and rational way, you have tremendous influence over your feelings. Victor Frankl's book *Man's Search for Meaning* (1946) spoke to this issue. Frankl was a survivor of a Nazi concentration camp during the Holocaust. Out of that horrendous experience, he found that our greatest freedom, the one freedom that can never be taken away, is the freedom to choose our attitude about every situation we encounter.

Learn to think calmly and rationally and you will gain control over your anger outbursts. Remember that feelings are caused by what goes on between your ears, not what goes on around you. Stop trying to control what others say and do, and start taking charge of what is going on in your own head. When core beliefs and automatic thoughts start to conjure up anger and anger-laden impulses, use self-talk to regain your emotional balance, reduce anger to manageable levels, and stay in The Box. That is how you stop hurting the people who love you.

Before going any further, let me clear up some common misconceptions about anger. First of all, it is not my goal to teach you how to avoid the feeling of anger. Anger is not a bad thing; it is just a feeling, and feelings by themselves are not dangerous. They are an important part of life. Even unpleasant feelings like sadness and anger add color and richness to our lives, and they are often an important source of information about our relationships. You will always experience bouts of anger, and that is as it should be. When you have been unfairly treated, when your partner callously hurts you, when people deliberately try to harm the people you love, you are going to get angry. There are times when you *should* get angry. The goal is not to stuff or avoid anger, but to manage it appropriately, to handle your anger in a way that makes the situation better rather than worse.

Another misconception is that people often confuse self-talk with *happy thoughts* (Gee whiz, isn't it a pretty day!), *self-affirmations* (Every day in every way, I'm better and better!), and *positive thinking* (Gosh it hurts being shot in the leg, but at least the bullet missed my vital organs!). I've nothing against it, but it's not self-talk. Self-talk is rational, logical, and most of all, *honest*. Self-talk only works if you believe the things you say to yourself are true. In other words, telling yourself that you are happy when you are mad really will not help. If you *know* it isn't so, you won't believe it. Self-talk is dealing with life rationally as it is, no better or worse:

I'm angry, but I don't want to make things worse. Yelling and shouting will definitely make things worse. Watch for my warning signs - I'll call a time-out if I see them. Stay in the box and attack the problem, not my partner. I love my family, so keep the Big Picture in mind, and don't say things I will regret later. Don't blow things out of proportion. Just focus on the problem and use the skills I've learned to get back to the OK Zone. I can handle this – just stop and think before I say anything. My partner is my ally, not my adversary. The game is on, and we will win or lose as a team.

That is how self-talk works. It will not make anger disappear, but it will keep you in the box. Self-talk is your defense against impulsive verbal or physical abuse. It keeps your anger in check and keeps you thinking. There is nothing wrong with anger, but anger should never run the show. Anger, unrestrained by sensible thought, can destroy everything. Anger-laden impulses only care about immediate gratification, not about long-term consequences or who gets hurt. That is why you should never stop reasoning with yourself when you are angry. Self-talk keeps anger at manageable levels, and keeps your behavior sensible. The story below is an example of how lives can be ruined when reason stops and blind rage takes over.

Rage Visits the Elderly Man

An elderly man entered our program after his release from prison. He was required to participate in domestic violence counseling as a condition of his parole. As is the custom of our program, new members tell their story in their first counseling session. Before the incident, he told us, he was a happy man. He owned his own business and was a prominent member of his community and his church. He was married and had one child, a son of whom he was very proud.

His domestic violence incident started, he told us, with a verbal dispute between him and his 25 year-old son. The fight grew more intense, and they quickly crossed the "I don't care what I say" line and got out of the box. Both of them said disrespectful things. The son became more and more disrespectful to the father, and in turn, the father's insults to his son became more cutting. In a fit of anger, they tried to inflict the deepest possible wounds. The father ordered his son to leave the house, but the son only grew more belligerent. Anger swelled to rage. They started physically threatening each other. Enraged that his son disrespected him, the father went to his bedroom and returned with a handgun. Storming back to confront his son, the father brandished the pistol and ordered his son out of the house, threatening to kill him if he didn't get out! Rather than leave, the son took a step towards his father, and the father shot him. Paramedics arrived quickly, but his son was dead.

The old man wept openly as he told his story, and the rest of us were silent. He stopped to compose himself, and then continued. He said that his life would never be the same, and he often wished that it would end. He wished that he was dead. A day never went by that he did not think about his son, and he felt only contempt for himself. Many years had passed since the murder, but even now he could scarcely believe that he had killed his only son. His life was an unending nightmare he lived every day. He wept again, haunted by the memory of that night. After a long pause he spoke again. When his wife looks at him, he sees loathing in her eyes. He is the man who shot her boy. She lives with him, but their marriage is over. He used to attend church regularly, but not now. He can't look the priest in the eyes. His son was married at the time of his death and his young wife was pregnant, but the man has never had more than a passing glimpse of his grandson. The daughter-in-law has not spoken to the old man since the killing, and she will not allow the grandson to visit him. After all, he will always be the man who killed the young boy's father. The elderly man sobbed and asked, *"What kind of man am I? What kind of man can kill his own son?"* The men in the group looked away.

This story is true. It's sad, but it isn't unique. Tragedies like this happen every day. How does a man kill his own son? It happened because reason stopped and blind rage took over. It started with the father's core beliefs. He came from a very traditional culture where the father of the family held absolute power. His own father and his grandfather were very authoritarian, and a core belief he developed as a child was that *a real man demands unquestioning respect and total obedience* from his wife and children. When the son fought with him and disobeyed his orders, this core belief was activated. Automatic thoughts relentlessly followed: *"I am not a man,"* he thought, *"if I allow my son to disrespect me in my own home! My son is disrespecting me - I must make him stop or I am not a man! I have to stop him."*

These automatic thoughts were present throughout the fight, causing his anger to swell past the *I don't care what I say* line, beyond the *I don't care what I do* line, and into depths of blind rage. Riding a cresting wave of anger, he did not stop to consider the consequences of his behavior. He was brimming with rage and beyond rational thought when he pulled the trigger. The sound of the gunshot brought him back. He said the sound of the shot woke him up, and he came suddenly to the awful realization of what he had done. His son was dead. He had killed him.

When anger becomes so intense that we start to act without the constraint of reason, we are in very dangerous territory. How different this story would be if the man had stopped to think and talk sensibly to himself. Suppose he stopped and said to himself:

Stop and think! What am I doing? My son has spoken disrespectfully to me, but he hasn't done anything bad enough to die for! My son is young and, in some ways, very immature. I need to be patient with him. He's a good son. Someday he will be embarrassed by the way he is acting here tonight. And what might happen if I threaten him with a gun? Remember that he's my son and I love him. I won't become less of a man because he says things that are disrespectful. I only become less of a man by disrespecting myself or others. My manhood does not depend upon what other people say or do, but upon what I do. Consider the consequences of my actions. Self-respect comes from living my life with honor and making wise decisions, not from harming those who behave childishly. Nothing good can come from threatening my son's life.

Had he stopped to think, his life and the lives of his family would have been very different. He could have stopped to think, but he didn't. When he stopped reasoning with himself, he surrendered to his blind rage, and his son paid the price with his life. Perhaps he never dreamed that he was capable of doing such a thing, but he was wrong. His son is dead. There is a lesson to here for all of us, a lesson that his son will never get a chance to learn. Self-control comes from your dogged determination to stop, think, and keep reasoning with yourself. Never stop thinking when you are angry. The next time you get mad, what will you do?

HOMEWORK ASSIGNMENT
CHAPTER 7

This assignment will help you use "self-talk" to think rationally when problems come up between you and your partner. Write *situation, automatic thoughts, and self-talk* on a piece of paper, like the example below.

SITUATION	Automatic Thoughts (ANGER)	SELF-TALK

Your job is to find everyday situations in which you feel angry. In the "Situation" column, describe what was going on. Who were you with? What was going on between you and the other person? In the "Automatic Thoughts" column, write down the thoughts you had just before and during the feeling of anger. In the "Self-Talk" column, record your rational, common-sense responses to the automatic thoughts. Self-talk will help you feel calmer and less angry.

This exercise may be difficult at first, but it gets easier with practice. Describing the situation is usually easy. Identifying the automatic thoughts behind your anger takes a little more work, but it is worth the effort. By identifying these automatic thoughts, you will eventually understand the core beliefs that drive them. Recording your self-talk is also important. Everyone is different, and it's necessary to know the self-talk that is effective for you in reducing your anger. To help you in this exercise, I have included homework assignments from past clients as examples for you to follow. The first example is from Elliot. He described the situation, the automatic thoughts that made him mad, and the self-talk that reduced his anger.

SITUATION	Automatic Thoughts (ANGER)	SELF-TALK
Another driver cut me off on the freeway, causing me to slam on my brakes.	He did that deliberately! He doesn't care if he kills me! He's taking advantage of me! I'm not going to let that jerk get away with that! I'll teach him!	Calm down. This isn't a big deal. It wasn't personal, so don't take it personally. He just didn't see me. Everyone makes mistakes. I've done things like that before. No one was hurt, so let it go.

Here is another example from Rebecca's homework. Rebecca and her boyfriend had a high comfort level with verbal abuse before she started counseling, and she's trying to change that. She is taking a leadership role in stopping the verbal abuse, and leading by example. Rebecca was proud of the way she handled this incident. Because of her determination to apply the concepts she had learned, she and her boyfriend were able to solve the problem rather than fight about it. Rebecca did a good job of recognizing her warning signs and using self-talk. Although her self-talk did not eliminate all of her anger, she did reduce it below the *"I don't care what I say"* line, allowing her to stay in The Box. Secondly, Rebecca kept her focus on the problem. Third, she did a good job of getting out of the "you mode." A person is in the "you mode" when they jab their finger in their partner's face, and start every sentence with YOU . . . YOU . . . YOU! Problems cannot be solved in the "you mode."

SITUATION	Automatic Thoughts (ANGER)	SELF-TALK
We didn't have enough money to pay the rent, and my boyfriend was blaming me for our financial problems. I got mad and saw my warning signs.	This isn't fair! Who the hell are *you* to criticize me? *You're* the one who can't get a decent job! You're nothing but an ass-hole! You don't appreciate anything I do. You're asking for it! You're pushing my buttons! This whole thing is *your* fault!	I see my warning signs – I'm "in his face," I'm starting to yell, and I want to hit him. Calm down. In group they say the best way to deal with criticism is to find something in the criticism to agree with. Is there some truth to what he's saying? I'm not the only one to blame, but I'm partly to blame for this problem and I'll take responsibility that. I don't want to win a fight. I want to solve this problem. He's scared because we're in trouble and he doesn't know what to do. I'm scared too. I'll tell him how I feel, but don't yell or say hurtful stuff. What can I do to show leadership – to help solve the problem?

Elliot and Rebecca's homework assignments gave them insight into their core beliefs about anger and aggression. When he looked over his homework assignment, Elliot discovered a core belief of his: *"When something bad happens, it is always deliberate and directed at me personally. People always try to take advantage of me. I have to get angry and aggressive or they will walk all over me."* These core beliefs kept Elliot stressed and on edge, and caused him a lot of trouble over his lifetime.

Elliot modified his core beliefs and made them more realistic: *When something bad happens, it doesn't always mean that someone did it deliberately or that it was directed at me personally. Sometimes it's just an accident, and it doesn't always mean that someone is trying to take advantage of me. Everyone is not a threat to me, or trying to take advantage of me, and I don't have to get angry and aggressive every time something goes wrong.*

Rebecca also identified the core beliefs behind her automatic thoughts: *It's awful and terrible when someone criticizes me. No one should ever criticize me. When they do, I have to get angry and aggressive and blame them back. Accepting criticism is a sign of weakness. If they push my buttons I should hurt them to teach them a lesson and make them leave me alone.*

She worked to make her core beliefs more rational: *It's uncomfortable to be criticized, but it's not awful. There's usually some truth behind criticism. Accepting criticism isn't a sign of weakness. If handled the right way it can be an opportunity to show leadership, grow as a person, and solve a problem that threatens my relationship. A strong person can even invite constructive criticism. I don't have to get angry and aggressive, and hurting my boyfriend only makes things worse. If I set an example by accepting criticism, my boyfriend will be more likely to do the same.*

When people identify problem core beliefs and make them more sensible, they experience big changes in their feelings and behavior. Everyone benefits.

Homework Summary

Step one: Every day for the next week find situations in which you feel anger or some variation of anger (frustration, irritation, jealousy, etc.). Describe the situation you were in, the automatic thoughts that were behind the anger, and the self-talk you used to reduce your anger. Write your thoughts down on a paper like the one below:

SITUATION	Automatic Thoughts (ANGER)	SELF-TALK

Step Two: After you have collected several situations on your paper, look them over. Are there any similarities among the types of situations? For example, are they situations where you think people are trying to take advantage of you, like Elliot, or where you think people are blaming you, like Rebecca? Next, read your automatic thoughts. What are the core beliefs behind the thoughts? Record your core beliefs in a box like the one below:

Core Beliefs:

[   ]

Step Three: After you have identified some of your core beliefs, evaluate each belief for accuracy.

- *Is the belief logical and realistic?*
- *Is this a belief or a fact?*
- *How does this belief make me feel?*
- *How does this belief affect me and the people I care about?*
- *What is the evidence for and against the belief?*
- *Are there situations in which the belief might not be true?*
- *Can I modify the belief to make it more accurate and rational?*

Write down any changes to your core beliefs in the box below:

Modified Core Beliefs:

[   ]

Take your time with this homework assignment. Developing the skill of self-talk, identifying core beliefs associated with anger and aggression, and modifying problem beliefs are important steps in maintaining an abuse-free lifestyle. They can change your life.

Chapter 8
Skill Building

Key Concepts: Reaching your goal of an abuse-free lifestyle requires both knowledge and practice. This chapter helps consolidate the material in the last three chapters and apply the concepts and skills in your relationships. Apply the skills and concepts in your daily life daily until they become second nature to you. It's what you do, not what you know, that gets results.

Skill Building: Complete the following quiz to test your knowledge and review the skills and concepts discussed in the last three chapters. Also, provide a detailed example of applying what you have learned to make better choices in your relationships.

The last three chapters introduced you to important skills and concepts. You learned that thoughts cause your feelings, and that if you think like an abuser you will act like one. You know that thinking in rational and sensible ways will help you take control of your emotional life. You are now familiar with the "cognitive set" of an abuser, and the role that core beliefs play in your automatic thoughts, feelings, and behavior. The short quiz below will evaluate your knowledge in these areas. If you have a trouble with any of the questions, go back and review the concepts that you're struggling with.

You will also find a new *Skill Building Log* to help you apply the concepts from the last three chapters to real-life situations. Once again, I cannot overstate the importance of practicing your skills. Knowledge of the concepts and skills in this book is important, but the ability to apply them in your relationships requires constant effort and practice. It's not just what you know, but what you do that matters. Lastly, the *Personal Progress and Self-Evaluation* form will help you evaluate the progress you have made so far and set goals for personal growth.

When you are ready, take the quiz and check your answers in the appendix. If any of the questions give you trouble, read those sections again. Stick with it until you have a solid understanding of the concepts in Chapters 5-7.

Quiz
Chapters 5-7

1. Anger is not caused by what others say and do. Rather, the way you _____ about what others say and do determines whether or not you get angry, and how angry you get. *(Chapter 5)*

2. You should never get angry.   True   False   *(Chapter 5)*

3. Anytime you think you should abuse a family member, your thinking is _____. *(Chapter 5)*

4. You have the freedom to choose to think in ways that escalate feelings of anger, or to think in ways that _____ it. *(Chapter 5)*

5. Abusive behavior is always a personal _____. *(Chapter 6)*

6. Just as your thoughts determine how you feel, your thoughts also determine how you _____ when you are angry. *(Chapter 6)*

7. At the moment of abuse, people think the same way about _____, _____, and _____. *(Chapter 6)*

8. The first step toward turning yourself into an abuser is to deny personal _____ for your abusive behavior. *(Chapter 6)*

9. Another step toward abuse and violence is to convince yourself that you are the boss, that you have the right to _____ your partner. *(Chapter 6)*

10. Whenever you find yourself instantly angry and aggressive, core _____ are at work. *(Chapter 7)*

11. Thoughts that flow automatically and without effort from your basic core beliefs are called _____. These thoughts come instantly when the core beliefs are activated. *(Chapter 7)*

12. By applying rational adult _____, your beliefs will become less child-like and more mature. *(Chapter 7)*

13. By taking time to stop and _____ before you react, you minimize the power of core beliefs and increase your chances of staying in The Box. *(Chapter 7)*

14. Self - _____ is an important tool used by clients in our program to challenge core beliefs, stay in the box, and keep anger below the "I don't care what I say" and the "I don't care what I do" lines. It lowers anger levels during time-out periods, and to increases analytic thinking when deciding how to react to a bad situation. It is the act of taking charge of your thoughts. *(Chapter 7)*

15. You should never stop _____ when you're angry. *(Chapter 7)*

Skill Building Log

Step 1: Select one or more skills from the list below that you want to practice. Selecting the right skills to practice is easy. Just answer this sentence: *"It would help me and my family the most if I would _____."*

Step 2: On a separate sheet of paper, write a detailed example of how you put the skills to use. Describe (1) who you were with, (2) the problem you struggled with, (3) any of your warning signs that came up, (4) the skills you used to handle the problem, (5) how things turned out.

TOOLBOX FOR CHAPTER EIGHT

Tools from Chapters 1-3:
- Memorize The Box
- Use The Box to guide my decision making
- Stay focused on problem-solving during an argument
- Learn and memorize my warning signs
- Recognize my warning signs when I start to feel angry
- Take a time-out
- Memorize the rules to the time-out procedure
- Explain time-out to my partner
- Never cross the "I don't care what I say line"
- Never cross the "I don't care what I do line"
- Stop using any form of verbal abuse
- Recognize and avoid denial, blame, and minimizing

Tools from Chapters 5-7:
- Whenever I feel angry toward my partner, stop and ask myself, *"Is my thinking rational? Am I making a big deal out of a small problem?"*
- Whenever I feel angry remind myself that I can choose to think in ways that escalate these negative feelings, or I can choose to think in ways that reduce them.
- Accept responsibility for everything I say and do.
- Lower my comfort level with violence. Don't minimize, call abuse something other than what it really is, or tell myself that such behavior is OK.
- Don't try to be my partner's boss or force my will on him or her. See my partner as my equal.
- Stop and think *before* I react.
- Is my partner being malicious? Will getting angry help solve the problem?
- Never "Awfulize."
- Stay out of the *"YOU MODE."*
- Use self-talk to reduce and prevent anger.
- Identify my core beliefs about anger and aggression

PERSONAL PROGRESS AND SELF-EVALUATION

1. Evaluate the progress that you have made so far in your counseling. Are you satisfied with the progress you are making? Are you putting forth your best effort? Is there anything you need to do to make your counseling experience more successful?

2. Select a relationship that is important to you. What can you do to make the relationship better? Set a specific goal for improving yourself. What do you want to accomplish over the next month?

3. Have you seen changes in your thinking or behavior since starting this program? If so, provide an example of how your thinking and behavior have changed.

4. Are there skills from your counseling that you use on a daily basis? If so, what are they? Give a recent example of using them. If you are not using the skills you have learned on a daily basis, why not?

5. Select a skill or concept from the book that is important for you to use. What skill did you select? How can using that skill benefit you and the people who love you?

Chapter 9
Solve Your Problems
(And Stop Fighting About Them)

Key Concepts: When partners respect each other and work together as a team they can solve almost any problem. However, blaming, controlling and hurtful behaviors block problem solving. These behaviors cause fights, build walls between partners, and make it almost impossible to resolve their differences.

Skill Building: Create a relationship that is conducive to problem solving. Put an end to your blame, control, and hurtful behaviors. Watch the way people react to you, and ask your partner to tell you when you are blaming, controlling, or hurtful.

This chapter, and the three chapters that follow, will provide you with the concepts and skills needed to solve problems successfully. One of the cornerstones of *The Choices Program* is helping you become a skilled problem solver. To understand why problem solving skills are so important, let's revisit *The Box* and some of the concepts you learned in Chapter One. Life is good until a problem comes up that shakes you and your partner out of the safety and comfort of the *"OK"* zone. The problem gives rise to *"Tension"* in the form of annoyance, resentment, anger, jealousy, or similar feelings, which grow and linger until you and your partner solve the problem. Solve the problem successfully, and you return to the *"OK"* zone. Fail to solve the problem and the tension will intensify and threaten to push you and your partner out of The Box, as illustrated below.

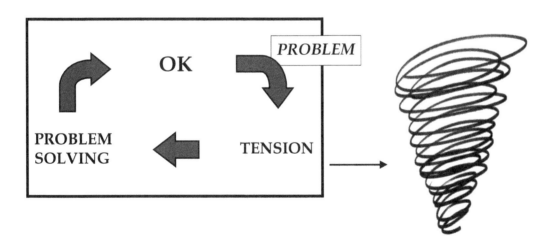

TENSION GROWS UNTIL
THE PROBLEM SOLVED

Some people are natural problem solvers. They resolve their relationship problems quickly and with minimal tension. But many people find problem solving a daunting task. They usually end up outside the box (verbally or physically abusing each other) when a problem comes up. If you're reading this book, this is probably what's been happening in your relationship. In the next few chapters I'll teach you what's been going wrong, and how to fix it. It will take a lot of work on your part, but it is worth it. You will become an intelligent and proficient problem solver, spend more of your time in the comfort of the OK zone, and *never* get out of The Box.

Why Problem Solving Fails

Think about the last time you tried to talk about a problem and ended up in a fight. What happened? Most likely, you opened the door to one of the *Three Bandits*. When the Three Bandits get into a conversation, they rob people of their chance to solve problems. They're known as *Blaming, Bossy, and Hurtful*. (I know this is corny, but it works. Read on.)

Blaming, Bossy and Hurtful — they're the most common hazards to problem solving. They block communication and build walls between partners, making it impossible to solve their problems. They make verbal abuse and domestic violence more likely because they escalate anger, frustration, and defensiveness between you and your partner. Even worse, they have the power to turn the two of you from allies into adversaries. The thing to remember about *Blaming, Bossy and Hurtful* is this: *if you let them into your conversation you're sure to get into a fight*. *Blaming, Bossy and Hurtful* always trigger fights. Whenever you are having a fight with your partner, the chances are that you are coming across as *Blaming, Bossy or Hurtful*. Let's look at how these behaviors block problem solving and cause fights.

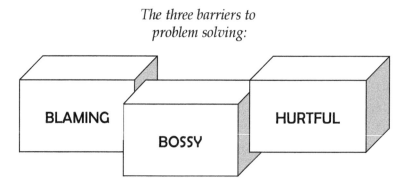

The three barriers to problem solving:

Blaming, Bossy, and Hurtful behaviors build walls between you and your partner and keep you from solving your problems.

Blaming

It's easier to solve problems when you and your partner work together as a team. When you cooperate and work together as allies you can solve almost any problem. Blaming, however, destroys the feeling that you and your partner are on the same team, causing you to become adversaries. Now it's you against your partner, rather than you and your partner working together against the problem. The blamed person feels attacked and defensive, and problem-solving comes to a standstill. Cooperation and teamwork is lost as you and your spouse blame each other for the predicament. That is why you should never blame your spouse for a problem, *even when you think he or she is clearly at fault.* Whether your partner is to blame for the problem or not, the result is always the same - defensiveness and fighting about whom is to blame. Before you say anything about a problem ask yourself, *"Do I want to make my partner acknowledge blame for a problem, or do I want to work together to solve the problem?"*

It's always easier to blame someone for a problem than to solve it. But problems aren't solved by pointing fingers and fixing blame. When you blame someone for a problem, you're asking the wrong question: *"Whose fault is it that we have this problem?"* You should be asking, *"What is the problem that needs to be solved?"* and, *"How can we work together to solve it?"* Good problem solvers don't waste time trying to fix blame. Like a dog chasing its tail, you and your partner will argue endlessly about where blame lies. Even if you do finally agree on who caused the problem, the problem will still be there, unsolved and building tension. It's better to focus on how the two of you can work together to solve the problem, rather than who should be blamed for it. Skip the blame game and you will have fewer arguments (and fights) and solve problems more effectively. In the problem solving steps that come later in this book, the question of blame never comes up. You don't have to fix blame to solve a problem. In fact, problem solving is easier when the issue of blame never comes up. The goal is not to assign blame. The goal is to solve problems and get back to the *OK* zone.

To avoid the blame game, you have to stay out of the *"you mode."* You know what I mean by the "you mode" - just point your finger at someone and shout, YOU, YOU, YOU, YOU! An angry and defensive reaction from the person you're pointing at is almost guaranteed. It quickly turns a loving partner into an angry adversary. It's a terrible way to problem solve.

Bossy

No one likes bossy and controlling people. In previous chapters you learned that abuse-free relationships are based on equality. There are no bosses in egalitarian relationships, and for good reason. Bossy people cultivate adversaries, not teammates. Good problem solvers know better than to come across to their partner as bossy. When you come across as bossy and controlling, your partner will resist what you have to say, even if your solutions make sense. If you find that your partner constantly rejects your solutions to problems, it may be your attempts at control that are being rejected rather than your suggestions themselves. That's why you should never try to force a solution on your partner, no matter how good you think your solution is. Approach your partner as an equal and seek solutions through *communication, negotiation, and compromise.* Allow yourselves to be influenced by each other. It is more important to stay on the same team than to solve a problem. Allies eventually solve their problems peacefully. Adversaries endlessly fight about them. Don't turn your partner into an adversary by being bossy.

A simple experiment illustrates what happens when one person tries to control another. Grab a person (someone you know well) by the wrist and slowly drag them towards you. They'll resist and pull away. Attempts to control others is always met with resistance. It's in our nature to resist bossy people. This is *not* the dynamic that you want to create when you're trying to work with your partner to solve a problem. You want to develop a spirit of friendship, cooperation and teamwork.

Hurtful

Hurtful comments are things said to hurt, offend, or humiliate your partner. They have no place in problem solving, and they should have no place in your relationship. When hurtful things are said anger spirals upward, battle lines are drawn, and the fight is on. Don't say hurtful things, even in retaliation for something said to you. After all, you can't be part of the solution when you are contributing to the problem. If you're looking for a fight and just can't help making irresponsible and hurtful comments, take a time-out and pull yourself together. Until your attitude improves, no one will want to talk to you anyway. To summarize:

- *Choose not to blame, even when your partner is blameworthy.*
- *Choose not to control, even when you are sure what your partner should do.*
- *Choose not to hurt, even when you think your partner deserves it.*

Watch Your Partner's Reaction

Sometimes you may come across to your partner as blaming, controlling, or hurtful when you are not trying to be. Other times, you may not be aware of how blaming, controlling, or hurtful your words really are. *The best way to screen your blaming, bossy, and hurtful behavior is to watch your partner's reaction to what you say.* If your partner responds to your words with anger, defensiveness, and non-cooperation, you're probably coming across as hurting, blaming, or controlling, and you need to change your approach.

It doesn't matter whether you *intend* to be blaming, bossy, or hurtful. The reaction you get from your partner is the same whether you mean to come across that way or not - problem solving comes to an end and the fight is on. Anytime you find yourself in a fight, the odds are good that your partner perceives you as blaming, bossy, or hurtful. The following table is a rough guide to use when you're talking about a problem. It tells you whether you're blaming, controlling, or hurting by watching your partner's reaction to your comments.

When I:	My Partner Feels:	And Reacts By:
Blame	Defensive	Blaming back
Control	Rebellious	Rejecting all my suggestions
Hurt	Angry	Hurting back

The decision not to blame, control, or verbally hurt your partner has nothing to do with who's right and who's wrong. Choose not to engage in blaming, controlling, or hurting behavior because they are harmful to your relationship and block problem solving.

Become a Leader

If you and your partner constantly fight about problems rather than solve them, someone needs to step up and start showing leadership. But let's be clear about what I mean by leadership. Leadership does not mean telling your partner what to do or acting like the boss. Leadership means leading by example. It means putting the welfare of your relationship first. Leadership means showing respect to your partner, handling your anger responsibly, and showing a willingness to look at yourself and make meaningful changes in your own behavior to make your relationship better. It means handling problems skillfully and staying in The Box.

You may ask, "But what do I do if my partner blames, bosses, or hurts me? What do I do then?" When that happens, your first impulse will be to blame back, refuse to cooperate, or hurt back. *Don't do it.* Times such as these are opportunities to make the relationship better by exercising skill and leadership. Every time your partner attempts to blame, control, or hurt you, you have a chance to lead your relationship in a better direction by putting your ego aside and responding in a positive and constructive way. Be a leader, not a follower, and choose your response wisely. Choose *not* to retaliate by blaming back, rebelling, or hurting back. These reactions only escalate anger and make problem-solving impossible. As they say, you can't get ahead when you're trying to get even.

Remind yourself that the blaming, controlling, and hurting in your relationship won't stop as long as you're a willing participant in it. It is not that what you are saying is untrue. It's just that this approach is not skillful or effective. It doesn't work well. Instead, think of your partner as your ally rather than an adversary. Be willing to tell your partner how you feel, but speak in a spirit of friendship and listen like a sponge. Stay positive and refuse to engage in destructive behavior. Change has to start somewhere. Rather than showing your willingness to fight, demonstrate your willingness to accept responsibility for your role in things, stay in the box, and cooperate in finding solutions to your problems.

The following table can be used as a guide when you feel blamed, bossed around, or attacked by your partner.

When I Feel	My Attitude Will Be	I Will
BLAMED	I'll listen without getting defensive. I'll keep an open mind and accept responsibility for my role in the problem.	Say how I feel, but I won't play the Blame Game. I'll let my partner know that I'm willing to make reasonable changes in my behavior to help solve the problem.
CONTROLLED	I won't be controlled, but I won't be non-cooperative either. I'm more interested in finding solutions to our problems than rebelling against my partner.	I'll say how I feel about bossy behavior, but I'll also try to understand my partner's concerns and seek solutions through negotiation and compromise.
HURT	I won't return abuse with more abuse. The hurting has to stop somewhere. This is the time to show leadership by example.	I'll tell my partner that I won't be verbally abused. I'll stay focused on the problem. I will let my partner know that I'm willing to listen, and that we need to respect each other to solve the problem.

The first step in effective problem solving is to create an environment that is conducive to solving problems. Learning to discuss problems without blame, control, or hurtful behavior, responding appropriately to your partner's blaming, controlling, and hurtful comments, is a big step in the right direction. As long as destructive behaviors persist in your relationship, you have an environment that is more conducive to fighting than problem solving. You will find that getting back to the *OK* zone is easy once you learn to avoid the barriers to problem solving that blame, bossy, and hurtful behaviors produce. Just remember this: whenever an argument turns into a fight, blaming, bossy and hurtful behaviors are in the room.

As illustrated below, blaming, bossy, and hurtful statements create a wall between you and your partner.

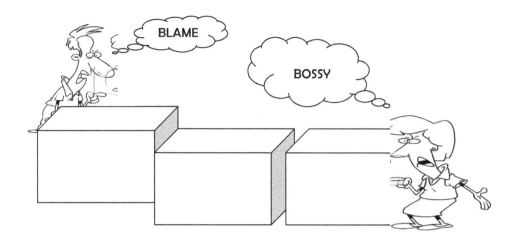

HOMEWORK ASSIGNMENT
CHAPTER 9

Years ago, before these concepts were organized into a book, my clients and I spent a lot of time trying to understand why their problem solving efforts failed. As time passed, we recognized that the failures were nearly always linked to blaming, controlling, or hurtful statements. When they occurred, a fight inevitably started. One brave soul in the group, whom we will call Bill, offered to conduct an experiment. "When I go home tonight," he said, "I'll ask my wife if I ever come across as controlling and see what she says." The group thought that was a good idea, and Bill offered to tell us how the experiment went the following week.

When the group met the following week, we were all curious about Bill's experiment. How did it go? "Well," said Bill, "the first thing I can tell you guys is this: if you don't want to know the answer, DON'T ASK!" Bill went on. "When I asked my wife if I was controlling she rolled her eyes and exclaimed, "All the time! You're ALWAYS trying to tell me what to do!" Bill was surprised, to say the least. "No I don't!" he said defensively. "Oh, yes you do," his wife countered, "and I hate it!"

As the week went on, Bill and his wife talked a lot about his controlling behavior and how it made her feel. To his credit, he eventually accepted her criticism. "She was right," he told us in the group. "I've been pretty bossy to her all these years, and I didn't even realize it. No wonder we fight so much."

We asked him how he was going to stop his controlling behavior, since much of the time he didn't seem to know that he was doing it. "I'll do two things," Bill promised. "First, when we start to get mad and fight, I'll ask myself if I'm trying to solve a problem by telling her what to do. If I'm being bossy, I'll apologize and start over. I'll also ask her to tell me whenever she thinks I am being bossy to her. That way, I'll see my controlling behavior quicker and stop it before we get into a fight." As the weeks came and went, we followed Bill and asked how his "experiment" was going. "Great!" he'd say. "We're actually talking about our problems instead of fighting all the time. I can't believe the difference!" Bill got such good results with his experiment that it became an important part of our counseling program.

Your task this week is to remove blaming, controlling, and hurtful statements from your problem solving strategy. Change has to start somewhere; it might as well start with you. As a first step, ask your partner each of the three following questions

1. *Do I ever boss you around and tell you want to do?*
2. *Do I blame you for our problems?*
3. *Do I ever say things just to hurt you?*

If you're not with your partner anymore, ask the questions to another family member or someone who knows you well. If your partner answers "yes" to any of the questions, follow Bill's example and follow up with the question below:

The next time you feel like I'm being bossy (or blaming or hurtful) will you tell me?

Start recording incidents in which your partner tells you that you're coming across as blaming, controlling, or hurtful. Write down what your partner said to you, how you responded, and how the situation turned out. A chart like the one below can be useful to record these interactions. If a few days go by without anything to record, remind your partner that you need his or her help in order to change.

Did your partner say you were blaming, controlling, or hurtful?	What was your response to your partner? What did you say to your partner after you were told that you were acting in a blaming, controlling, or hurtful way?	How did things turn out? Did you work through the problem? What was the feeling between you and your partner?

Have the courage and humility to follow Bill's example and you'll go a long way towards creating a good problem solving environment. When your partner tells you that you're being controlling, blaming, or hurtful, stop and apologize, then start over. Don't get defensive. Instead, thank your partner for helping you. You'll soon find that you are working together and solving your problems rather than fighting about them.

Chapter 10
The Problem Solving Steps

Key Concepts: Problem solving is the only way to remove tension between you and your partner and get back to the "OK Zone." As you start resolving your problems, the tension between the two of you will begin to lift, and you will enjoy your relationship more. Problem solving skills are an essential part of maintaining an abuse-free relationship.

Skill Building: Develop your problem solving skills by learning the six-step method described in this chapter. Practice your skills daily by applying them to the problems that arise in your relationships.

In the last chapter, you were encouraged you to rid yourself of blame, control, and hurtful statements. As you rid yourself of those negative behaviors, the walls between you and your partner will come down and you will start to build an environment in which problem solving is successful. This chapter provides a step-by-step guide to successful problem solving that leads you away from common mistakes and guides you back to the "OK Zone" of The Box.

We begin with a review of "The Box." Conflict usually follows a predictable path. At first, everything is "OK" between you and your partner. That is, there are no major problems or stressors, and you are both generally satisfied with the way things are going. Then a problem arises, causing tension between you. If you are not able to identify and solve the problem, the tension continues to grow. Tension may escalate until you get out of the box and engage in verbal abuse or domestic violence. On the other hand, if you solve the problem successfully, the tension disappears and you return with your partner to the "OK Zone." It is important to become a skilled problem solver.

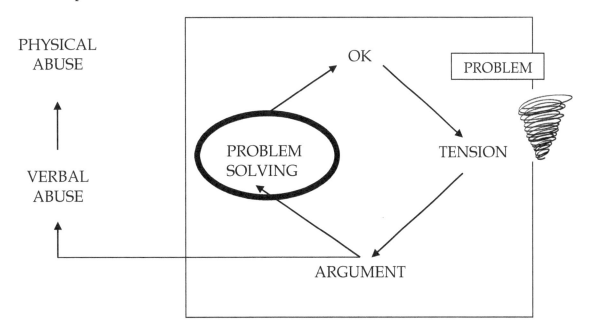

In this lesson, you will learn a 6-step method for solving problems. The steps may feel unnatural at first, but that is only because they are new to you. The steps will feel more natural as you get accustomed to them. These steps work. They solve problems and get you back to the "OK Zone." As with any of the other skills discussed in this book, however, they take time and practice to master. But then, no great achievement comes without effort. As you learn the steps in this problem-solving procedure, maintain a positive attitude and keep the following points in mind:

1. <u>Some problems cannot be solved quickly</u>. Some problems are more challenging and complex than others. Sometimes, the best you can do is own up to the fact that you don't know the answer to a problem, but that you will keep working on it. Don't get frustrated if you cannot solve a tough problem the instant it comes up. Be patient.

2. <u>Sometimes there is no perfect answer</u>. People often want a solution with no down side. Yet there are times when best solution comes down to choosing the lesser of two evils. You and your partner may have to go along with a solution that you are not completely comfortable with simply because it is the best solution you can come up with at the time. At times like these, you have to be content in knowing that you are doing the best you can with a difficult problem.

3. <u>Stay on the same team</u>. *It is more important for you and your partner to stay on the same team than to solve a problem!* We went into this at length in the last chapter. Do not create a bigger problem by turning your partner into an adversary by blaming, saying hurtful things, or trying to coerce your partner into agreeing to something he or she does not want to do. These tactics cut the lines of communication when you need them most. Remember, problem solving requires teamwork. It should be *you and your partner against the problem*. If it starts to become *you against your partner*, stop and do whatever it takes to get back on the same team before you go on.

4. <u>Stay focused on the problem</u>. Do not ask, *"Who is to blame for the problem?"* That question is divisive and creates defensiveness. Better to ask, *"What is the problem?"* and, *"How can we work together to solve it?"* Also, stay focused on one problem at a time. If another problem comes up, agree to talk about it another time.

5. <u>Pick the right place and time</u>. Pick a time and place to discuss the problem when you can both give the best you have to offer. Bringing up a problem the minute your partner returns from a long day at work or during his or her favorite television show is not a good idea. You may have to schedule a time to talk that works for both of you. Saying, *"I need to talk with you about our budget. How about talking after supper?"* is better than demanding immediate attention. Don't expect your partner to drop everything the moment you bring up a problem. Likewise, if your spouse brings up a problem at a bad time for you, propose a better time. Say, *"I want to talk about this when I can give you my full attention. I'll be free in an hour. How about then?"*

Problem Solving Steps

The "Problem Solving" area of the box is exactly six steps wide – no more, no less. If you successfully complete each of the six steps, you will return to the peace and harmony of the "OK Zone." But be advised that there are hidden mines along the way, and if you step on one the whole problem solving process will blow up and end in disaster. "Mine fields?" you ask. "What do you mean by mine fields?" The road to problem solving is covered with hidden mines (potential mistakes) that can derail the entire problem solving effort. You have to know where the mines are to avoid them. Relax – I will tell you where the mines are located each step along the way. Each step will be explained in detail, as well as the "mine fields" that surround them. To begin, familiarize yourself with the six problem solving steps below.

1. *Identify the real problem.*
2. *Tell your partner how you view the problem.*
3. *Demonstrate understanding of your partner's point of view.*
4. *Working together as a team, create as many solutions as possible.*
5. *Mutually pick solutions to the problem.*
6. *Evaluate your progress one week later, and make changes as necessary.*

Step One: Identify the Real Problem

Have you ever had a fight with your partner, but could not remember what the fight was about the following day? Or, did you ever feel that the problems you wanted to talk about were different from the problems your partner saw as important? If so, chances are the problem was never clearly defined to begin with. Before you bring up a problem, be sure that you understand what the *real* problem is. *You have to know what the real problem is before you can work together to solve it.* Take time to think about what is really bugging you (or your partner), and be clear in your own mind what the problem is before you start fixing things. Like a carpenter, you need to know what you want to build *before* you pick up your tools and start hammering away.

 CAUTION: MINE FIELD

The need to identify the real problem brings you to the first mine on the problem solving road. When the wrong problem is identified, problem solving ends before it gets started. Even worse, couples fight the same battle repeatedly without finding a solution, continuously increasing the tension between them. That is what happened to Jamil and his girlfriend Carla, who repeatedly failed to identify the real problem. Here is their story.

Jamil liked to go out with his long-time buddies for drinks and laughs from time to time. He didn't do this often; he met his friends at a club once a month or so, and he always let Carla know about his plans ahead of time. One day in group Jamil said, "I don't understand my girlfriend. We have been fighting all weekend. It's the same old problem. Every time I go out with the guys she gives me hell, and I'm sick of it!" He went on:

"I hardly ever go out with the guys, but every time I do, Carla gets mad. She says I go out with the guys, but I never take *her* anywhere. She *knows* that's not true! I always come home right after work, and we do stuff together almost every weekend. Just last week we went to Las Vegas! We've been fighting all weekend about whether I spend enough time with her. I've even asked her to go with me when I see the guys, but she won't go. We go through this every time, and I'm sick of it!"

Despite all their arguments and fights, the *real* problem was never identified. The real problem became clear later, and it had nothing to do with the amount of time that Jamil and Carla spent together. The real problem had to do with Carla's insecurity. It turns out that Danny, one of Jamil's friends, was a real womanizer, and Carla knew it. Danny chased women in the singles clubs, and Jamil would be with Danny on those nights when he went out with the boys. The thought of Jamil being part of this scene made Carla angry and insecure, but she was reluctant to say this to Jamil. She eventually opened up. Once the real problem came out, Jamil and Carla were able to talk about it openly and find a solution by following the rest of the problem solving steps. Jamil still spends time with his buddies, but he participates in activities that are more sensitive to his girlfriend's concerns. More importantly, the fighting has stopped.

In order for that to happen, the real problem had to be identified. Sometimes the problem that you and your partner are arguing about is not the real problem. Make sure you know what the real problem is before you try to solve it. Uncovering it may take some digging, but once it is in the open, a solution can usually be found. Here of some other examples of couples arguing about the wrong problem:

The supposed problem:	The real problem:
John was mad that his wife planned to take the kids to Disneyland. He accused her of spoiling the kids. She argued back, telling John that she was a good mother, and that there was nothing wrong with the occasional trip to Disneyland.	*John's boss told him there might be layoffs at work, and John was worried about it. What would they do if he got laid off? John had not told his wife about the situation at work.*
Pam complained that Greg worked too much. He often stayed at the office after everyone else had left. Pam accused Greg of being a workaholic. Greg argued that he had to stay longer to get his work done.	*Pam was very demanding of Greg's time. He often stayed at the office to have time to himself. He had never explained to Pam how badly he needed some personal space.*

 CAUTION: MINE FIELD

A second mistake is to use a "machine gun approach" when identifying problems. Sometimes couples rapidly throw up problem after problem, one upon the heels of the other, without waiting for any of them to be solved. The experience is usually a frustrating one, and problems usually go unresolved. Focus on one problem at a time.

Step Two: Tell Your Partner How You See the Problem

After you identify the real problem, you need to bring it to your partner's attention. This sounds easy, but this is the step where problem solving often goes wrong. Don't make your partner defensive — you are not looking for a fight. Bring up the problem in a way that encourages cooperation and a feeling that you and your partner are working together to solve the problem. Remember, your partner is not the problem. Your partner is your most important ally in resolving the problem. Attack the problem, not your partner.

 CAUTION: MINE FIELD

A common mistake people make is asking their partner the wrong question. People ask "Who's to blame for this?" rather than "How can we work together to solve the problem?" Nothing derails problem solving quicker than bringing up a problem with an accusing and blaming attitude. As you learned in the last chapter, that approach puts you and your partner on opposite sides of the fence. You become adversaries rather than allies, and that's not a useful thing to do if you really want to solve your problems. You can argue for years without agreeing about who's to blame for something. The argument just goes around and around, like a dog chasing its tail. It's better to avoid the whole question of blame, because *it is not necessary to assign blame for a problem to solve it*. In the problem solving steps you are learning, the question of blame never comes up. Blame is unnecessary, counter-productive, and usually derails the problem solving process.

To avoid stepping on the "blame mine," avoid using the word *"YOU"* when telling your partner how you see a problem. Choose words that build unity, like *"WE"* and *"OUR."* Words like *"you"* and *"your"* are used to blame your partner for the problem. They're divisive. In contrast, words like *"we," "us,"* and *"our"* are inclusive and foster a feeling of teamwork.

Here's an example. Dan received a bill from the bank for a bounced check that his girlfriend Kelly had written. This is how he brought up the problem: "*You* have a problem, Kelly. *You* bounced another check! I don't understand how *you* can be so irresponsible. Do *you* have any idea how much *you* cost us in fees? What are *you* going to do about it?"

Dan's accusations may be factual and accurate. Perhaps Kelly *is* to blame. Yet Dan's approach may make it hard for them to work as a team to solve the problem. When you bring up a problem, ask yourself whether you want to fix blame or solve the problem. If you want to solve the problem, it is best to work as a team. Nothing will be resolved if the situation deteriorates into a fight. Here is a more skillful approach to the same problem. Dan says to Kelly, "*We* have a problem. *We* don't have enough money in our account to cover all the checks *we* write. *We're* getting bounced check charges, and it's costing *us* money. Let's think about what *we* can do to about it."

Which problem solving approach do you think will work best for Dan and Kelly? The approach that is most likely to work is the approach that keeps them on the same team and fosters a spirit of cooperation. The words you use to bring up a problem matter. Do not be afraid to talk to your partner about a problem, but avoid blaming. *Stay focused on the problem, rather than who to blame.* Assigning blame is provocative and irrelevant once you have become a skillful problem solver.

Also, stay in control of your voice and your words. Don't shout or yell. Never swear, threaten, or verbally attack your partner. Body language is also important. *How* you say something is just as important as *what* you say. If you find yourself struggling with these concepts, read the section on avoiding blame in the previous chapter again. Avoiding blame is the key to avoiding the mine fields in the second problem solving step. If you have been fighting about your problems rather than solving them, this mine may be derailing you.

Step Three: Demonstrate Understanding of Your Partner's Opinion

Ask your partner how she or he sees the problem, and demonstrate understanding of your partner's opinion. The goal is *not* to reach agreement or change your partner's mind. Just ask for your partner's opinion and show that you understand it. See the problem through the eyes of your partner. Use words such as, "*Let me be sure I understand you. The way you see it is . . . Is that right?*" Keep reflecting (mirror back what your partner said using your own words) until you get it right. You want to understand your partner exactly, because the better you understand each other, the easier it will be to find a solution that you both find acceptable, and the more effective you will be at problem solving.

Demonstrating understanding of another person's opinion does not mean that you agree with their opinion. It only shows that you understand and respect it, and that's important. Feeling understood reduces anger and defensiveness. Again, the better you understand each other's concerns, the better you will be able to find workable solutions to your problems.

 CAUTION: MINE FIELD

During step three, derailment of the problem solving process usually happens when one partner invites the other to give their opinion, and then tells them how stupid their opinion is. A *"who's right"* argument follows. A *"who's right"* argument is one in which you are trying to "win" the fight by making your partner admit they are wrong. I have known "who's right"

arguments that have gone on for many years without resolution. When this occurs, the real problem is often forgotten and unsolved.

During a "who's right" argument, each partner dregs up dozens of issues, past and present, trying to prove their point. Did you ever get into an argument and, thirty minutes later, find yourself arguing about a totally unrelated problem, or an incident that took place years ago? Did you ever start to argue about one problem, get into a big fight, and afterwards couldn't remember what started it? That's a "who's right" argument. The illustration below show what happens in this type of argument.

During step three, derailment of the problem solving process usually happens when one partner invites the other to give their opinion, and then tells them how stupid their opinion is. A *"who's right"* argument follows. A *"who's right"* argument is one in which you are trying to "win" the fight by making your partner admit they are wrong. I have known "who's right" arguments that have gone on for many years without resolution. When this occurs, the real problem is often forgotten and unsolved.

During a "who's right" argument, each partner dregs up dozens of issues, past and present, trying to prove their point. Did you ever get into an argument and, thirty minutes later, find yourself arguing about a totally unrelated problem, or an incident that took place years ago? Did you ever start to argue about one problem, get into a big fight, and afterwards couldn't remember what started it? That's a "who's right" argument. The illustration below show what happens in this type of argument.

What happens during a "Who's Right" argument

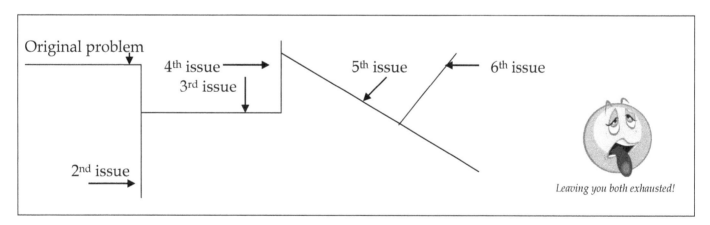

As discussed earlier in this chapter, it is a good policy to talk about one problem at a time. If you get too many problems in the air at the same time, it will be difficult to focus on all of them and you will both feel overwhelmed. If your partner brings up a different problem or concern, offer to deal with it later, but ask to work on one problem at a time. And remember, the goal is to demonstrate understanding of your partner's opinion, not to change it or decide whose opinion is right.

Step Four: Create As Many Solutions as Possible

Working with your partner, make a list of possible solutions to the problem, listing as many solutions as you can. This is a time to be playful and creative, so don't be afraid to include solutions that seem silly or unworkable. Do not evaluate solutions as "good" or "bad" at this point. Right now, you need a lot of possible solutions - as many ideas as possible. Write down all of them, no matter how unlikely the ideas seem at first. (Remember, it's alright to have some fun here.) Make sure that both of you get a chance to contribute to the list of solutions. Your list should include ten or more potential solutions to the problem.

 CAUTION: MINE FIELD

When things get fouled up in step four, it's usually because one partner tries to control what goes on the list by insisting the other partner's solutions are silly or unworkable. When that happens, the other person gets frustrated and doesn't feel like an equal partner, causing the problem solving process to break down. Every suggestion should make it on the list, and each partner has an equal opportunity to contribute. If you don't like your partner's suggestions keep your opinion to yourself for now.

Step Five: Mutually Pick Some Solutions

Now that you have a list of solutions, pick a solution (or a combination of several solutions) upon which you both agree. Key words to remember here are *communication, negotiation, and compromise*. Fairness and the willingness to experiment and compromise gets the job done, while bullying your partner into accepting unwanted solutions derails the process. *A solution forced on someone else won't work in the long run.* For this reason, solutions must be chosen together. It may take time and effort, but keep working with each other until you come up with a set of solutions that you can both live with. Write the solutions down so you have a record of what you've agreed to do.

Everything you read in the last chapter about controlling behavior comes into play here. Sometimes a partner is pretending to be flexible, but has already decided that there is only one solution on the list that he or she will accept. If you attempt to control your partner and have your way, if you refuse to be flexible and compromise, you will step on a major land mine.

Below is an example of how negotiation and compromise work. Suppose the illustration below is the list of possible solutions to financial problems that you and your partner came up with in step four.

Solution 1:	*Make a budget*	Solution 6:	*Look for another job*
Solution 2:	*Hold weekly meetings*	Solution 7:	*Ask for a raise*
Solution 3	*Get a second job*	Solution 8:	*Reduce expenses*
Solution 4:	*Ask for more hours*	Solution 9:	*Get rid of credit cards*

| Solution 5: | Have a yard sale | Solution 10: | Meet with financial planner |

Maybe you start by suggesting solutions 3, 4, and 7. Your partner doesn't like solution 4 at all and thinks solution 1 is a better choice. You don't like solution 1, but you're willing to compromise. You'll accept solution 1 if your partner will try solution 4 for a month. Your partner says "no way," but how about solution 9 instead. Solution 9 wasn't the first choice for either of you, but it's something you're willing to try. In the end, you both agree to experiment with solutions 3 and 9 for a month. Get the idea? Mutual negotiation and compromise win the day when it comes to problem solving.

Step Six: Evaluate Your Progress

This is perhaps the most overlooked step in the whole process. After you come up with your solutions, set a time to sit down with your partner to evaluate how successful (or unsatisfactory) your solutions turned out. Often times, your solutions will need adjustment and continued experimentation before the best solutions are found. Problem solving is really a series of ongoing experiments. Keep experimenting with solutions until you solve the problem.

 CAUTION: MINE FIELD

When partners don't evaluate their progress they tend to slip back into their old behaviors. The problem returns. This can be a frustrating experience for both partners. Be sure and set a time to review your progress and make any needed adjustments to the problem solving plan.

When Problem Solving Succeeds

When you and your partner successfully work through a problem, you will feel good about it. The tension the problem caused will disappear, and you'll feel even closer to each other than you did before the problem came up. When you feel the tension disappear, you know you have made your way back to the *"OK Zone"* of The Box. You know problem solving was successful because the tension caused by the problem ceases to exist. It's simply not there anymore, and your relationship feels healthier and stronger. You worked as a team and solved a problem. You both feel confident that you can do it again the next time a problem arises.

HOMEWORK ASSIGNMENT
CHAPTER 10

Start building your problem solving skills by going through the six steps below with your partner. Identify a problem and work on it one step at a time.

Step One: Before you bring a problem to your partner's attention, take some time to think about the real problem. *The problem I want to work on is:*

Step Two: Next, think about the words you will use when you approach your partner. Be sure to avoid words that foster defensiveness like "you" and "your." Try to include words that build teamwork like "we" and "our." Write down the words you plan to use when you bring the problem up. Avoid the land mines! *These are the words I will use to describe the problem:*

Step Three: Describe how you demonstrated understanding of your partner's opinion. Did you do a good job of reflecting his or her point of view? Record what you said to your partner. *I demonstrated understanding of my partner's opinion by saying:*

Step Four: List of the potential solutions that you and your partner developed. *The possible solutions we thought of were:*

Step Five: Write down the solutions that you mutually agreed upon. *The solutions that we both agreed to try were:*

Step Six: How did you do? Describe your and your partner's evaluation of progress on the problem. *Our progress on the problem so far is:*

Chapter 11
Letters That Get You Talking Again

Key Concepts: When a couple is unable to resolve their problems, the tension between them intensifies. When anger is the only emotion expressed, tension can grow so fierce that they stop talking altogether. Letters that openly convey a range of feelings can open communication, bring you closer together, and make problem solving possible.

Skill Building: Open the lines of communication with your partner by writing a structured letter that reveals feelings other than anger, such as sadness, fear, regret, understanding, and love.

The skills and concepts from the last two chapters can help you resolve problems in your relationship. You and your partner will spend more time in the *"OK Zone"* if you remember that tension is not the opening bell for a fight, but a signal to start working together to solve a problem. At least, that is what you should do if you and your partner are still talking to each other. But what if the anger and animosity between you is so intense that you stopped talking? How can you work on problems when you are not speaking to each other? When that happens, write a letter. In this chapter, you will learn to use letter writing to get you talking again. Letter writing will not solve your problems, but it often gets you talking again, and that makes problem solving possible.

Letters can help you express what you think and feel in a constructive way. The great thing about letters is that you can think about what you want to say before you say it. You can choose your words thoughtfully, then set the letter aside and read it again later to make sure it is just right before you give it to your partner. You can work on the letter at your own pace without being emotionally flooded. But what makes this letter effective is that it helps you express feelings that need to be expressed, but rarely are.

How the Letter Works

When a couple cannot solve their problems, the tension between them intensifies as time goes by. Softer feelings of affection and trust become buried beneath a blanket of anger, resentment, hurt, and frustration. Tension can grow so strong that talking only makes matters worse. Everything is misinterpreted, and every attempt to bring up a problem triggers a defensive response. The fighting grows more and more hurtful. Finally, the partners stop talking altogether.

When couples experience chronic conflict, they express anger clearly and loudly, but gentler feelings such as affection and appreciation go unexpressed. It may not feel safe to express affection. In this environment of angry withdrawal, neither partner trusts the other well enough to reveal feelings that might be seen as weakness and make them vulnerable to attack or rejection. Affection is hidden, if it's still experienced at all, and neither partner trusts the other. Neither wants to be the first to take a chance and open up. Neither wants to get hurt. An oppressive silence permeates the home.

If your relationship has become similar to the one described above, your partner already sees you as angry, abusive, uncaring, unwilling to listen, and unable to deal with problems in a mature way. Every hurtful thing you have ever said or done confirmed your partner's opinion of you. That has to change. If you want to start talking to your partner again (and you must talk to resolve your differences – there is no other way), you have to start giving voice to feelings other than anger. Venting anger during conflict has made you your partner's adversary. It's time to end the war.

The structured letter in this chapter will help you break the silence and start talking again. Through the letter, you will reveal feelings other than anger, feelings like sadness, fear, regret, and appreciation, feelings you may not be aware you harbor. Expressing these feelings to your partner will help break through icy silence by creating a new atmosphere – one of warmth, openness and trust. The feelings that you express in this letter may offer a new start for you both.

Six Key Feelings

The six key feelings that you will express in your letter are *anger, sadness, fear, regret, understanding, and love*. For each of the six feelings, there are three sentences for you to write. I will start each sentence for you, and you complete it by "filling in the blank." The author John Gray suggested a similar letter in his popular book, *Men Are From Mars, Women Are From Venus*. The six key feelings in the letter are:

ANGER	SADNESS	FEAR
REGRET	UNDERSTANDING	LOVE

The sentences you will complete, three sentences for each feeling, are in the box below. But before you get started on your own letter, take time to read the examples of other letters that are included in this chapter. The letters were written by former clients who were in counseling at the time they were written. They will help you understand how your letter should be written.

The examples vary widely in quality. Some of them were very good, some are average, and one of them is, well, *terrible!* I have included examples of the good, the bad, and the ugly for you to read so that you can tell the difference between a well-written letter and a poorly written one. It's important to know the difference. A poorly written letter can make things worse than they already are.

ANGER

I'm angry that _____

I get mad when _____

I feel frustrated _____

SADNESS

I'm sad that _____

It hurts me when _____

I'm disappointed that _____

FEAR

I'm afraid that _____

I'm worried that _____

I don't want _____

REGRET

I'm ashamed _____

I was definitely wrong _____

I apologize _____

UNDERSTANDING

I understand _____

I see your point about _____

I know you feel _____

LOVE

I love _____

I appreciate _____

I thank you for _____

Bob's Letter

The first sample letter was written by Bob to his girlfriend Alison. Alison was surprised by the letter. It brought them closer together, and allowed them to talk about their issues. This was the first time that Bob took responsibility for his abuse, and he openly expressed remorse to Alison for his behavior. Bob still had a lot of work to do and many changes to make, and he still had to prove that his words were sincere and not just a ploy to keep Alison from leaving. After all, words are cheap. But his letter was a good start for him.

Dear Alison,

I'm angry that . . . I put my hands on you and called you out of your name.

I get mad when . . . I think about what I did to you.

I feel frustrated . . . that I caused you to fear me and not trust me.

I'm sad that . . . instead of me talking to you I chose to hit you.

It hurts me when . . . I look in your face and see the pain I caused.

I'm disappointed that . . . I put my hands on you.

I'm afraid that . . . one day I will lose you.

I'm worried that . . . you think I'm going to hit you again.

I don't want . . . to lose my family.

I'm ashamed . . . that I hit you.

I was definitely wrong . . . for ever putting my hands on you.

I apologize . . . for all the wrong I caused.

I understand . . . why you don't trust me.

I see your point about . . . my big mouth and your fear.

I know you feel . . . hurt and betrayed.

I love . . . you and the kids.

I appreciate . . . the way you hang in there and have hope.

I thank you for . . . all that you ever did and never walked out on me.

Bob openly acknowledged the hurt that he caused Alison. He admitted the shame he feels when, in his words, "I look in your face and see the pain I caused." He acknowledged that he had "hurt and betrayed" Alison, and that he was ashamed of himself for hitting her. Good. These are things that Alison needs to hear – and things that Bob needs to say.

Also, notice that Bob told Alison that he loved her, and that his greatest fear was that "I will lose you." This emotional honesty and opening up to Alison was new ground for Bob. As you will see, the fear of losing one's partner is a common theme in these letters. Some people react to that fear by becoming even more abusive and controlling, hoping to make their partner too afraid to leave. Other people realize that their abusive behavior is pushing their partner away, and that realization motivates them to stop the abuse. Which type of person are you?

Donald's Letter

Donald had just started counseling when he wrote this letter to his wife, Emily. Even though they were legally separated, they continued to see each other every week. Donald and Emily still seemed to care for each other, but they continued to have verbal sparring matches and there was a high level of anger and conflict in the relationship. Here is the first draft of Donald's letter to Emily.

Dear Emily,

I'm angry that . . . we argue every other week.

I get mad when . . . you leave there are rude messages on my answering machine.

I feel frustrated . . . because we are not on the same page.

I'm sad that . . . our marriage hasn't worked out like it should.

It hurts me when . . . we go days without seeing or talking to each other.

I'm disappointed that . . . I haven't been more responsible towards my family.

I'm afraid that . . . if I get close to you I will get hurt.

I'm worried that . . . we might not stay together forever.

I don't want . . . us not to be together.

I'm ashamed . . . that I have pushed you and verbally abused you.

I was definitely wrong . . . for all the times I didn't tell you I loved you.

I apologize . . . for not being more supportive.

I understand . . . your frustration and feelings of resentment.

I see your point about . . . how spending more time together will bring us together.

I know you feel . . . a little scared, nervous, and unsure.

I love . . . that you have stood by me through thick and thin.

I appreciate . . . you and how you have raised my kids.

I thank you for . . . not jumping ship when the going has gotten tough.

Donald was deeply emotional as he read the letter to his group. After he wrote the letter, he told us, he went to Emily and asked her, "Why are you still with me after all the things I've done?" Emily replied, "Because I love you." Donald told us how touched he was by Emily's response and how ashamed he felt. He said he was determined to change himself. Emily deserved better.

Notice that Donald crossed out the words *"you leave"* in the second sentence of his letter. Although he was relatively new to our counseling group, he was applying what he had learned about staying out of the *"You Mode."* He also opened up to Emily in ways that were new to him. For example, he told her about the ambivalence and fear he felt about getting too close to anyone. He told her that it hurt him when they *"go days without seeing or talking"* to each other, but that he was afraid that *"if I get close to you I will get hurt."* This was an important insight for both of them, and it helped explain the mixed messages that Emily often got from Donald, and in his words, *"all the times I didn't tell you I loved you."*

Donald also expressed his shame about his abusive behavior toward her, and the fear that she might leave him. Donald's letter wasn't perfect. His expression of gratitude towards Emily for *"how you have raised my kids"* (instead of *our* kids) suggests that male privilege issues may have to be addressed. But overall, Bob did a good job in his first letter writing exercise. He discovered a lot about himself, and he revealed it openly to Emily, the most important person in his life. With communication established, problem solving could begin.

Jose's Letter

Jose wrote the following letter to his girlfriend Veronica. He didn't follow the structured format for the letter, so many thoughts and feelings were not discussed. Jose liked to go his own way. I've included it here so you can compare it to the previous letters.

Dear Veronica,

I'm angry that I have put ourselves in such an awful position and the abuse I've caused you. I'm hurt that I have lost the trust you once had in me. I'm sad we don't make love the way we used to. I'm afraid the happiness we once shared got lost and I'm going to work very hard to get it back and more. I'm happy you are here more than anything else. I appreciate all your patience and understanding, your kindness and most of all your love. I love you so very much, the last thing I want to do is lose you. We will overcome these obstacles and have a happy home once again.

"This stuff really works!" told us cheerfully as group started. He said he left the letter out for Veronica to find and read. Veronica cried when she read it, then she came to his room, kissed him, gave him a hug, and they made love. Jose was all smiles at group the next morning, and he thought letter writing was a *great* homework exercise!

Jose should have put more effort into his letter. On the positive side, he did acknowledge that his actions had cost him Veronica's trust and their happiness, and that he was committed to working hard to get it back. Also, Veronica seems to have appreciated the letter. But Jose is not specific about what he did to *"put ourselves in such an awful position"* or what he intends to do to *"get it back and more."* He does not talk about worries or show understanding of Veronica's needs. Nor does he say how he plans to change himself to "have a happy home once again." He is not specific about his past abusive behaviors. However, Jose is clear that he is *"sad we don't make love the way we used to."* Maybe it's just me, but I suspect that Jose had other motives in mind when he wrote the letter.

Peter's Letter

Peter was confronted strongly by the more experienced men in his counseling group when he read his letter. See if you can identify some problems with the letter as you read it.

> *Dear Sandra,*
>
> *I'm angry that . . . my girlfriend and I argue about everything.*
>
> *I get mad when . . . my girlfriend calls me names.*
>
> *I feel frustrated . . . when she don't stop when I ask.*
>
> *I'm sad that . . . we get into it so much.*
>
> *It hurts me when . . . she doesn't like to talk.*
>
> *I'm disappointed that . . . when I get upset.*
>
> *I'm afraid that . . . if this keeps on we will break up.*
>
> *I'm worried that . . . my son will suffer the most.*
>
> *I don't want . . . visitation of my son only on court ordered days.*
>
> *I'm ashamed . . . for going to court.*
>
> *I was definitely wrong . . .*
>
> *I apologize . . . for the name calling.*
>
> *I understand . . . your feelings.*
>
> *I see your point about . . . arguing.*
>
> *I know you feel . . . bad.*
>
> *I love . . . you.*
>
> *I appreciate . . . you being such a good mother.*
>
> *I thank you for . . . understanding.*

When Peter read his letter, my first impression was that he put as little effort and thought into the assignment as possible. *I know you feel bad. I'm disappointed when I get upset. I understand your feelings.* Sentences like these lack substance. They suggest that Peter had little motivation for counseling or to work through problems with his girlfriend.

My second impression was that Peter blamed his partner for their problems. The letter is full of information about things he resents, but he doesn't have much to say about his own history of abuse towards her (there was an extensive history of abuse). For example, he didn't even bother to respond to the sentence that begins, *"I was definitely wrong..."* He couldn't think of anything. In another sentence, Peter apologizes for name-calling but doesn't mention his acts of physical abuse. The only thing he's ashamed of is going to court. This is an example of the type of letter that can do more harm than good. But the worst is yet to come. Meet Martin.

Martin's Letter

Here's Martin's letter to his wife. It speaks for itself.

> *Dear Donna,*
> *I'm angry that . . . you lied.*
> *I get mad when . . . you quit your jobs.*
> *I feel frustrated . . . when you lay around all day.*
> *I'm sad that . . . you took my daughter away from me.*
> *It hurts me when . . . you lie.*
> *I'm disappointed that . . . that you lied.*
> *I'm afraid that . . . our relationship is doomed.*
> *I'm worried that . . . you will never understand.*
> *I don't want . . . you to be my wife anymore.*
> *I'm ashamed . . . that I had to go to jail.*
> *I was definitely wrong . . . to marry you in the first place.*
> *I apologize . . . for nothing.*
> *I understand . . . that I can't change you.*
> *I see your point about . . . getting a divorce.*
> *I know you feel . . . bitter.*
> *I love . . . someone else.*
> *I appreciate . . . our separation.*
> *I thank you for . . . our beautiful daughter.*

Martin is an angry man. He's too angry to communicate without trying to hurt and abuse. He's too angry to solve problems, or to look at his own behavior objectively. Rather than talk to his wife, Martin used his letter to vent hostility and heap more destruction on an already battered marriage. His letter is included an example of what *not* to do in your letter. Martin's letter is an example of many of the behaviors that you have learned to avoid: blame, avoidance of responsibility, the "You Mode," and attacking your partner rather than the problem. Thankfully, Martin's spouse never read the letter – a court protective order spared her that. Before you start working on your own letter, take a moment to compare the first letter in this chapter with the letter that Martin wrote. You'll see that letters can be used as a powerful tool for good, or as a weapon to destroy what little is left of a struggling relationship.

HOMEWORK ASSIGNMENT
CHAPTER 11

Write a letter to your partner using the questions in this chapter as a guide. After your letter is finished, set it aside for a while. Read it again later, and as you do, think about how your words sound to your partner. Ask yourself if you are being fair to him or her. Try to avoid the "You Mode," and follow the other guidelines for effective problem solving.

When you write your letter, remember that it is as important *how* you say something as *what* you say. Anger can be expressed with consideration and respect, or in a way that is hurtful, demeaning, and mean-spirited. You can be truthful without being hurtful, and open without being malicious. While it is appropriate to express anger, remember that it is not the purpose of the letter to vent, but to get you and your spouse talking again. Don't use the letter to hurt or open old wounds. It's sometimes hard to express anger without hurting your partner, and it is equally hard to remain respectful when your feelings have been hurt. But a successful relationship requires that you learn to do both of these things reasonably well. A couple must be able to listen to their partner's feelings in a loving and respectful way, and they must also express feelings of their own with respect and sensitivity.

You might want to invite your partner to write his or her own letter. If so, respond to your partner's letter in a respectful manner. Don't punish him or her for expressing thoughts and feelings you don't like. If you get angry and defensive now, your partner will have a hard time trusting you in the future. Take some time to cool down if you need it, and tell your partner, "Thanks for writing this letter. I need some time to think about what you told me. Let me think it over, and then we'll talk about it some more." Remember, the goal of the letter is to open lines of communication and get you talking again. Write in the spirit of friendship, and let your letter bring you closer together.

Chapter 12
Skill Building

Key Concepts: Reaching your goal of an abuse-free lifestyle requires both knowledge and practice. This chapter will help you consolidate your understanding of the material in the last three chapters and apply the concepts and skills in your relationships. Remember, to build your skills you must commit to applying them in your daily life. It's what you do, not what you know, that gets results.

Skill Building: Complete the following test to review any gaps in your knowledge of key skills and concepts. Provide detailed examples of your efforts to apply them in your Skill Building Log.

The problem solving skills discussed in the last three chapters are important. They provide reliable strategies for solving problems and reducing tension in your relationship. A sound approach to problem solving is essential for anyone who wants to maintain an abuse-free relationship. Practice your problem solving skills daily and re-read the previous three chapters until you thoroughly understand them. Don't get discouraged if you step on "land mines" when you start applying the problem solving steps. If that happens, learn from the experience. Review the chapters to find out which mine you stepped on so you can avoid it next time. Use the quiz below to review important concepts and identify areas that need additional work.

There is also a new *Skill Building Log* to help you apply the concepts and skills from the last three chapters. The importance of the *Skill Building Logs* cannot be overstated. They give you an understanding of these concepts that only comes from practicing them in real situations. Effective and skillful problem solving requires a *lot* of practice, but it's one of the most important skills you'll ever acquire.

Quiz
Chapters 9-11

1. When partners respect each other, cooperate, and work together as allies they can solve almost any problem. However, blaming, _____, and _____ behaviors cause fights, build walls between partners, and make it almost impossible to resolve problems. (Chapter 9)

2. Tension grows and lingers until you and your partner solve the problem. Solve the problem successfully, and you'll remove the tension and return to the _____ zone of The Box. (Chapter 9)

3. Good problem solvers don't waste time trying to assign _____. In fact, problem solving is easier when the issue of _____ never comes up. (Chapter 9)

4. To avoid the Blame Game, you have to stay out of the _____ Mode. (Chapter 9)

5. When you come across to your spouse as _____, your partner will probably resist what you have to say even if your solutions make sense. (Chapter 9)

6. Always approach your partner as an equal and seek solutions through negotiation and _____. (Chapter 9)

7. Never say _____ things to your partner, even in retaliation for something hurtful said to you. You can't be part of the solution when you are contributing to the problem. (Chapter 9)

8. The best way to screen your blaming, bossy, and hurtful behavior is to watch your partner's _____ to what you say. (Chapter 9)

9. Leadership does not mean telling your partner what to do. Leadership means focusing on _____ and leading by _____. (Chapter 9)

10. Problem solving requires teamwork. It is more important for you and your partner to stay on the same _____ than to solve a problem.

11. The Six Problem Solving Steps Are: (Chapter 10)

    a) Identify the _____.

    b) Tell your partner how you _____.

    c) Understand your partner's _____.

    d) Working together as a team, create as many _____ as possible.

    e) _____ pick a solution or a combination of solutions.

    f) Evaluate your _____ one week later.

13. A letter will not _____ your problems, but it may open the door to communication and get you talking again, and that makes problem solving possible. (Chapter 11)

Check your answers in the appendix and move on to the Skill Building Log.

Skill Building Log

Step 1: Select one or more skills from the list below that you want to practice. Selecting the right skills to practice is easy. Just answer this sentence: *"It would help me and my family the most if I would _____."*

Step 2: On a separate sheet of paper, write a detailed example of how you put the skills to use. Describe (1) who you were with, (2) the problem you struggled with, (3) any of your warning signs that came up, (4) the skills you used to handle the problem, (5) how things turned out.

TOOLBOX FOR CHAPTER TWELVE

Tools from Chapters 1-3:
- Memorize The Box
- Use The Box to guide my decision making
- Stay focused on problem solving during an argument
- Learn my own Warning Signs
- Watch for my Warning Signs when I start to feel angry
- Take a Time Out whenever I see my warning signs
- Memorize the rules to Time Out and follow them
- Explain Time Out to my partner
- Never cross the "I don't care what I say line"
- Never cross the "I don't care what I do line"
- Stop using any form of Verbal Abuse (stay in The Box)
- Recognize and avoid using Denial, Blame, and Minimizing

Tools from Chapters 5-7:
- Whenever I feel angry toward my partner, stop and ask myself, *"Is my thinking rational and logical right now? Am I making a big deal out of a small problem?"*
- Whenever I feel angry (or frustrated, jealous, etc.) I'll remind myself that I can choose to think in ways that escalate these feelings, or I can choose to think in ways that reduce them.
- Accept responsibility for everything I say or do.
- Lower my comfort level with violence. Don't minimize, call abuse something other than what it really is, or tell myself that such behavior is OK.
- Don't try to be my partner's boss or force my will on him or her. See my partner as my equal.
- Allow my partner the right to express his or her thoughts and feelings openly and without intimidation.
- Always stop and think *before* I react.
- Never "Awfulize."
- Stay out of the *"YOU MODE."*
- Self-talk to prevent or reduce anger.
- Identify my core beliefs about anger and aggression and modify them.

New Tools from Chapters 9-11:
- See tension as a signal to problem solve rather than the opening bell to a fight.
- Remove all controlling, blaming, and hurtful language from my problem solving.
- Ask my partner if I come across as bossy, blaming, or hurtful.
- Ask my partner to tell me whenever he or she feels controlled, hurt, or blamed.
- Use the six problem solving steps.
- Whenever I step on a land mine, find out which mine it was and avoid it the next time.
- Write a letter to my partner expressing all of the feelings described in the letter writing exercise.

- Invite my partner to write a letter back to me.

PERSONAL PROGRESS AND SELF-EVALUATION

1. Evaluate the progress that you have made so far in your counseling. Are you satisfied with the progress you are making? Are you putting forth your best effort? Is there anything you need to do to make your counseling experience more successful?

2. Select a relationship that is important to you. What can you do to make the relationship better? Set a specific goal for improving the relationship. What do you want to accomplish over the next month?

3. Have you seen changes in your thinking or behavior since starting this program? If so, provide an example of how your thinking and behavior have changed.

4. Are there skills from your counseling that you use on a daily basis? If so, what are they? Give a recent example of using them. If you are not using the skills you have learned on a daily basis, why not?

5. Select a skill or concept from the book that is important for you to use and develop at this time of your life. What skill did you select? How can using that skill benefit you and the people who love you?

Chapter 13
See the Big Picture

Key Concepts: Keeping the Big Picture in mind can make a big difference in the way you choose to behave when you are angry. Having a Big Picture allows you to see past small day-to-day annoyances and focus on long-term relationship goals.

Skill Building: Write your own Big Picture. When problems come up and tension starts to build, keep your Big Picture in mind until the problem is resolved. Think about the Big Picture during time-out periods to help you put things into perspective. Remember who you're talking to, how important your family is to you, and what you want your relationships to become as the years go by. With your Big Picture in mind, you will be more likely to act in a way that is consistent with your long-term goals.

What would you do if you won a million dollars in the Lotto? People answer the question very differently depending on whether they have a *"Big Picture."* Imagine that through incredible good fortune, Sally and Sue both won a million dollar cash Lotto prize. The day after she received her money, Sally quit her dull job and launched herself on a world-class shopping spree. She bought expensive luxury items, an expensive car, a boat, diamond jewelry, a trip around the world, and threw lavish parties. The first year after winning the Lotto was an amazing dream come true for Sally, a dream she wished would never end. But her dream came to an abrupt conclusion when the cash ran out. A couple of years later, Sally was back at her dull job struggling to make ends meet.

Sue handled her money differently. After paying off some debts, she invested the balance of her winnings wisely. She used part of her money to put herself through college so she could earn a higher income and enjoy the satisfying career she always wanted. A few years later, Sue was enjoying financial security and earning a salary that allowed her have many of the finer things in life she had always dreamed of. What's the difference between Sally and Sue? Sue had a Big Picture, Sally did not.

It is also important to develop a Big Picture for your relationships. People without a Big Picture are without long-term relationship goals. Easily caught up in everyday quarrels irritations, they drift from moment to moment, not thinking about the long term effects of their words and behavior. Unable to "see the forest for the trees," they say and do things that no relationship can long withstand. Reason tells us that we need to avoid verbally and physically abusive behavior because it destroys relationships. We know that we cannot swear at the people we care for, call them demeaning names, physically assault them, and expect that they will still love, trust, and respect us. Yet otherwise reasonable and responsible people do just that. In giving vent to anger over some perceived slight, they foolishly assault their partners with words and behaviors that are sure to antagonize, hurt, and offend. In time, the feelings of affection, tenderness, and hope that were once a source of happiness for the couple turn to resentment, bitterness, and disappointment.

The daily news talks about war, crime, violence, and brutality in the world. But not all warfare is waged between nations. Too often, the home becomes a battlefield in which family members wage vicious verbal and physical combat that erodes love and inflicts lasting emotional scars. Brutality and violence occur not only on dark streets at the hands of strangers, but also in our own homes at the hands of family members. Sometimes people are aware of the destruction they are causing but keep doing it, sometimes as a matter of stubborn pride, sometimes because they smugly believe that they're "right" and their partner is "wrong," until there is no hope at all that the relationship can be saved. All the while, they sooth their guilty conscience by telling themselves that it was all their partners' fault, that others "pushed my buttons," that there was nothing else that they could have done. The result is one of the greatest sicknesses in the world today, the feeling of being unwanted and unloved.

Why do perfectly reasonable adults do and say things that they know will destroy their relationships? Part of the answer is that people lose sight of the Big Picture. The Big Picture means seeing past the day to day squabbles and problems that are an inevitable part of two people trying to adjust to each other's differences. It is being mindful of the reasons you got into a relationship with your partner in the first place. It means keeping sight of how you want your relationship to grow, and what you want it to become as the months and years go by. It means letting the power of love replace the love of power.

In this chapter you will create your own Big Picture. Start by asking yourself why you chose to be in a relationship. What are you looking for? What do you want it to grow into? How do you see you and your partner five years from now, twenty years from now? We will be talking a lot about family and way family relationships are important. To start, let's define what "family" means to some people. In fact, let me give you my own Big Picture. This is what my family means to me:

My Own Big Picture

To me, forming a family means doing something great and noble. My family is where "I love you" is expressed sincerely and often. It is the only place on earth where I know that the most powerful force in the universe is not hate, greed, or some other vice, but love. It's where I experience what it means to love and to be loved. It's where I learn that it is not how much I give that is important, but how much love I put into the giving.

In my family I find support and relief from the pressures and problems of life, and gain courage from the knowledge that at home there are people who will always be there for me, and that I can always count on. Family is where I experience what it means to be a husband and father. My family is the greatest source of happiness that's within my power to reach. While the work that I do brings me happiness for a time, my family will be a source of joy for my entire life. It is the most important work I'll ever do. Through my shared experiences with my family I'll build a storehouse of contentment and glad memories to draw upon. Long after I leave this earth I'll leave something of myself behind – something good that just may, if I set a good example and do my best as a husband and a father, continue to have a positive effect on the lives of my children, and of their children after them.

These are more than just words. It's my Big Picture. This is what I want my relationships to grow into as the years go by. Being far from perfect I sometimes forget, and when I do I act foolishly. Sometimes I say and do things that I regret. But I keep coming back to this Big Picture of mine, and I try to keep it in mind when I feel angry or frustrated about something. I stop and remind myself that these people I'm speaking to are my wife and children, and I remind myself what they mean to me. I remind myself that my relationship with these people, my connection to the people I love, is all that really matters to me in this world. Then I try to act accordingly. And while I don't dwell on it, I know that one day I'll leave this world. When that day comes I want my wife and children to know beyond doubt that they were loved deeply and profoundly. I regret that I fail at this far too often, but I'm trying to improve. I try to keep my Big Picture in mind every day.

I believe Henry W. Longfellow, the great American poet, had a Big Picture. He articulated his Big Picture long ago in one of my favorite poems, *The Children's Hour*.

Between the dark and the daylight,
When the night is beginning to lower,
Comes a pause in the day's occupations
That is known as the Children's Hour.

I hear in the chamber above me
The patter of little feet,
The sound of a door that is opened,
And voices soft and sweet.

From my study I see in the lamplight,
Descending the broad hall-stair,
Grave Alice and laughing Allegra,
And Edith with golden hair.

A whisper, and then a silence;
Yet I know from their merry eyes
They are plotting and planning together
To take me by surprise.

A sudden rush from the stairway,
A sudden raid from the hall!
By three doors left unguarded
They enter my castle wall!

They climb up into my turret,
O'er the arms and back of my chair;
If I try to escape, they surround me,
They seem to be everywhere.

They almost devour me with kisses;
Their arms about me entwine,
Till I think of the Bishop of Bingen
In his Mouse-Tower on the Rhine!

Do you think, O blue-eyed banditti,
Because you have scaled the wall,
Such an old Mustache as I am
Is not a match for you all?

I have you fast in my fortress,
And I will not let you depart,
But put you down in the dungeon,
In the round-tower of my heart.

And there I will keep you forever,
Yes, forever and a day,
Till the walls shall crumble to ruin,
And moulder in dust away.

Longfellow had the Big Picture. He knew what his relationships meant to him. Many others have written in a similar fashion. One such man was Sullivan Ballou, who served as a Major in the 2nd Rhode Island Volunteers during the American Civil War. An ardent patriot, Major Ballou believed deeply in the cause for which he was fighting. But he wasn't a fool; anyone could see that many men from both sides would soon die on this battlefield. Preparations had been underway for some time, and by July of 1861 over 60,000 Union and Confederate soldiers were gathered along the banks of Bull Run for the imminent battle. Nearly 5,000 men were to lose their lives.

On a summer evening one week before the battle started, Major Ballou's mind was on his two children and his wife, Sarah. As sometimes happens on the eve of battle, he had a premonition that he wouldn't survive. There were things he wanted to tell Sarah, things he wanted her to know before he died. On July 14, 1861, in the calm of a summer night, the Major opened his heart to her in a letter.

July 14th, 1861
Camp Clark

My very dear Sarah,

The indications are very strong that we shall move in a few days – perhaps tomorrow. Least I should not be able to write you again, I feel impelled to write a few lines that may fall under your eye when I shall be no more.

Our movement may be one of a few day's duration and full of pleasure – and it may be one of severe conflict and death to me. If it is necessary that I should fall on the battlefield for my country, I am ready. I have no misgivings about, or lack of confidence in, the cause in which I am engaged, and my courage does not halt or falter. I know how strongly American Civilization now leans upon the triumph of the Government, and how great a debt we owe to those who went before us through the blood and suffering of the Revolution. And I am willing – perfectly willing – to lay down all my joys in this life, to help maintain this government, and to pay that debt.

I cannot describe to you my feelings on this calm summer night, when two thousand men are sleeping around me, many of them enjoying the last, perhaps, before that of death – and I, suspicious that Death is creeping behind me with his fatal dart, am communing with God, my country, and thee.

Sarah, my love for you is deathless, it seems to bind me to you with mighty cables that nothing but Omnipotence could break; and yet my love of Country comes over me like a strong wind and bears me irresistibly on with all these chains to the battlefield.

The memory of the blissful moments I have spent with you come creeping over me, and I feel most gratified to God and to you that I have enjoyed them so long. And hard it is for me to give them up and burn to ashes the hopes of future years, when God willing, we might still have lived and loved together, and seen our sons grow up to honorable manhood around us. I have, I know, but few and small claims upon Divine Providence, but something whispers to me – perhaps it is the wafted prayer of my little

Edgar – that I shall return to my loved ones unharmed. If I do not, my dear Sarah, never forget how much I love you, and when my last breath escapes me on the battlefield, it will whisper your name.

Forgive me my many faults, and the many pains I have caused you. How thoughtless and foolish I have oftentimes been! How gladly would I wash out with my tears every little spot upon your happiness, and struggle with all the misfortune of this world, to shield you and my children from harm. But I cannot. I must watch you from the spirit land and hover near you, while you buffet the storms with your precious little freight, and wait with sad patience till we meet to part no more.

But, Oh Sarah! If the dead can come back to this earth and flit unseen around those they loved, I shall always be near you; in the garish day and in the darkest night – amidst your happiest scenes and gloomiest hours – always, always; and if there be a soft breeze upon your cheek, it shall be my breath; or the cool air fans your throbbing temple, it shall be my spirit passing by.

Sarah, do not mourn me dead. Think I am gone and wait for thee, for we shall meet again.

Major Ballou was killed one week later. Major Ballou, like many soldiers moving toward the field of battle, had the Big Picture when he wrote his letter to Sarah. People in life and death situations often do. Unfortunately, there were times when he lost sight of the Big Picture. The lines, *"Forgive me my faults and the many pains I have caused you. How thoughtless and foolish I have oftentimes been!"* suggest that there were times when Major Ballou forgot how important Sarah was to him. It often works that way. We don't appreciate what we have until it's gone. It's not until we've lost the people we love that we realize how much they mean to us. Far too often, that realization comes in divorce court, in a child custody hearing, or with the death of a loved one. When the Big Picture comes, it's too late to do anything about it.

Regret is a terrible thing – regret about things we should have said but didn't, regret about wounds we wish we could undo but can't. As the Major wrote to Sarah, *"How gladly would I wash out with my tears every little spot upon your happiness . . . But I cannot."* How much better life would be if we always kept the Big Picture in mind? Losing sight of it always leads to regrets. Let me tell you about one of Arturo's regrets. Like Major Ballou, Arturo was a good man, but sometimes he lost sight of the Big Picture.

Arturo and the Towels

Arturo loved his daughter Julia, and she loved her father. Julia was soon to be married to a fine young man of whom her father approved. Arturo came home one day and found that his daughter and several of her friends had left their towels by the pool. Arturo was annoyed that they hadn't put the towels away, and he scolded Julia. Jabbing his finger at her he yelled, "If you can't get your friends to clean the place up, then *you* do it!" It wasn't so much his words as the harsh tone of his voice, with her wedding only days away, that upset Julia. She didn't say anything, but excused herself and went to her room. A while later, Arturo's wife told him that Julia was in her room crying. Arturo's only response was a shrug of his shoulders.

When Arturo told me this story I asked him why he didn't go to Julia to talk with her. "I never apologize," Arturo said. "That's one thing I never do." Knowing how he adored Julia, I asked him to consider the Big Picture. "Is this the last memory you want Julia to have as your daughter in your home?" "What do you mean?" Arturo asked. I reminded him that his and Julia's lives were about to change forever. In a few days she would be married with a husband and a home of her own. Did he really want to bring this phase of their lives to an end with such an ugly memory? Were the damn beach towels worth even one of his daughter's tears?

"Try to see the Big Picture, Arturo," I said. "Remember who Julia is and what she means to you. When you react to small problems with an aggressive attitude you may give her the impression that the towels are more important to you than her feelings. Julia is about to take a big step in her life. In her few remaining days with her father she needs to feel your love and support. She needs to know that she can turn to you for advice and relief from the problems and pressures that she will face over the years to come. This is a time to let her know that you'll always be there for her, and that she can confide in you without fear that you'll yell at her. Isn't that part of your Big Picture, Arturo?"

Arturo regretted having lost sight of the Big Picture. Beneath his gruff exterior he cherished Julia, and he set about the job of putting things right between them. This is a relatively minor incident when compared to the other stories in this book, but it illustrates the hurt we inflict upon people we love when we lose sight of the Big Picture. Keeping the Big Picture in mind when we're angry can make a big difference in the way we react to things, as shown by the client who was scratched by his cat. His cat had a habit of jumping up on a chair and pawing at him every morning when he left for work. One day the cat scratched him badly enough to draw blood. His first reaction was to hit the cat, but he stopped himself and thought, "I'd rather have the cat try to stop me from leaving each day than have it run from me when I come home." That's using the Big Picture. By keeping sight of the Big Picture of our relationships, we avoid saying and doing things that hurt the people we care about.

The Big Picture is also an important part of the time-out procedure. When a problem comes up and tension starts to build, keep the Big Picture in mind until the problem is solved. Thinking about the Big Picture during a time-out helps you keep things in perspective. Remember who you're talking to, how important they are to you, and what you want your relationship to become as the years go by. With your Big Picture in mind, you'll be more likely to act in a way that's consistent with it.

Whenever you experience negative feelings toward a loved one, use it as a cue to think about your Big Picture, as in the following illustration:

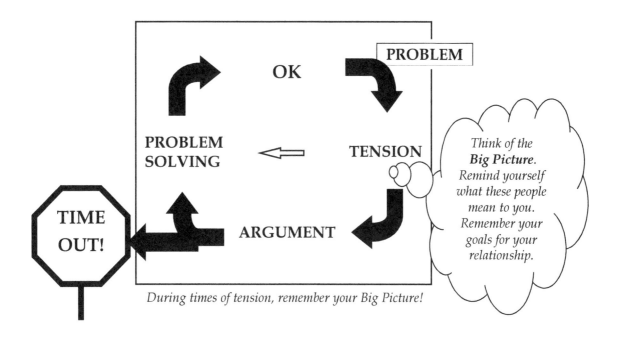

During times of tension, remember your Big Picture!

Emotional Numbness

Why do so many relationships fail? How do people who love each other lose their way and drift apart as the years go by? One reason is that many people are taught from childhood how to be tough and strong, but not how to give and receive love. Uncomfortable with any strong emotion other than anger, they tune out their emotions and develop "emotional numbness." Expressing feelings like love, fear, and sadness cause nervous tension and make them feel vulnerable, so they pretend not to feel anything. The mere mention of the word "emotion" causes some of the most brave and courageous among us to "cut their cables" and run. Uncomfortable giving or receiving strong expressions of love, they stumble over the words "I love you" and avoid real intimacy in their relationships. They tell themselves their partner and children know how they feel, it's not necessary to say the words. As one man said, "I would never hug my son! I might shake his hand - but I'd never hug him!" His son was eight years old.

Typically, people who suffer from emotional numbness don't see it as a problem. Rather, they see their spouse as the problem, claiming they are "too emotional." Everything would be fine, they tell themselves, if their partner would stop talking about feelings so much. They don't understand that their inability to express any emotion but anger isolates them from others. Their relationships lack warmth and closeness, and they live emotionally disconnected from others and from themselves. Expressions of love and affection, the feelings that build strong connections and secure attachments to others, are rare.

If you don't tell people you love them, how are they to know? Your partner and your children need to hear you say the words. I'm not saying that you need to wear your feelings on your sleeve. I am saying that you should be at least as comfortable expressing love as you are expressing anger. The words "I love you" need to be a said, and said often. Make sure the words are part of your Big Picture.

Destructive Anger

Expressing anger destructively also causes relationships to fail. It has been said that "anger doesn't solve anything, but it can destroy everything." Freely venting anger without regard for the pain it causes and the harm it does to your relationship is childish and irresponsible. The things you say when you're angry matter, and they can't be taken back once you say them. Vicious verbal attacks scar your partner and can wound your relationship deeply, possibly beyond repair. As the poet Claire Thomas wrote:

> *Cold steel may penetrate the flesh,*
> *The wound may throb and smart,*
> *But far more painful are the wounds*
> *Inflicted on the heart.*
>
> *Yes - marks upon the flesh will fade,*
> *Forgotten with the pain,*
> *But when the heart is wounded thus,*
> *The scar will long remain.*

What can you do if your relationship has already been damaged by things you have said and done? The skills and tools in this book can help. You also need a Big Picture. A large part of the Big Picture is learning to give and receive love. As Karl Menninger wrote: *"Love cures people – both the ones who give it and the ones who receive it."* In your words and behavior toward your partner, act as though you were as deeply in love as you wish you could be, and keep at it. Don't expect to undo all the hurts overnight, but persist in showing your love through words and actions. Stay in The Box when angry and let time pass. In time, if not too much damage has been done, you will see a change in the both of you. The important thing is to begin to really give and receive love, and when problems come up, to keep your eyes on the Big Picture.

The choice is up to you. You have the power to make your relationship a heaven or a hell. For better or worse, our relationships will always be what we make them. They will be as poor or as great as our own Big Picture. As Alfred Grant Walton penned:

> *We make the world in which we live*
> *By what we gather and what we give,*
> *By our daily deeds and the things we say,*
> *By what we keep or cast away.*
>
> *What is the place in which we dwell,*
> *A hut or a palace, a heaven or hell*
> *We gather and scatter, we take and we give,*
> *We make our world – and there we live.*

HOMEWORK ASSIGNMENT
CHAPTER 13

<u>Step One</u>: Write your own Big Picture. Take your time and put thought into this exercise. Why are you in a relationship? What do you want to get out of it? Why did you choose this person as a partner? How do you want your relationship to grow over the years to come? How are you willing to change to reach your relationship goals? How will you talk and act during times of conflict? How do you want your relationships with your children to develop over the years? If you're not in a relationship now, describe the kind of relationship you hope to have one day. Avoid the temptation to talk about how big your house will be, or about the expensive car you will drive. The Big Picture is about the quality of your relationships with the people you love.

<u>Step Two</u>: Describe three changes *you* are willing to make to turn your Big Picture into a reality.

1.

2.

3.

Chapter 14
Social Influences and Violence

Key Concepts: As adolescents we asked ourselves whether we were tough enough. As adults we need to ask whether tough is enough. To be successful in adult relationships we need to redefine what it means to be strong, and what it takes to be a successful adult.

Skill Building: Examine your beliefs about what it means to be tough and strong. Develop a more mature understanding of the qualities needed to be a strong and successful adult.

Why are people so violent? Watch the local news, see a movie at the theater, or pick up a local newspaper and you'll see how pervasive violence is in our society. Authorities tell us that most violent crime is carried out by men against other men. However, much of the violence in our society is of the domestic variety, between partners in their own home. To get a picture of the extent of the problem, look at the number of domestic violence cases filed in the first four years of a dedicated domestic violence court located in Long Beach, California. The chart below shows the number of felony and misdemeanor domestic violence cases filed in Long Beach Superior Court between 1991 and 1994.

Year	Felony	Misdemeanor	Total Cases
1991	39	1,652	1,691
1992	73	2,303	2,376
1993	97	2,787	2,884
1994	155	3,875	4,030

Notice that from 1991 to 1994 the number of domestic violence cases seemed to increase 238% in the city of Long Beach. (The number of felony cases increased by 397% over the same period.) Was there a spectacular spike in domestic violence in the early 1990's? Probably not. The apparent increase in domestic assaults may be due to other developments that occurred in the early 1990's. During these years there were timely changes in domestic violence laws, changes in the way enforcement agencies responded to domestic violence calls, and an increased public awareness of domestic violence issues among the public. There was the O.J. Simpson trial with all its controversy and media attention. After 1991, batterers who would once have walked free were more likely to be reported, arrested, and prosecuted. However, there would be no report, no arrest, and no prosecution if partners were not subjecting each other to domestic abuse in the first place.

Let's take these numbers one step further. Research by Straus, Gelles, and many others suggests that about 10% of domestic violence incidents are reported to the police. If the 10%

report rate holds true for Long Beach, and there's no reason to think it doesn't, the total number of spousal abuse incidents in the City of Long Beach between 1991 and 1994 is closer to 110,000, or about 27,500 incidents per year. That's an estimate of 27,500 incidents of domestic violence per year in one city in America. Whatever the reason for the increase in domestic violence cases from 1991 to 1994, the sheer number of cases shows the extent of the problem of violence in American homes.

Two nationwide studies of American families (*Straus & Gelles, Physical Violence in American Families: Risk Factors and Adaptations to Violence in 8,145 Families, 1990, 2nd printing 1999*) indicated that in the average American household, 8,700,000 couples experience at least one incident of domestic violence per year, and that's probably an underestimation of the actual numbers. A large portion of the violence was relatively minor in nature (not likely to cause severe injuries that require medical attention). However, 3,400,000 of those couples experienced the more severe levels of violence (kicking, punching, choking, hitting with an object, using a weapon) that *are* likely to require medical attention. One-third (33%) of the couples in the study experienced at least one domestic assault during the course of the marriage. The same survey found that about 1,500,000 children per year are severely assaulted (kicked, punched, beaten up, burned) in their homes.

To their surprise, the authors also found that the violence was not confined to male on female violence. Women in the study were full and equal partners in the violence. By their own report, the men and women who participated in the 1985 survey (84% of those contacted agreed to participate) revealed the following rates of violence in their relationships:

1985 Survey Results (Straus & Gelles)

Violence Rates Between Partners	
Any violence by the husband	11.6%
Any violence by the wife	12.4%
Severe levels of violence by the husband	3.4%
Severe levels of violence by the wife	4.8%

Domestic assaults reported to the police:	
Minor violence	3.2%
Severe violence	14.4%

In other words, women in the studies reported that they carried out domestic assaults at about the same rate as men did. In an effort to find out how many of the women acted in self-defense during assaults initiated by men, Straus (1980) found that among couples reporting one or more domestic violence incidents, about half of them reported mutual violence (they were hitting each other). In a quarter of the cases, only the man committed violent acts, and in a quarter of the cases only the woman was violent. In cases were the violence was mutual, women hit first half the time, and men hit first half the time.

The incident rates reported by Straus and Gelles were highly controversial when first reported, but similar rates have been found in dozens of studies (for example, O'Leary, Malone, & Tyree, 1994). In their book *Domestic Violence: The Criminal Justice Response (Third Edition, 2003)*, Eve and Carl Buzawa reviewed spousal abuse research in depth and concluded, *"The preceding recent studies collectively suggest that female-on-male violence is a widely underreported phenomenon . . . . [The research] also simply does not fit into the image that many authors, activists, and politicians have of a crime that is almost exclusively within the province of men."* Researchers Williams and Frieze (2005) found that female violence occurs at the same rate as male violence, and occurs independently of their male partner. They concluded that women's use of violence against their partners cannot be dismissed as self-defense. Women get violent too, and at a higher rate than people thought.

Men reading this chapter should not use this information to justify their acts of violence towards female partners. No act of spousal abuse is justifiable, not a single one. And there are important differences between men's violence and women's violence. As Eve and Carl Buzawa acknowledge, *"the impact [of violence] in the form of actual injuries and death is demonstrably less [with female violence] than [with male violence]."* In other words, male-on-female violence is much more likely to result in severe injury or death. Men inflict far more severe injuries on women. If someone is seriously injured due to domestic violence, the majority of the time the victim is a woman. Women are far more likely than men to receive emergency room attention due to domestic violence, and women are far more likely to be murdered by their partners in domestic violence situations. In 1994, 78% of the people killed by their partners or ex-partners in California were women (source: *Los Angeles Times* article referring to data from the California Department of Justice). In 2013, 76% of domestic violence homicides in North Carolina were committed by men (source: North Carolina Department of Justice).

Male violence is also more likely than female violence to induce fear in the victim. With fear comes the potential to use violence or the threat of violence to intimidate and control the partner. Studies of couples who report mutual violence in the relationship (both the husband and the wife have been violent towards each other) show that, for the most part, only the wives are fearful during arguments (Jacobson, et al., 1994). While there are exceptions, it is generally true that male violence induces fear in the female victim, while female violence usually produces anger in the male victim.

Women reading this chapter should not use that fact to minimize the abusive nature of their own violence. You do not have to inflict severe injury on your partners to abuse them. The point I want to make is this: domestic violence is not a male or a female issue. It's not a straight, gay, or lesbian issue. It's not a racial or class issue. It's a human issue. *All domestic violence, regardless of the gender of the person doing the hitting, and regardless of the gender of the person being hit, is an abusive, destructive, and in nearly all instances, a criminal act.*

Social Pressure

So why are people so violent towards their partners? To understand violence we must understand how we are socialized. From a very young age, boys (and an increasing number of girls) are taught that certain characteristics are strong and admirable, while other characteristics are weak and contemptible. Try to remember what it was like to be a 13 or 14-year-old adolescent. How did you want to be seen by your peers? What kind of characteristics did you want to develop, and what characteristics did you want to keep away from?

As an adolescent,

I wanted my peers to see me as:	*I did not want to be seen as:*
Strong	Weak
Tough	Easily pushed around
Confident	Unsure of myself
Unafraid	Frightened
Experienced, Street smart	Naive, Gullible
Don't take any bull from others	Cowardly
Don't show feelings (except anger)	Emotional
Sexually experienced	Sexually inexperienced

If you put the characteristics you thought were good in a box, you have the adolescent idea of what it means to be a real man. To most young men, this box can be called the "adolescent idea of a *Real Man*." Many young women also come to see these characteristics as those belonging to a strong woman.

The Adolescent Idea Of "A Real Man"	
STRONG	UNAFRAID
TOUGH	EXPERIENCED, STREET SMART
CONFIDENT	TAKE NO CRAP FROM ANYONE
IN CONTROL	AVOID FEELINGS (EXCEPT ANGER)
AGGRESSIVE	SEXUALLY EXPERIENCED

When I was an adolescent, the characteristics associated with "real men" were very sought-after. Examples of "real men" seemed to be everywhere - in movies, sports, and among my peers. The social rewards for being a "real man" were obvious. My favorite film and sports heroes got the respect of other real men, dated beautiful women, and make lots of money by being tough. In movies and sports I watched them solve their problems with strength and aggression. They never cried, they were never afraid, they never let themselves be pushed around by others, and I wanted to be just like them. I didn't realize it at the time, but my adolescent idea of a real man was based on two lies:

Lie One: *A real man can solve all his problems with violence. In fact, the stronger, tougher, and more violent you are the better you will be at solving your problems.*

Lie Two: *A real man doesn't have to pay negative consequences for his violence.*

If you want to see examples of these two lies in action, go see the latest action movie at your local theatre. The action hero on the screen will be tough and strong, live totally inside the adolescent "real man" box, and solve all his (or her) problems by shooting someone, bashing them around, or blowing something up. The hero won't get in serious trouble for this violent behavior – no jail, probation, court-martial, ruined relationships, or mandated court counseling – and he will never die.

Most of the training on how to act like a "real man" came from our peers. We trained each other to always be tough and strong. While the rewards for being strong and tough seemed wonderful, punishment from peers for "weak" behavior was swift and terrible. Weak behavior was any behavior outside the adolescent "real man" box. We put tremendous pressure on ourselves and on each other to act tough and strong, like the "real man" we all wanted to be. Those who dared act in ways we thought "weak" or "effeminate" were attacked and ridiculed. We called them names that suggested they were not "real men" or tough enough. Special names were reserved for those who appeared fearful or timid, were easily intimidated and pushed around by others, or who showed too much emotion in front of their peers.

Names we called each other when we got outside the "Real Man" box:	
wimp	punk
sissy	fag
mama's boy	pansy
pussy	crybaby
queer	pussy-whipped
bitch	girl

Do you see what these names have in common? They all attack your manliness. They accuse you of acting like "a girl" rather than a "real man." These names apply social pressure to get you to act tough and strong, to stay inside the "real man" box. The name-calling, ridicule, physical attacks, and rejection usually last until you conform to the narrow adolescent ideal of what a "real man" should be. In ridiculing others in this way, we try to ease our own insecurities about being tough enough. When attacks were directed at us, this type of ridicule hurt deeply. Fear of ridicule motivated us to appear tough and strong to our peers, no matter how we felt inside. When we did feel hurt, sad, frightened, or unsure about ourselves, we tried to cover it up and hide it because we feared ridicule and rejection. We were all subjected to this type of socializing and training by our peers. For example, raise your hand if as an adolescent you ever:

- *Exercised or worked out to get stronger.*

- *Took turns trading punches on the arm with another guy. (Or any other game where the goal is to get the other guy to show fear or hurt while hiding your own.)*

- *Done something you didn't really want to do because a peer "dared you" to do it.*

- *Covered up feelings of fear, sadness, or insecurity because you did not know how your peers would react.*

- *Did something you did not really want to do to appear tough or brave to others.*
- *Were called names listed in the box above, or called others those names.*
- *Got in a fight you could have avoided because you were afraid people would think you were afraid if you walked away.*
- *Refrained from showing affection to another guy because you were afraid he might think you were gay.*

Let's take a short quiz to see how well you have learned your lessons about being a "real man." What is a "real man" supposed to do in the following situations?

1. On the way home from school a bully gets in your face, pushes you, and calls you a pussy. The adolescent idea of being a "real man" says you should:

    a) *Ask him to stop annoying you.*
    b) *Ask a teacher for help.*
    c) *Tell him how his behavior makes you feel.*
    d) *Punch him in the face.*

2. You really hurt yourself sliding into home plate during a baseball game. The adolescent code of being a "real man" says you should:

    a) *Cry.*
    b) *Tell the coach you quit.*
    c) *Show no outward signs of pain and "walk it off."*
    d) *Ask someone to go get your mom.*

You knew the answers, didn't you? You were well trained. As an adolescent, what kind of reaction would you have received from your peers if you took any course but the "approved" one? Can you see how thoroughly you were trained to act like a "real man?" As a man, you were trained to prove your toughness by following the manly rules of adolescence, some of which are shown below:

1. *Show no feelings except anger.*
2. *Don't show when you are hurt.*
3. *Never cry or show weakness.*
4. *Never show affection for other men, even those you love.*
5. *Avoid talking about personal problems with other guys or turning to them for emotional support.*
6. *Take no crap from anybody.*

As a teenager, I lived scrupulously by these adolescent rules of conduct. Living like a "real man" helped minimize ridicule and rejection from my peers. But when I entered the world of adults, I found that these adolescent rules were not enough to solve the grown-up problems I had to contend with. Rather than avoiding problems, these rules from our adolescent lives cause bigger problems, some of which are shown below.

- *Because men are accustomed to hiding most of our feelings, our partners think we are uncaring and distant. They think we don't love them.*
- *We try to handle problems by getting angry and being tough, but this only makes the problems between you and your partner worse.*
- *Because we are used to avoiding personal problems, our partner is frustrated in her or his attempts to discuss problems with us. No one told us how to "open up" and talk problems through.*
- *We don't show feelings of hurt until we explode like a volcano.*
- *We see our children and spouse moving away from us, but are helpless to stop it.*
- *We are more comfortable with sex than with intimacy.*
- *Because we have learned to get aggressive when pressured, we resort to violence when we feel threatened. Sometimes we get arrested for our aggression against our partner. We are surprised when we get arrested, because we were only behaving like we learned to behave as adolescents – like "real men."*

Real Men and Their Children

One of the saddest and most destructive aspects of adolescent thinking about manhood is the effect it has on the relationship between a father and his children. Too often, fathers think that what children (especially sons) need is "toughening up." In reality, what they need most from us is understanding, love, compassion, respect, and patience. They need to know that we understand what they are going through, and that we are proud of them. They need to be taught that manhood means being strong at times, but it also means being gentle, kind, and loving. They need to be shown by our example to control their anger and solve problems non-violently.

Far too often, what they receive instead are harsh words and physical ill-treatment. Many fathers feel uncomfortable demonstrating affection, even to their own sons. They think that showing affection is a woman's job; a father's job is to make them "tough." If they show affection to their sons it might make them "soft." Because of this attitude, the myths of adolescence are reaffirmed to our children, and they perpetuate the cycle with their own children.

The Adolescent Man Falls Short

The main point of this chapter is that we learned as young men to adopt an adolescent idea of what it means to be strong. Due to pressure from our peers and others, we were afraid to act any other way. The problem is that the adolescent man is woefully unprepared to handle the complex problems and issues that adults must face in their relationships. How do I get these bills paid? I don't know if my partner loves me anymore. I'm afraid my daughter's using drugs. My son's failing school. Is my partner having an affair? My boss doesn't like me. My doctor told me I have a serious illness. Why don't my kids want to be around me? These are adult problems that require adult skills to handle them. If all we have in our toolbox is being tough, strong, aggressive, and showing no feelings but anger, we're going to fail.

As adolescents we often asked ourselves: *"Am I tough enough?"* As adults, we have to ask ourselves a different question: *"Is tough enough?* The answer is no. Being tough is not enough to be successful in adult relationships. Success in the adult world requires a set of skills that weren't in the Adolescent Box. What are the skills needed? Many of them are in this book, but there are others as well. You know what they are. Just ask yourself this question: *"When I was an adolescent, what did I need more of from my father?"* If you're like most of my clients, your answers will be like those below:

What I Needed More Of From My Father	
Love	Support
Time	Understanding
Advice	To know he was proud of me
Listen to me	Talk to me about stuff I was going through
Do things with me	Patience

These are the things you need to be successful in the adult world. They're the things your partner and your children will need from you to make your relationships work.

Does this mean that all of the characteristics in the Adolescent Box are of no value to you? No, it doesn't. There's nothing wrong with being tough sometimes. When you're raising a gaggle of teenagers, you may need to be tough in setting limits and rules of conduct. There's nothing wrong with being physically strong and controlling emotions. How could children's burn clinics operate if the people who work there couldn't turn off their emotions at times? There's nothing wrong with being a good sexual partner. All of these things are part of the characteristics that make a successful adult. *But they're not enough. You also need to develop patience, the ability to listen and show understanding, the ability to give support and receive it from others, and the willingness to show feelings other than anger. Taken together, these characteristics provide the flexibility and range of skills that strong adults need.*

If violence in your home is to stop and if your relationships are to be successful, you must break free from adolescent thinking. Adolescent thinking must be replaced with mature, adult thinking and behavior. Adult thinking about being strong includes the following principles. The principles apply to both men and women, but some are especially important for men:

- *A strong person does not have to hide feelings from his or her partner. A strong adult has the courage to share not only anger, but all of his feelings appropriately and honestly, including feelings such as love, hurt, and insecurity.*

- *A strong person is not afraid to ask, "Am I doing right or wrong?" or, "Am I acting responsibly towards my family?"*

- *A strong person maintains strong standards of behavior and takes responsibility for mistakes without blaming others or making excuses.*

- *A strong person never resorts to violence to resolve problems with his or her partner. A true adult understands the negative effects of abuse, and knows that verbal and physical aggression make matters worse. Self-control is more valued than controlling others.*

- *A strong adult is willing to talk about problems with his or her partner, and does not avoid them. Mature strategies for solving problems are used, such as communication, negotiation, and compromise, rather than intimidation and bullying.*

- *Strong adults do not blame their partner for their own mistakes. A strong adult accepts full responsibility for handling their anger responsibly, and takes whatever steps are needed to stop his or her own abusive behavior.*

- *A strong adult can tolerate the anxiety that comes from trusting and opening up to his or her partner, so that they can be truly intimate.*

- *A real man has the courage and self-confidence to give and receive emotional support.*

- *A real man can show affection for his children without fear of making them "soft." He teaches them through his example that being strong also includes traits like kindness, patience, understanding, and love.*

HOMEWORK ASSIGNMENT
CHAPTER 14

1. Write the characteristics you believe it takes to be a strong adult man or woman. Take your time, and try to write at least a full page.

2. How do your current beliefs differ from the adolescent idea of a "real man" discussed in this chapter?

3. Circle any characteristics from your paper that you need to develop more fully.

4. During the week to come, record examples of the things you did to practice those characteristics with your partner and your children.

Chapter 15
Changing the House Rules

Key Concepts: Every relationship has unspoken rules about the way anger is expressed. In the beginning, the rule is that no hostility is ever allowed. Over time, rules change allowing verbal hostility and physical hostility into the relationship. You can learn to change the rules back to the no-hostility rule.

Skill Building: Learn the process by which the rules in your relationship changed over time. Apply your skills to remove hostility from your relationships and return to the no hostility rule.

Every relationship has rules about how anger is expressed. Generally, the rules are unspoken. No one actually says, "From now on, this is how we will act when we get angry." But you and your partner understand the rules. These unspoken rules determine how you express your anger to each other. This lesson will help you understand the rules that exist in your relationship now, how the rules changed over time, and what to do if you don't like the rules that currently exist.

When relationships are in the honeymoon period, the rule is that you can be angry with each other, but you *cannot be hostile towards each other*. Hostility is not allowed in a new relationship. It will help you understand this concept if we define the difference between *anger* and *hostility*.

Anger: *Anger is a feeling, not a behavior. It describes the way you feel, not the way you behave. For example, you can be angry about something but not let it show.*

Hostility: *Hostility involves a certain way of acting. Hostile behavior is openly aggressive, abusive, and destructive. Examples of hostile behavior are yelling, swearing, name calling, threats of violence, and violence itself. Everyone recognizes a hostile attitude when they see it.*

The Honeymoon Period

In the beginning, there was a honeymoon. When you first started to date your partner, how did you act when you were angry about something? Most likely, you were always on your best behavior because you wanted to create a good impression. You were attracted to your partner, and because you wanted him or her to like you, you wanted your partner to like you. When you were angry about something, you probably just blew it off. If you're like most people, statements like, *"That's OK, don't worry about it"* were common. You instinctively knew that if you were openly hostile toward your partner on your first date, there wouldn't be a second date. Let's face it, no one goes out for a movie, dinner, and a beating later. The rule is, "No hostility allowed!"

This is the unspoken rule of all new relationships, if you want them to last. How did you act the first time you met your boss? You were on your best behavior, right? How did you act the first time you met your neighbors or your in-laws? Same thing – if you want any relationship to continue past the first few minutes you have to avoid a hostile attitude. The rule about anger during the honeymoon period is this: *no hostility is allowed.*

Unfortunately, the rule forbidding hostility between you and your partner didn't last. Do you remember the first time you yelled at your partner, or your partner yelled at you? There was a first time. Can you remember the first incident of swearing or name-calling? There was a first time for that, too. What about the first time you said something cruel or hurtful to each other? You may not remember it, but there was a very first time. If you're reading this book, I assume that those incidents were handled in a way that changed the rules about the way anger is expressed in your relationship. Hostility was introduced, accepted, and a new rule emerged.

The First Rule Change

To change the rules in a relationship, the consent of both partners is required. There are no victims here. It only takes one partner to suggest a rule change, but both partners must agree to it before the rule can be changed. As you have read, your relationship started with the unspoken rule that *no hostility is allowed*. At some a new rule came into effect: *verbal hostility is OK*. Let's see how you and your partner changed the no-hostility rule to a new rule that allowed hostility to become a part of your relationship.

It probably happened this way. A problem came up, and you and your partner started to argue. The tension caused by the problem grew to a level never reached before. As the tension grew higher and the argument became more heated, either you or your partner crossed the *"I don't care what I say line."* One of you became verbally hostile – one of you started to yell, swear, insult, call names, or engage in some other form of verbal hostility.

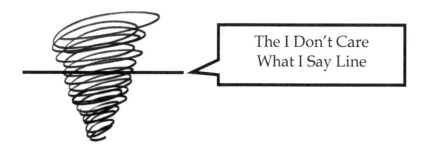

This open expression of hostility was reckless and irresponsible. It did two things. First, it greatly escalated the anger between the two of you, making it harder to solve the problem. Second, it created a *"pull"* on the other partner to join in the hostilities. When someone yells at you, what do you want to do? If you and your partner are like most people, you want to yell back. The first occurrence of verbal abuse is an invitation from one partner (the person yelling) to the other partner (the one being yelled at) to change the no-hostility rule, like the invitation below.

The Invitation

> ### An Invitation to My Partner
>
> *Dear Partner of Mine,*
>
> *This is a formal invitation to join me in changing the rules we live by. From now on, I want to get verbally hostile when I'm mad at you. If you care to join me in this rule change, please respond by:*
>
> *1. Participating in the hostility with me, or*
> *2. Passively accepting my hostility without objecting to it in a meaningful way.*
>
> *Lots of love,*
>
> *Me*

It doesn't matter who offers the invitation. As far as rule changes go, the important thing is whether the invitation is accepted. That's what seals the deal. Any expression of verbal hostility is a request to change the rule about how you treat each other when you get angry. Once again, it's not important which person started it. Let's say that your partner was the first to yell. Does that mean that the rule change was all his or her fault? No, it does not. *A rule change is not complete until the partner who is yelled at accepts it by (1) giving in to "the pull" and participating in the hostility (yelling back), or (2) passively accepting the other person's hostility toward you.*

Either course of action is a way of saying: *I accept this rule change. From now on hostility can be a part of our relationship.* If you chose to participate in the verbal hostility you're saying, *"I'll show you that I can't be pushed around! I'll give back as good as I get. I'm OK with this change in our relationship. I'm willing to change the rules."* If you passively accept the hostility without assertively objecting to it in a clear and decisive manner, you also tell your partner (through your behavior) that you accept the rule change. By accepting the invitation, whether by getting verbally hostile back or through passive acceptance, the process is complete. The unspoken no-hostility rule has changed. Hostility will now become an increasing frequent part of your lives. Your relationship is going to be very different from now on.

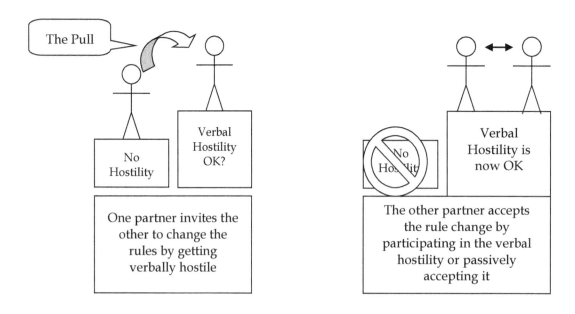

The rule change unlocked a door that was closed during the honeymoon period. Once unlocked, it became easier to go through that door again. The next time you get angry with each other, the yelling comes a little quicker and grows a little louder. From now on the rule is: *"When we are angry with each other, verbal hostility is acceptable."* The hostilities increase in frequency and in severity as you and your partner grow to be comfortable with hostility in your relationship. After a while it even seems normal. As the comfort level develops, so does the anger and frustration between you. On the other hand, expressions of love and affection come less frequently than before. Problems aren't being solved. Your relationship is in trouble.

Before the rule change, the average tension level between you was low. The "average tension level" is the amount of tension between you when you wake up in the morning, before you even say anything to each other. There was a time when it took a lot to get you or your partner anywhere close to the *"I don't care what I say line"* and out of The Box. But allowing hostility into your relationship changed that. With every expression of hostility between you, the average tension level grew higher. Now, any small problem or minor increase in tension can push you over the line.

The Second Rule Change

Living with such a high level of tension is no fun for anyone. It's no fun for the partners who find themselves in constant verbal combat. It's certainly no fun for the children, who have to endure the unrelenting tension between their parents. They can't escape it, and may try to cope by discharging their anger with hostility of their own. Extended family and friends see what's happening, and they're upset by it. With every new insult and shout, the tension grows higher.

Problems are unsolvable in this environment. As you've read, problems are solved when partners work together as a team against the problem. But in this atmosphere, teamwork is impossible. With all the yelling going on, the partners spend more time attacking each other than attacking their problems. Like ghosts that refuse to go away, old problems that were never resolved continue to haunt them, and new problems give rise to ever higher levels of hostility. This is the new normal. Every word between the partners is laced with animosity and anger.

Sooner or later, a second invitation is made to change the rules: *from now on, let's get verbally **and** physically hostile with each other.* This doesn't happen in every relationship where the door is opened to verbal abuse, but as you read in the last chapter, at least eight million couples a year take this next step. Here is the second invitation:

An Invitation to My Partner

Hey Asshole,

This is a formal invitation to join me in changing the rules we live by. From now on, I want to physically hurt you when I am mad at you. If you care to join me in this rule change, please respond by:

1. *Participating in the physical hostility with me, or*
2. *Passively accepting my physical hostility without objecting to it in a meaningful way.*

I hate you,

Me

The second rule change happens the same way as the first. The average tension level between the partners may already be well above the *"I don't care what I say line,"* and dangerously close to the *"I don't care what I do line,"* with one or both partners spending a lot of time outside of The Box. One day, there is an incident of open verbal hostility, but this time one partner escalates beyond verbal hostility to physical hostility. The first incident of physical hostility may be relatively minor (a punched wall, a thrown dish, a pushed partner), or it may come as a vicious physical assault like an exploding volcano. Either way, the invitation to change the house rules has been offered.

Any physical assault upon a partner is inexcusable and outrageous. But how does the partner respond to it? An invitation to change the rules once more has been made, but will the victim of the assault accept the invitation? *Remember, the rule change is not complete until the second partner accepts the invitation by (1) giving in to "the pull" and participating in the physical hostility, or (2) passively accepting the other partner's physical hostility.*

Either course of action is a way of saying: *I accept this rule change. From now on physical hostility will be a part of our relationship. I'm OK with this change in our relationship. I'm willing to change the rules. From now on, when we are angry with each other, physical hostility is OK."* Once again, if you participate in the violence or passively accept it without assertively objecting to it in a clear and decisive manner (calling the police, following the advice of a woman's shelter, separating, etc.) you show through your behavior that you accept the new rule change. By accepting the invitation by getting physically hostile back or through passive acceptance (I don't like what you are doing to me, but I'm not going anywhere), the process is complete. The unspoken rule that forbade violence has changed. Physical hostility will become a part of your lives. As with verbal abuse, the comfort level with physical hostility grows with each new incident. Once the door to physical hostility is unlocked, it usually becomes more frequent and severe over time.

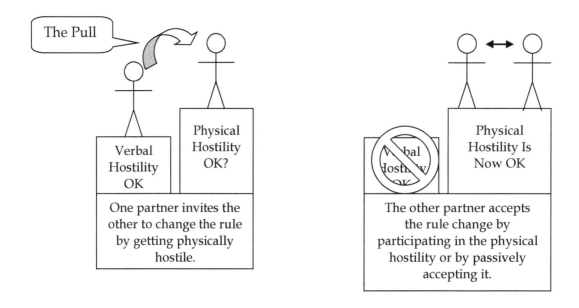

Many men and women are surprised when they are arrested during one of these incidents of physical hostility. In their first session, they express dismay that anyone thinks that they need counseling. Because their comfort level with hostility in their relationship had grown so high, their behavior didn't seem serious to them: *"After all, it was just a little slap."* They also have a hard time seeing their part in the rule changes, and why they're wrong to only blame their partner for the hostility in the relationship. The rules that exist between the partners would not be there if they had not accepted the invitations offered.

More about Passive Acceptance

As you've seen, participating in the verbal and physical hostility is not the only way that rules are changed. Rules are also changed if one partner becomes passive and submissive when the other partner is abusive. When one partner abuses the other, and their partner passively accepts it, the rule change is complete. The abusive partner will continue to be abusive. This is commonly seen in the "battered woman's syndrome," in which the battered woman continually forgives and submits to the abusive partner. If accepted passively, abuse is likely to escalate in frequency and severity. The two stories below are drawn from my client files. The names are changed, but the stories are true. They show how passive acceptance of hostility can actually promote it.

Flora and Carlos

There is a disturbing scenario that is often seen among clients in our program. Consider Flora and Carlos. Flora arrived in this country to marry Carlos, an older man whom she did not know very well. The marriage was arranged by the families of Flora and Carlos. Soon after a short honeymoon period, Carlos began to verbally abuse Flora, who accepted the abuse silently and passively. She was new to the country and its ways, and her culture and religion prohibited divorce. The abuse continued for several years, and the anger and frustration grew in the loveless relationship. Flora was miserable but saw no escape from the situation in which she found herself.

One evening, Flora was preparing dinner and as she chopped vegetables with a large kitchen knife, Carlos began to verbally abuse her. On and on he went. Flora's anger escalated past the *"I don't care what I do line."* Without a word Flora suddenly turned and threw the knife at Carlos. The knife struck deep into Carlos' belly. Carlos survived, but Flora was convicted of serious felony charges.

Jermel and Tisha

Jermel was extremely overweight. So much so that he passively accepted Tisha's constant verbal ridicule and occasional physical abuse. Tisha started her verbal hostility soon after their marriage, but Jermel accepted it passively. He was so insecure about his weight that he was, in his words, "just grateful that someone would have him." He was afraid that if he said anything back to Tisha or stood up for himself she would leave him, and he would be alone for the rest of his life. The verbal and physical abuse continued. Tisha would insult and humiliate Jermel in public, and often used her angry tirades to control and manipulate him. Sometimes she would physically assault him. All this Jermel passively accepted for seventeen years. But the anger and resentment grew inside, Jermel was a volcano waiting to explode.

One hot summer day, Jermel and Tisha were returning home after a trip out of the city. At the airport Jermel struggled alone with their heavy luggage, and Tisha was yelling at him about one thing or another. Suddenly, he dropped the luggage, clenched his fists, and punched Tisha hard in the face. Jermel could see a police officer watching him, but he didn't care. He was past the *"I don't care what I do line."* Blinded by seventeen years of rage, he saw the policeman but punched her anyway. Like Flora, Jermel expressed shock, dismay, and shame about what he had done. He never believed that he could behave in such a manner.

What role did the passive acceptance of abusive behavior play in the behavior of Flora and Jermel? What should they have done? Getting hostile back isn't the answer to their problems, and neither is passive submission to their partners' abuse. The answer is assertive behavior.

Assertive Behavior

Assertive behavior differs from both hostile and passive behavior. Take a moment to read the following descriptions of hostile, passive and assertive behaviors.

HOSTILE BEHAVIOR: "I have rights but you don't." It's OK for me to express my anger in an aggressive, contemptuous, and hurtful way. I don't have to take responsibility for my behavior toward you, because you deserve it. I don't care if my behavior is harmful to you and to our relationship. I want the immediate gratification of going off on you. *Example: "I hate you! You're a fat bitch and I wish I'd never met you!"*

PASSIVE BEHAVIOR: "You have rights but I don't." It's OK for you to express your anger in an aggressive and hostile way. You don't have to take responsibility for your words and behavior towards me. I don't like it, but I'll take it from you. You don't have to worry if your behavior is harmful to me and to our relationship. You can go ahead and get immediate gratification by going off on me. I'll hold on to my own anger and find a way to stuff it. *Example: Say nothing when abuse is directed at you; just keep silent. Apologize even when you've done nothing wrong.*

ASSERTIVE BEHAVIOR: "We both have rights." I can express my anger to you, but I'll do it in a way that is respectful and non-abusive. I take responsibility for my words and behavior towards you, and I expect you to do the same. I will not abuse you, and I will not allow myself to be abused. We must both take responsibility for the way we express ourselves, and do so in a way that does not harm our relationship. I will put the long-term good of our relationship over the immediate gratification of expressing my anger inappropriately.

Example: "I don't appreciate the way you're talking to me. Yelling and insulting each other isn't going to help. I don't talk that way to you, and I want the same consideration. I'm willing to listen to you and work with you on this problem, but I'm not going to be yelled at. Let's calm down and talk."

To better understand the difference between hostile, passive, and assertive behavior, imagine yourself in the following situations. Try to imagine a hostile, passive, and assertive response to both scenarios.

1. *You are in a long line at a store. You're growing inpatient when a person cuts in line ahead of you. Give examples of hostile, passive, and assertive responses.*

2. *You've agreed to pick up your partner from work, but for one reason or another you are late. When do finally arrive, your partner starts to yell at you and calls you an inconsiderate jerk. Give examples of hostile, passive, and assertive responses.*

Turning Back the Clock

The goal of this book is to remove verbal and physical hostility from your relationship. The skills and concepts presented in these chapters are designed to help you change the rules once again – to return to the time when you expressed anger without hostility. To be successful, you must make a personal commitment to avoid hostile speech and behavior in the future. Remind yourself that the hostility will not stop as long as you're a willing participant in it. *Making a personal commitment to remove hostility from your own behavior is the first step.*

Because hostility has been a part of your relationship for so long, it's going to take some time to remove it. Meaningful change doesn't happen overnight. Removing hostility from your own behavior will not immediately heal the wounds you have inflicted in your partner. Also, you may find that when you stop your hostile behavior, your partner does not. What do you do if your partner continues to abuse you? Suppose a problem comes up, and your partner starts to yell and insult you. What do you do? *The first thing you will feel is that familiar "pull" to yell or hit back.* You must not give in to it.

You can't always choose the situation that you find yourself in, and you certainly don't control the way your partner behaves. But you *do* choose how you respond to your partner. If you choose to respond with hostile or passive behavior to your partner's hostility, you will fail to change the rules. Be assertive when confronted with hostility. For example, respectfully but assertively address the issue of the yelling by telling your partner how it makes you feel, how you are trying to change your own behavior, and why it's important that the yelling stops. This is the time to use all of the skills you have learned so far. Warning signs, self-talk, problem-solving, the box, time-out, keeping the big picture, all of the homework assignments you have done; every lesson in this manual has prepared you for this. Apply what you have learned and lead by example. Use self-talk and stay focused on the problem. *Do whatever you have to do to keep yourself from responding in a hostile or a passive manner.*

When you handle the situation respectfully, assertively, and without hostility, it creates a different kind of pull on your partner. If you apply your skills and abide by the "No Hostility" rule, it creates a pull for your partner to stop the yelling and join you in STOPPING THE HOSTILITY. That's how you turn back the clock.

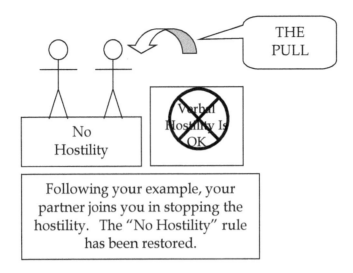

Once again, the change won't happen overnight. Meaningful change takes determination and work; it won't come easily. You will have to resist "the pull" over and over again. But every time you successfully resist the pull, you come one step closer to removing hostility from your relationship for good.

HOMEWORK ASSIGNMENT
CHAPTER 15

1) Your partner accuses you of not doing your share of the chores. You disagree. As you talk, tempers rise and your partner insults you. Give examples an assertive response, a hostile response, and a passive response.

2) Over the week to come, provide an example of how you resisted "the pull" to become hostile. Describe the situation and the skills that you used to avoid hostility and stay assertive and in The Box.

3) What is the rule that governs your relationship now? Do you live by the "No Hostility Rule" or, is verbal or physical hostility OK? What rule governed your relationship in the past? What rule do you want to govern your relationships in the future?

Chapter 16
Skill Building

Key Concepts: Reaching your goal of an abuse-free lifestyle requires both knowledge and practice. This chapter will help you consolidate your understanding of the material in the last three chapters and apply the concepts and skills in your relationships. Remember, to build your skills you must commit to applying them in your daily life. It's what you do, not what you know, that gets results.

Skill Building: Complete the following test to review any gaps in your knowledge of key skills and concepts. Provide detailed examples of your efforts to apply them in your Skill Building Log.

You've learned a lot of new concepts in the last three chapters. Understanding The Big Picture, the social influences that affect your behavior, and the way unspoken rules affect your relationships will help you make the changes that you're working towards. Take some time to review the concepts in the last few chapters before going on, and take the quiz to check for any gaps in your knowledge. Be sure to go back and review any items on the quiz that give you trouble. You'll also find a fresh *Skill Building Log* to use as you apply the concepts and skills you've learned.

Quiz
Chapters 13-15

1) Chapter 13 dealt with something called "The Big Picture." Pretend that you're talking to someone who hasn't read this book and describe The Big Picture to them. (Chapter 13)

2) How does having a Big Picture help self-talk? (Chapter 13)

3) You should bring the Big Picture to mind during a _____ period to help you put things into perspective. (Chapter 13)

4) It has been said that anger doesn't solve anything, but it can destroy _____. (Chapter 13)

5) For the most part, our relationships will always be what we have made them. They will be as poor or as great as our own _____. (Chapter 13)

6) What is meant by "emotional numbness? (Chapter 13)

7) It is estimated that more than _____ million couples experience at least one incident of domestic violence per year, and that more than _____ million children per year are severely assaulted. (Chapter 14)

8) Two lies that are commonly told in the media are that a real man can solve his problems with _____, and that a real man doesn't have to pay negative _____ for his violence. (Chapter 14)

9) As adolescents we often asked ourselves: "Am I tough enough?" As adults we have to ask ourselves a different question: "_____." (Chapter 14)

10) Describe the "Adolescent Idea of a Real Man." (Chapter 14)

11) How is the adolescent idea of a strong person different from the adult idea of a strong person? (Chapter 14)

12) The rule about anger during the honeymoon period is this: no _____ is allowed. (Chapter 15)

13) Relationships start with the unspoken rule that no hostility is allowed. In many relationships this doesn't last. At some point a new rule comes into effect: _____ hostility is OK. (Chapter 15)

14) Open expressions of hostility create "The _____" on the other partner. (Chapter 15)

15) A rule change is not complete until you accept it by (1) giving in to "the pull" and _____ in the hostility yourself, or (2) _____ accepting the other person's hostility toward you. (Chapter 15)

16) Generally, the first rule change involves _____ hostility. The second rule change involves _____ hostility. (Chapter 15)

Check your answers and move on to the Skill Building Log.

Skill Building Log

Step 1: Select one or more skills from the following list that you want to practice. Selecting the right skills to practice is easy. Just answer this sentence: *"It would help me and my family the most if I would _____."*

Step 2: On a separate sheet of paper, write a detailed example of how you put the skills to use. Describe (1) who you were with, (2) the problem you struggled with, (3) any of your warning signs that came up, (4) the skills you used to handle the problem, (5) how things turned out.

TOOLBOX FOR CHAPTER SIXTEEN

Tools from Chapters 1-3:
- Memorize The Box
- Use The Box to guide my decision making
- Stay focused on problem solving during an argument
- Learn my own Warning Signs
- Watch for my Warning Signs when I start to feel angry
- Take a Time Out whenever I see my warning signs
- Memorize the rules to Time Out and follow them
- Explain Time Out to my partner
- Never cross the "I don't care what I say line"
- Never cross the "I don't care what I do line"
- Stop using any form of Verbal Abuse (stay in The Box)
- Recognize and avoid using Denial, Blame, and Minimizing

Tools from Chapters 5-7:
- Whenever I feel angry toward my partner, stop and ask myself, *"Is my thinking rational and logical right now? Am I making a big deal out of a small problem?"*
- Whenever I feel angry (or frustrated, jealous, etc.) I'll remind myself that I can choose to think in ways that escalate these feelings, or I can choose to think in ways that reduce them.
- Accept responsibility for everything I say or do.
- Lower my comfort level with violence. Don't minimize, call abuse something other than what it really is, or tell myself that such behavior is OK.
- Don't try to be my partner's boss or force my will on him or her. See my partner as my equal.
- Allow my partner the right to express his or her thoughts and feelings openly and without intimidation.
- Always stop and think *before* I react.
- Never "Awfulize."
- Stay out of the *"YOU MODE."*
- Self-talk to prevent or reduce anger.
- Identify my core beliefs about anger and aggression and modify them.

Tools from Chapters 9-11:
- See tension as a signal to problem solve.
- Remove all controlling, blaming, and hurtful language from my problem solving.
- Ask my partner if I come across as bossy, blaming, or hurtful.
- Ask my partner to tell me whenever he or she feels controlled, hurt, or blamed.
- Use the six problem solving steps.
- Whenever I step on a land mine, find out which mine it was and avoid it the next time.
- Write a letter to my partner expressing all of the feelings described in the letter writing exercise.

- Invite my partner to write a letter back to me.

<u>New Tools from Chapters 13-15:</u>
- Develop a Big Picture and keep it in mind when problems come up.
- Let go of the adolescent idea of what it means to be strong.
- Recognize and avoid "The Pull."
- Live by the no-hostility rule.

PERSONAL PROGRESS AND SELF-EVALUATION

1. Evaluate the progress that you have made so far in your counseling. Are you satisfied with the progress you are making? Are you putting forth your best effort? Is there anything you need to do to make your counseling experience more successful?

2. Select a relationship that is important to you. What can you do to make the relationship better? Set a specific goal for improving the relationship. What do you want to accomplish over the next month?

3. Have you seen changes in your thinking or behavior since starting this program? If so, provide an example of how your thinking and behavior have changed.

4. Are there skills from your counseling that you use on a daily basis? If so, what are they? Give a recent example of using them. If you are not using the skills you have learned on a daily basis, why not?

5. Select a skill or concept from the book that is important for you to use and develop at this time of your life. What skill did you select? How can using that skill benefit you and the people who love you?

Chapter 17
Personality, Acceptance, And Encouragement

Key Concepts: Much of the fighting that goes on has its source in basic personality differences – differences that aren't going away. Accepting differences rather than striving to control or change each other can reduce conflict in your relationships.

Skill Building: Understand the significant personality traits that are a source of conflict between you and your partner, and develop ways to show acceptance and willingness to compromise.

The other day I watched a television commercial advertising a vacation resort on a romantic island in the Caribbean. In the commercial a young couple on their honeymoon walked hand-in-hand along a beautiful beach at sunset. The man was handsome, the woman lovely. They smiled as they strolled along and gazed lovingly into each other's eyes. Obviously, this couple was in love. They have no problems between them of any consequence, and looking at them as they walked hand-in-hand along that beach it's easy to believe they never would. It seemed that their life was perfect, and having found the perfect partner their future together would always be perfect.

Unfortunately, life isn't like that. Sooner or later the romantic honeymoon period ends. How long will their fairytale honeymoon period last? I hate to say this, but the honeymoon period usually ends – well, it ends as soon as they get to know each other better, which is usually somewhere between six and 18 months. Sometimes the honeymoon doesn't even last through the honeymoon. I remember a cruise that my wife and I took to Mexico a few years ago. As we checked into our cabin we happened to meet the young couple checking into the cabin next to ours. They told us they were on their honeymoon. They had the same loving look as the couple in the commercial for the vacation resort I just told you about. Before long, the sound of angry voices could be heard in their cabin. Their angry voices intensified to shouts and obscenities as the couple, who seemed so in love a few hours earlier, verbally battered each other. The honeymoon was over, and the ship hadn't yet cleared Los Angeles harbor.

What Happened to the Honeymoon?

Why does the honeymoon period end? How does our romantic couple on the beach go from loving gazes to, well, reading a book like this? To answer that question, let's follow the course of a new relationship from its beginning to the end of the honeymoon period. When relationships are new, it's natural to feel overly optimistic about the future. Infatuated with our partner, we feel the wonderful emotional high that comes from romantic love. We think about our lover constantly, and even brief separations are difficult to bear. We call from work to leave intimate love messages, we buy small gifts as tokens of love, and we demonstrate affection in infinite ways. Attentive to their every mood, we use pet names such as "darling," "honey," and "sweetheart." It is the nature of infatuation that we see only the qualities in our new partner that are attractive, and ignore or minimize the less attractive traits. (We can always change those little annoying habits of theirs later, right?) No, we can't change our partner, and the belief that we *can* marks the beginning of the end for the honeymoon period.

As time goes by, each partner is faced with a disconcerting and indisputable fact: *my partner is different from me!* My partner is too emotional, or doesn't show enough feeling. My partner spends too much time socializing, or never wants to go out. My partner always wants to try new things, or never wants to do anything different. My partner forgets to pay the bills, or has to plan everything. My partner is grumpy and rude to people, or is too nice and always gets taken advantage of by others. My partner wants different things, likes different things, has different opinions, and acts in ways that annoy me. *Why can't my partner just be more like me?*

The discovery that you and your partner are different is inevitable because you're both individuals with your own personalities. There are *always* differences between people. People differ in personal habits, ideas about the way money should be spent, their choice of friends, beliefs about the way chores should be distributed, and even expectations about the way a husband or wife should act. The specific differences vary from couple to couple, but because no two people are ever exactly alike, differences are always there. Even if you leave your partner (which many people do when the honeymoon ends) and find a new partner, you will discover a new set of differences between you and your new partner. The problems may be different, but there will still be problems. *Having to cope with individual differences is the price you pay for being in a meaningful relationship.*

The success of your relationship does not depend on whether you have differences. Every relationship has them. *The success or failure of your relationship depends upon how you and your partner handle your differences.* If differences are handled wisely, the feeling of affection will grow. You will experience a renewed confidence in the strength of the relationship, and lay the foundation for real love to flourish. But if differences are handled unwisely, *by trying to change each other*, anger and resentment will flourish instead of love.

Marital discord is correlated with domestic violence – couples with more marital conflict have more incidents of domestic violence. Studies also suggest that younger couples have higher rates of domestic violence than older couples. This isn't really surprising. Young couples are just starting to struggle with their partner's differences, and they don't have a clear strategy for dealing with them. They often simply expect their partner to change in order to make them happy and resent their partner if they don't. If your relationship is to be free of abuse you need to develop a strategy for dealing with the differences between you. A fundamental part of this strategy should be **acceptance** and **encouragement**.

Acceptance

If you choose to live with someone, the sooner you can learn to accept each other the better. Unfortunately, as soon a couple gets together they usually set about trying to change their "perfect" partner into something else. He should be more this way; she should be less that way. I'm not suggesting that you accept behaviors like infidelity, substance abuse, or domestic violence – there are some things that no partner should tolerate. But I am saying that you should accept your partner as a separate individual. You need to accept that you are different in some ways, and stop trying to change or control each other. When you accept your partner as he or she is you send a powerful message: *"You are O.K. as you are. You don't have to change. I accept you as you are. You don't have to meet my standards or be just like me for me to love you."* Acceptance is an important and powerful message for partners to send to each other. It helps couples feel intimate. Feeling free to be themselves, they're able to open their innermost thoughts and feelings to each other. You demonstrate acceptance of your partner when you do the following things:

- *Choose not to point out your partner's faults.*
- *Focus on your partner's strengths.*
- *Choose not to criticize when your partner makes a mistake. Instead, offer your support and understanding.*
- *Show faith in your partner's decisions.*
- *Give your partner positive messages every day.*
- *Avoid telling your partner how he or she should or must do things.*
- *Listen to your partner's thoughts and feelings respectfully, even if you disagree.*
- *Don't blame your partner for your unhappiness.*
- *Don't demand that your partner think and feel the same way you do.*
- *Be emotionally available to your partner.*
- *Be willing to say "I'm sorry" when appropriate.*
- *Control your anger and accept responsibility for past abusive behaviors.*
- *Learn to enjoy the ways that your partner is different from you.*

Group members often ask what to do about a partner who consistently does something that irritates or annoys them. Often, the partners have had repeated arguments about some issue, but the annoying behavior continues. First, realize that *you don't have to have everything your way in order to have a happy and satisfying relationship.* Whenever two people choose to live together, there will always be differences that annoy and irritate. You won't always want the same thing or see things the same way. It would be foolish to expect it to be otherwise. Understand that there are also things that *you* do that irritate and annoy your partner. You each must learn to accept each other's annoying behaviors in order to share your lives. Don't allow yourself to turn a minor annoyance into a major problem. Sometimes people get so focused on a relatively minor annoyance that they forget what attracted them to their partner in the first place. Ask yourself: "Do the good things about this relationship outweigh the bad?" If so, you may have to learn to accept some of your partner's annoying habits, just as your partner may have to accept yours.

It is also important to be able to tell the difference between a real problem and an annoyance. Too often, partners treat small irritations or annoyances as serious problems. They *"awfulize."* Annoyances are just a part of life, and should be accepted as such. Don't demand perfection from your partner, don't let small annoyances rob you of the good things about your relationship, and don't sweat the small stuff. Endless bickering about the small stuff will drain the joy from your relationship.

Personality Traits

Here's another reason why you should learn to accept your partner as he or she is: *your partner isn't going to change much, whatever you do*. So what does this have to do with acceptance? Just this: with all the complaining, cajoling, and criticism in the world, your partner isn't going to change much – and neither are you. That's because personality traits, the enduring characteristics that define our personalities and make us the person we are, are very stable. For the majority of people, their basic personality traits don't change much over their entire lifetime.

This does *not* mean that couples shouldn't try to work through their differences and resolve their problems. People can and do make meaningful changes in their behavior. But the changes that can and will take place are usually constrained, or limited, by each person's basic personality. For example, it's unreasonable to expect John, a life-long introvert, to become the unfailing "life of the party," no matter how much Jill, a life-long extrovert, wants him to. He may work to become a bit more outgoing, but it's unlikely that he'll change to the extent that a real party animal might like. If Jane is a dedicated hedonist (she cares mostly about the pleasure and fun she can have today), she's never going to turn into as conscientious a person as her CPA husband John, no matter how much they fight about it. Jill will never care as much as John whether the bills are paid on time, and all his lecturing about credit ratings won't change that. If they're wise, partners can find ways to compromise on some issues. But many couples launch headlong into vicious fights without any regard or appreciation for the fundamental differences in their personalities.

To illustrate my point, let me tell you more about personality, and how personality differences can be a source of unceasing conflict in relationships. One prominent theory of personality is called the five-factor model. The five-factor model identifies, as you can guess, five major parts to every personality: Neuroticism, Extraversion, Openness, Agreeableness, and Conscientiousness. Every person in the world, including me, your neighbor, and you and your partner, can be measured on each of these five dimensions of personality. Here's a general idea of what the scales mean. A score of 1 is on the low side, 5 is on the high side, and a score of 3 would be somewhere between the two extremes. Keep in mind that there are no "good" or "bad" scores. One score isn't better than any other.

NEUROTICISM

LOW   HIGH
1   2   3   4   5

Calm and relaxed, doesn't show a lot of emotion, seldom sad, worried or upset by things. Rarely experiences anxiety or depression. Emotionally stable.	Hot-tempered, sad, worries a lot and easily upset by stress. Easily frustrated. Can be prone to anxiety, depression, and anger outbursts. Very emotionally reactive.

     Where would you rate yourself on the "Neuroticism" scale? Are you low, high, or somewhere in the middle? Where would you rate your partner? Can you imagine how differences between partners on this personality trait can lead to conflict? Suppose that John is low on the scale, and Jill is on the high side. John may be baffled why Jill is so emotionally reactive, and Jill may see John as emotionally detached and unavailable. John says, "why do you have to get so emotional all the time? Can't we just once have a calm conversation?" Jill responds, "How can you just sit there show no feeling? If you loved me you would show me your feelings." Mary, a patient of mine, was very high on this scale. She often criticized her husband, who was on the low end of the scale, for rarely showing strong emotion. One night at a restaurant, the waiter was very slow to take their order. Mary was boiling mad, but her husband seemed not the least upset. Her only explanation was that he must be stuffing his anger. "Why," Mary asked him, "do I always have to experience your anger for you? It's not fair!" It never occurred to her that his personality is such that he just does not experience strong anger as frequently as she does.

     Personality differences can be easily misinterpreted, and that can lead to a lot of conflict unless they understand that, in some ways, they are fundamentally different. If they're wise, John will see that Jill brings a lot of emotion and color to his life that he might otherwise miss, and Jill will understand that John can be a calming influence that adds stability to her life. In truth, that's probably what attracted them to each other in the first place. *The choice is this: accept your differences and appreciate the positive contribution that the differences bring to each of your lives, or reject each other's differences as bad and engage in endless, futile attempts to make your partner be more like you.*

     The next scale is Extraversion. It describes how important socializing is to people. If you are high on the scale, you enjoy being with others a lot. If low on the scale, you prefer more solitary activities.

EXTRAVERSION

LOW   HIGH
1   2   3   4   5

| Reserved and quiet, but not unfriendly. Independent, prefer to spend time alone or with a few close friends. Can be social, but prefers not to. | | | Sociable and talkative, enjoys large groups and social gatherings, outgoing and energetic. Can enjoy quiet time alone, but prefers socializing. |

Rate yourself and your partner on the Extraversion Scale. What type of conflict could personality differences on this scale lead to? John, who is low on the scale, has his heart set on spending their vacation in their cabin on a lake. Jill, who is high on the scale, craves the nightlife and action of Las Vegas. John says Jill never wants to stay home and needs to settle down. "Can't we ever have a quiet night at home?" Jill complains that John is a couch potato and that never wants to go out anymore. If they're wise, they will learn to accept their differences, find ways to compromise, and have the best of both worlds.

The next scale is Openness to Experience, which I've described below:

OPENNESS TO EXPERIENCE

LOW   HIGH
1   2   3   4   5

| Traditional and down-to-earth, conservative and conventional in outlook, likes familiar things. Not a lot of interest in unconventional ideas or experiences. | | | Untraditional, likes new experiences and a lot of variety. Unconventional and adventurous. Craves new and exotic places and experiences. Always willing to try something new. |

If you remember the old TV show *Dharma and Greg*, you'll have a good idea of what this personality trait is about. Greg is low on the scale, and Dharma is high. Their relationship works because they're able to accept their differences and appreciate the qualities that each gives to the other. Their lives are fuller because of the differences. In real relationships, acceptance of differences works the same way.

The next scale is Agreeableness. People high on this scale want very much to be liked. They are uncomfortable with direct expressions of anger. Those who are low on the scale generally don't trust or like others, express their anger easily, and can be rude to others.

AGREEABLENESS

LOW   HIGH
1   2   3   4   5

Don't trust others, uncooperative and irritable, can be rude and disagreeable, competitive and tough-minded.	Trusting of others, eager to be helpful, sympathetic, forgiving, and softhearted. Willing to sacrifice their own wants to get along.

You may think that it's better to be high than low on this scale, but that's not necessarily the case. I'd want a lawyer who is defending me in court to be on the lower side of this scale. On the other hand, I'd like my children's kindergarten teacher to be high on the scale. The best personality type depends on the situation you're in. Some situations are a good fit for your personality, and some are not. A person who is very low on the Extraversion scale would be miserable as the Activity Director on a cruise ship. A person who is very high on this scale would probably be unhappy as a Forrest Ranger in an isolated part of the country.

Differences between partners on the Agreeable scale can lead to conflict if they're unable to understand and accept each other, and find some way to be influenced by each other. For example, John is low in Agreeableness and Jill is on the high side. John accuses Jill of spoiling the kids and thinks she's foolish to spend so much time and money on charities. He thinks people walk all over her and take advantage of her kindness. Jill accuses John of being too gruff with their children and rude to others. She thinks John is uncaring about the plight of less fortunate people, and cares more about money than people. In reality, sometimes John is too hard, sometimes Jill is too soft. If they could be more accepting of each other, respect each other's point of view, and find ways to be influenced by each other, both would be better off. Where do you and your partner fall on the Agreeableness scale?

The last scale is Conscientiousness. People high on the scale are very conscientious. They are organized, pay their bills on time and arrive early for their appointments. They schedule their day and have long-term career goals. Disorganization is stressful for them. People low on the scale are hedonistic and pleasure-seeking. They like to live moment to moment, and rarely stress out. Being organized, staying on top of things at work, and meeting deadlines are not very important to them.

CONSCIENTIOUSNESS

LOW				HIGH
1	2	3	4	5

Lives for the moment, careless about deadlines and appointments, unmotivated, pleasure seeking, lacks clear goals or direction in life. Likes to have fun.	Well organized and disciplined, always make appointments and pays bills on time, very reliable and well organized, neat and goal oriented.

Rachel and Joe were instantly attracted to each other. Rachel was on her way to a business meeting when she saw Joe sitting on his surfboard, soaking up the sun and laughing with his friends. She wished she had more time for fun. Joe noticed Rachel too. He thought she was sexy, and her new Mercedes was cool. They got together. Joe moved in, and at first it was fun for both of them. But now they fight a lot. Rachel expects Joe to "grow up" and get a serious job. Joe complains that Rachel worries too much and tries to "plan their whole lives." He thinks she just needs to "chill" and have some fun. Rachel calls Joe a lazy beach bum. Joe calls Rachel a control freak. They both need to stop trying to change each other.

Joe is never going to be as conscientious as Rachel, no matter how hard she pushes him. He's never going to become a CEO for a top corporation; he's probably not even going to become a great surfer. But he does bring a lot of fun and spontaneity to Rachel's life. Rachel is never going to be as "laid back" as Joe wants her to be. But with Rachel's conscientious ways she provides greater stability to Joe's life - great "digs," the bills get paid, and things get done. If Rachel and Joe are going to be happy together, they'll want to understand and accept each other, be willing to make some compromises, and appreciate the unique qualities they each bring to the lives of the other.

By including this chapter in the book, I hope to help you understand that a lot of the conflict in relationships is unnecessary and futile. Much of the fighting that goes on has its source in basic personality differences – differences that just aren't going away. Why not learn to accept your differences and stop trying to change each other? If you're going to stay together, you'll need to appreciate that your unique personalities can actually enhance your lives. The aim is not to change each other, but to accept each other and to look for ways to make each other happier by finding ways to compromise.

Encouragement

Life can seem pretty discouraging at times. There may be times when nothing seems to turn out the way you planned, when everything in your life seems a disappointment, failure, and discouragement. Life has a way of dealing out enough *discouragement* (literally, the loss of courage) for all of us. Our homes and relationships can be an oasis against discouragement, a place where we can count on receiving support, acceptance, and *encouragement* (literally, to give courage) from our partner. Below is a table that contrasts *discouraging* behaviors with *encouraging* behaviors.

Discouraging	**Encouraging**
Demands perfection	Recognize small improvements
Blaming	Understanding, patience
Demanding	Accept partner as he or she is
Controlling	Respect each other and enjoy differences
Pessimistic	Hopeful and confident in partner's abilities
Disapproving	Approving, respectful of partner
Focuses on failures	Focuses on successes

Encouragement is the greatest motivation for change that is available to you and your partner. It might seem contradictory, but the more you demand change from your partner, the less likely it is that change will happen. On the other hand, the more acceptance and encouragement you give your partner, the more likely it is that the changes you request will take place. If there is something that you and your partner want to change, try the following approach.

The secret to encouraging change:

1) Choose not to criticize when your partner does something that annoys you.

2) Actively look for times when your partner doesn't do the thing that annoys you, doesn't do it as much, or does something that you like.

3) Encourage your partner by acknowledging his or her effort and expressing your appreciation.

Use words such as: *"I noticed when you _____. I just wanted to tell you that I noticed, and to say thank you. I really appreciate it."* These words are much more effective than words that are angry, critical, and demanding. Major change in personality trait are unlikely, but you can better understand each other, and allow yourselves to be influenced by the person you love.

HOMEWORK ASSIGNMENT
CHAPTER 17

1) Using the personality traits discussed in this chapter, describe the most significant differences between your personality and the personality of your partner.

2) Have these differences led to conflict between you? Have you tried to deal with your personality differences by trying to control or change each other?

3) Describe ways that you can show acceptance of your differences, and ways that you can compromise in the areas where there is conflict.

4) Find opportunities to show encourage your partner this week. Use *"The secret to encouraging change"* strategy described in this chapter. Write down what you said and did to encourage your partner, and your partner's reaction to your encouragement.

Chapter 18
Fear and Respect,
Tyrants and Leaders

Key Concepts: The belief that a person can be feared AND respected is false. Leaders win the love and respect of others. Tyrants are feared, but not respected. You can tell the difference between leaders and tyrants by the tools they use. Leaders use the, tools of patience understanding, and self-sacrifice. Tyrants use intimidation and violence. Choose to become a respected leader.

Skill Building: Practice using leadership skills during times of conflict. Apply the tools that foster love and respect, and avoid the tools of the tyrant that create an environment of fear and resentment.

Would you rather be respected or feared? Do you want to be a leader or a tyrant? How are you now seen by your partner and your children – do they respect you or do they fear you? In their eyes, are you a trusted leader or a feared tyrant? Are you neither a leader nor a tyrant, or do you think you're little of both, depending on your mood? This chapter will discuss respect and fear, and leaders and tyrants. The hope is to clarify these concepts and help you decide the type of person you want to be in your relationships. This chapter can greatly enhance your Big Picture, which you started to develop in Chapter 13.

Let's start by looking at the way your partner and children behave around you when you get angry. Do they get anxious and shy away from you? Are they afraid? In Chapter Three, Aaron was aware of the fear he had caused his family and acknowledged it in his Anger Inventory: *"I physically and emotionally damaged my wife and caused my children inestimable pain and distress. I have seen fear in their eyes as they recognized my rage. I have noticed their avoidance of me at times and their timid demeanor with me."* To his credit, Aaron was ashamed of the fear he had caused his family and vowed to change. Do you see the same fear in the eyes of your family when they recognize your rage? If so, you need to read this chapter carefully.

The first thing to accept about respect and fear is this: *no person can be feared and respected at the same time.* In my work, I often hear people say, "I want to be feared and respected." That's not possible. *A person who is feared is not respected. Respect goes to different kinds of people who do different sorts of things. In the same way, a person who is respected is not feared. Respect is the exact opposite of fear. If you want to be respected, you must treat people in ways that engender respect – if you want to be feared, you must behave in ways that engender fear. You can have either fear or respect, but not both.*

Please go back and read that last paragraph again. Read it carefully. You can have *either* fear or respect, but not both. When I teach this concept it provokes an argument from at least one or two of the men or women in the group. From a young age, some people believe that *fear* and *respect* go hand in hand, like burgers and fries. They don't.

The following exercise illustrates how different fear and respect are. First, think of the person you feared most in your life. Take your time. This person whom you feared may be someone currently in your life, or it may be a person from your childhood – a bully in the neighborhood, an abusive step-parent, or some tormentor from your teenage years. The important thing is to think of a person whom you really feared. Understand that I'm not talking about the kind of fear engendered by a strict parent who would spank you if you cut school or stole candy. I'm talking about genuine fear. If you were exposed to a truly abusive parent or step-parent, you know the kind of fear I'm talking about. After you have a person in mind, make a list of the characteristics of the person you feared. What was the person like? What made you fear them? In my groups, people come up with a list that looks like this:

> *The Feared Person*
>
> *Got violent when they were angry*
> *They were angry most of the time*
> *Took advantage of people smaller and weaker than themselves*
> *Were unpredictable, especially when using drugs or drinking*
> *Couldn't be trusted*
> *Had no respect for the rights of others*
> *Liked to boss people around and order them about*
> *Only cared about themselves*
> *Had no self-control*
> *Were feared and hated by everyone*

Now think of the person in your life you respect most. Out of all the people you have known in your life, who do you respect the most? Make a list of the characteristics of the person you respected. What made you respect them?

> *The Respected Person*
>
> *Was never abusive*
> *Took time to listen to me*
> *Had good moral character, they did the right thing*
> *Cared about me as a person*
> *Respected the rights of other people*
> *Was willing to sacrifice for the good of others*
> *Had wisdom and knew right from wrong*
> *Had self-control, even when angry or disciplining me*

Notice the similarities between this list and the list in Chapter 14, "What I Needed More of from My Father." The lists are similar because children need parents that they can respect, not tyrants they fear.

Now compare the two lists side by side in order to show the difference between the feared person and the respected person.

The Feared Person	The Respected Person
<ul><li>Got violent when they were angry, and</li><li>They were angry most of the time</li><li>Took advantage of people smaller and weaker than themselves</li><li>Were unpredictable, especially when using drugs or drinking</li><li>Couldn't be trusted</li><li>Had no respect for the rights of others</li><li>Liked to boss people around and order them about</li><li>Only cared about themselves</li><li>Had no self-control</li><li>Were feared and hated by everyone</li></ul>	<ul><li>Was never abusive</li><li>Took time to listen to me</li><li>Had good moral character, they did the right thing</li><li>Cared about me as a person</li><li>Respected the rights of other people</li><li>Was willing to sacrifice for the good of others</li><li>Had wisdom and knew right from wrong</li><li>Could be trusted, and I could depend on them</li><li>Had self-control, even when angry or disciplining children</li></ul>

As you compare the two lists, can you see that they describe two very different people? Not only are feared and respected people different, they are the *exact opposites* of each other. The feared person is a tyrant. You can tell tyrants by the tools they use to get what they want: fear, intimidation, and violence. The tyrant often gets what he or she wants by bullying others, but they're fooling themselves if they think they can act this way and *also* be loved and respected. Tyrants have a core belief that fear, intimidation, and violence are the best ways to control others and get what they want out of life. If they persist in acting this way, they eventually find themselves alone, despised even by their own family, and very frequently, incarcerated.

A respected person is the opposite of a tyrant. They are not feared by the people who know them. They aren't avoided, and people don't have a "timid demeanor" around them, as Aaron described in his Anger Inventory. In fact, people want to be with people they respect, and look forward to their coming home. They make their family feel safe and secure. They have no desire to engender fear or to intimidate others even though they may be bigger and stronger, and because of that they're loved and respected. You can tell a leader by the tools they use: respect for others and self-control; they're trustworthy and self-sacrificing. They're true leaders in their home.

Fear and intimidation are the tools of a tyrant, while respect and trust are the tools of a leader. Whenever your partner does what you say out of fear of you, you have become a tyrant to them. Because it's so important, I'm going to repeat an earlier statement: ***A person who is*** *feared is not respected. Respect goes to different kinds of people who do different sorts of things. In the same way, a person who is respected is not feared. Respect is the exact opposite of fear. If you want to be respected, you must treat people in ways that engender respect – if you want to be feared, you must behave in ways that engender fear. You can have either fear or respect, but not both.*

As you read this you may be telling yourself, "Sometimes I act like a leader, and sometimes I get mad and act like a tyrant. Doesn't that mean I can be feared and respected at the same time?" No, it doesn't. As I've said, fear and respect are polar opposites. You can't have both. It works this way: to the degree that you've been acting like a tyrant you'll be feared. To the degree you start acting like a leader people will stop fearing you and slowly start to respect you. The diagram below illustrates the concept:

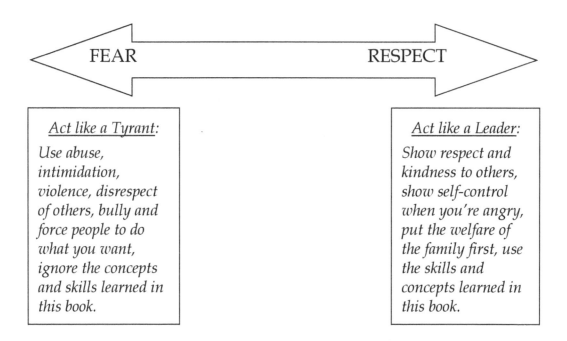

To the degree you behave like a tyrant, people's feelings toward you will move toward the *FEAR* end of the spectrum. To the degree you act like a leader, their feelings will move toward *RESPECT*.

What It Means To Be a Leader

There's nothing wrong with wanting to be a leader in your home. In fact, I encourage you to become a leader. If you and your partner are getting out of The Box, if there is abuse, if the verbal or physical hostility rule is in effect, your relationship is crying out for *someone* to start showing leadership. That person might as well be you. But before you take on the mantle of leadership, first be clear what's required of a leader. I've allowed myself to do a lot of talking about becoming a leader in your home, so I should make sure you understand what I mean by being "a leader."

> *Being a leader does not mean being the boss! Let me say it again: a leader and a boss are NOT the same thing. Being a leader does <u>not</u> mean controlling your partner. Being a leader does <u>not</u> mean getting power and control over others. Being a leader does <u>not</u> mean getting your way or telling your partner what to do.*

Being a leader means *leading by example*. It means mastering the skills and concepts in this book and applying them in your daily life. *It means making meaningful and lasting changes in your own behavior <u>first</u>, and then inviting others to follow your example.* It means respecting your partner at all times, staying in The Box from now on, living by the "no-hostility" rule, and abandoning efforts to control or manipulate others. If that's what you want (and you should want it), then you're on your way to becoming a skilled and trusted leader. In time you'll be loved and respected, rather than feared and resented. *Add it now to your Big Picture: I want to become the best leader I can be for my family.* To be a real leader, you'll have to give up any idea you had about controlling others. You'll have to accept your partner as an equal in every way, and the only influence you'll have over your partner will be through communication, persuasion, negotiation, compromise, and the example you set through your own choices.

I believe that women can be every bit as controlling as men. I also believe that women can become every bit the leader that men can. But men have centuries of cultural history to overcome that gave them complete control over their female partners. Roman law, for example, allowed men to sell their wives into slavery and even put them to death. Women were seen as the property of men, much as their farm animals were. English common law allowed men to beat their wives with a stick as large as the man's thumb (the rule of thumb law). The social and political system granted men control over all property obtained in the marriage, even if the property was obtained through the wives' inheritance. It wasn't until the late nineteenth century that America saw the first U.S. court decision that rescinded the common law rights of a husband to beat his wife (1871, Supreme Court of Alabama), and granted women some relief from physical abuse suffered at the hands of their husbands. Little wonder that so many men find it a hard thing to surrender control and accept their female partner as their full equal. In order to become a true leader, men must come to terms with the embodiment of power and control that is male privilege.

Male Privilege

Male privilege is the belief that any man has the right to be "the boss" in any relationship with a woman. It is the belief that *men should have special privileges, power and control over women, and that what a man wants, thinks, and feels is somehow more important than what a woman wants, thinks, and feels.* This attitude can be expressed in countless ways in a relationship, some subtle and others not so subtle. Below are some examples of male privilege. If you're a man reading this book, how many of these beliefs do you agree with? If you agree with any of them, you have some male privilege issues to deal with.

Men who believe in male privilege:

- *Believe that it is a man's right to be the boss of the house.*
- *Believe that it is worse for a woman to have an affair than it is for a man.*
- *Believe that a woman should ask the man's "permission" before she gets a job.*
- *Believe that it is the man's right to make all major decisions for the family.*
- *Believe that disagreeable chores like changing diapers, doing the laundry, and washing dishes are "women's work."*
- *Believe that the man has the right to demand sex from his partner whenever he wants.*
- *Believe that a man should always have the last word.*
- *Believe that a woman's place is in the home.*
- *Believe that men are natural leaders, and women are natural followers.*
- *Believe that women are naturally inferior to men.*

Some men argue that they have special rights over women because men are *supposed* to be the "head of the family." They argue that because men pay the bills, are the protectors of the home, because it has always been that way, and for a number of other reasons, men should have more power in a relationship than women have. They believe that they should be the "king of the castle," and demand that their female partners accept them as the boss. They believe men should always get their way, and they should have the final say about all the important decisions in the home simply because they are men. They do not feel guilty about their violence toward their partner because they believe that when their partner challenges their authority as head of the home, it is their privilege to use violence to maintain their power and control over her: *"I'm the boss, and if I have to get tough to control her I will, and if I get tough it's her fault for not doing what I said in the first place."*

Why should a man have any special rights or privileges in a relationship? The woman did not surrender her constitutional rights when she married. Is there any logical reason why a man should hold any power or authority over his partner? Why should his wants, thoughts, or feelings have more importance than those of his partner? In our groups, we often hear men say that it is a man's place to be the head of the home. Why? *Why should any man enter a relationship with the expectation that he should have special status as the head of the home?*

In my counseling groups I ask group members to give me all the reasons why they think a man should be the head of the home and write their responses on the board. We then go over their reasons one at a time. The typical reasons given, and my responses to them, are listed below.

Some say men should be the head of the home because:

<u>Men earn the money. They pay to have the say</u>. Actually, more and more homes depend on the income of both the wife and the husband to get by. In many instances, the woman is the sole

provider for the family. Even if the wife is not employed outside the home, her work in the home makes many of his outside activities possible. Her work in the home is of great value, even though she isn't paid for it. And further, would men change places with their partner and adopt the traditional female role if they lost their jobs, and the woman earned the family income? Not likely. It is more likely that equality in relationships would suddenly seem much more attractive to them.

Men are stronger. If being stronger makes a person a better leader, why don't we limit public office to weight lifters? Following this logic, a person who can bench press 300 pounds would surely be a better president than a person who can only lift 250 pounds. In reality, physical strength has nothing to do with the qualities that make a good leader in the home. Strength of character, intelligence, understanding, and good judgment are what count, and they have nothing to do with physical strength.

Men are smarter. Not true. There is no meaningful difference between men and women in intelligence tests scores. Women excel in every walk of life – in medicine, law, government, and business. History is full of examples of women who were great leaders of nations during times of crisis and war. If there are historically fewer women than men in the public eye, it is due more to lack of equal opportunity than to lack of ability.

In the past, men have always been the head of the family. Slavery, bleeding the sick with leeches, and child labor were also traditions at one time. Because a thing was once a tradition does not make it right, it just means that's the way things used to be. The old ways are not necessarily the best ways.

The truth is, there's no rational, moral, or legal reason why one partner should expect to have any special power or authority over another partner. When people strive to gain power and control over their partner they do harm to themselves, their partner, and their relationship. They harm themselves because they push others away through their attempts to dominate and control them. They waste time and energy trying to control others, rather than learning to gain control of their own lives. Their partners are harmed by the endless power struggles and the erosion of their self-esteem and self-confidence. Their relationships are harmed because their partners regard them with fear and resentment rather than love and respect.

Who should be the "head of the home?" *In the sense that being the head of the home means that one partner dominates or holds power over the other partner, there should be no head of the home.* Successful relationships don't have bosses, they have equal partners. To be successful, relationships must be based on mutual respect, freedom of choice, and equality. Every man and woman has a right to live their life according to their own lights. No partner surrenders that right when they voluntarily enter a relationship with another adult. Neither partner has the right to force their will on the other. Once that reality is accepted and an egalitarian relationship is established, the qualities of leadership in both partners can start to emerge.

Be a Leader

While there is no place for a tyrant, there is nothing wrong with a leader, a man or a woman, wanting to show good leadership in the home. Indeed, if you have been having marital problems, leadership is needed. But a leader must understand that leadership does not mean having your way all the time. Nor does it mean dominating or controlling your partner. You must understand that leadership does not come by birthright or gender, but by the example you set and by the respectful and caring way you treat your spouse and children. It comes from the way you meet your daily responsibilities and gain control over your own life. You become a leader by putting the good of the family before your own wants when necessary. Leadership comes from being willing to talk about and work on problems in the home, rather than avoiding them or blaming others for them. You become a leader when you demonstrate self-control, and go the extra mile to help your partner. If you have been a tyrant in the past, you need to stop. If you want to be a leader, start today. The following chart should give you some thoughts about where you can begin.

A Tyrant Asks:	*A Leader Asks:*
• Who is in charge?	• What can I do to help my partner?
• How can I make my partner do what I want?	• How can we compromise?
• How can I control my partner?	• Am I in control of myself?
• What is my partner doing wrong?	• What can I do better?
• Why doesn't my partner understand me?	• Do I truly understand my partner?
• Why does my partner complain so much?	• Am I meeting my responsibilities; am I being the best partner, friend, lover and parent that I can be?

If you want to be a leader, start by challenging yourself to be your best version of yourself. Lead by example, by doing the things that need doing in your relationship. Stop trying to get your partner to change, focus on yourself, and start setting a positive example for others to follow. If your relationship needs more respect, start respecting more. If it needs more tolerance, start tolerating more. If it needs more communication, start communicating more. If it needs more love, start loving more. Remember that leadership is like trying to move a string in a straight line: it has to be pulled from in front, not pushed from the rear.

HOMEWORK ASSIGNMENT
CHAPTER 18

Complete the following exercises on a piece of paper:

1) *Describe the difference between a leader and a tyrant.*

2) *Looking at your past behavior, have you acted more like a leader or a tyrant?*

3) *Do those close to you fear you or respect you?*

4) *How can you become more of a leader in the future?*

5) *Find the "Power and Control" wheel and the "Equality" wheels in the appendix. Using the "Power and Control" wheel, describe at least three examples of controlling behavior you have engaged in with your partner. Using the "Equality" wheel, describe the non-controlling behaviors you could have used to show leadership and acceptance of your partner as an equal.*

Chapter 19
The Children

Key Concepts: When children experience domestic violence it has devastating effects. Children who must live in a home where one or both parents are abused are denied the security and nurturing that they deserve. They live in an environment of fear, anger, resentment, shame, and guilt. Research on children who witness abuse between parents suggests that these children experience short-term and long-term developmental problems that are similar to those of children who are themselves the target of abuse.

Skill Building: Create a home for your children where they never witness or experience abuse and violence. Maintain a loving and supportive environment where your children feel safe and protected, and where their parents model consideration and respect for each other.

The following story was related to me by a staff member of a local women's shelter. A mother and her three young children were admitted into a woman's shelter after enduring years of horrific abuse at the hands of her alcoholic husband. Safe at last from their brutal father, the children were interviewed by a shelter staff member. "What was it like at home?" she asked. "My daddy would come home drunk at night," replied one of the children. "He would make us go to bed and turn out the light. Then he would beat up mommy. We were afraid to get out of bed, but we could hear him hitting her. We could hear mommy crying." The shelter worker asked, "Wasn't it awful laying there in the dark listening to your mommy being hurt?" "No," the child answered. "The worse part was when he stopped! Then it was quiet and we didn't know what happened to mommy."

Of all the different groups in our society, children are the most vulnerable to abuse and exploitation. Children are totally dependent upon the adults around them. They don't choose their parents and they have no control over the way their parents act. The adults in their lives have the power to make their world warm and safe – or brutal and frightening. But whether parents make their children's world a heaven or a hell, their children must live in it. They can't leave when things go wrong at home.

For many children, things at home are terribly wrong. Child abuse, in its various forms, is a fact of life for far too many children. One estimate (Carlson, 1984) is that over three million children witness acts of domestic violence in their home every year. Straus and Gelles (1990) estimate that at least one-third of American children have witnessed violence between their parents. Straus (1990) reported that of the 46 million American children who were living with both parents in 1975, approximately 1.7 million were subjected to "very severe violence" at the hands of their parents. You may be asking, *"Hey, I've never abused my children. What's this chapter doing here?"* This chapter is here because there are some things you need to know. Most importantly, you should know that you can't abuse your partner without hurting your children. Here is a brief review of research on the subject:

- In a 1983 study, sixty-five percent of the children who attempted to kill themselves had witnessed violence in their own homes (Kosky, 1983).

- Witnessing domestic violence between parents as a child has been found to be a stronger predictor of adult violent behavior than having been physically abused as a child. (Kolbo, Blakely, & Engleman, 1996).

- One study of violent teenage boys found that exposure to family violence was associated with a positive feeling about using violence to solve their problems (Spaccerelli, Coatworth, & Bowden, 1995). (Remember the discussion about the development of *core beliefs* about violence in Chapter Seven?)

- Compared to other women, battered women were six times more likely to have been subjected to physical violence when they were children (Kalmuss, 1984).

- Women who were abused by their husbands were twice as likely to abuse their own children, as compared to women who were not abused. The more violent a husband is to his wife, the more violent the wife is to her children. Women who are battered commit the highest rates of child abuse (Straus & Gelles, 1990).

- Seventy-six percent of children who were repeatedly abused by their parents repeatedly and severely assaulted their brothers or sisters. The more violent parents are to their children, the more violent children are to their own siblings (Straus & Gelles, 1990).

- Sons who witnessed battering between parents were ten times as likely to abuse their own partners. This does not mean that *every* child who witnesses abuse between their parents will eventually abuse their own partner. Many people who abuse come from non-violent homes, and some children from violent homes do not abuse. But witnessing abuse as a child does seem to increase the risk of becoming an abusive partner (Straus, Gelles, & Steinmetz, 1980).

- Exposure of a child to family violence is associated with a number of significant childhood problems, including antisocial behavior, depression, anxiety, and school problems (Adamson & Thompson, 1998).

The evidence is clear that parents who abuse each other also abuse their children, even if the children aren't the ones being hit. That's why children are sometimes referred to as the "hidden victims" of the violence between their parents. In this lesson, we will be discussing some fundamental issues about child abuse, beginning with the most basic question of all: *"What is child abuse?"* We will look at the various types of abuse and the effects of abuse on children. We'll also ask an important question for the readers of this book: *"Are children abused even when the abuse and violence is kept between the parents?"*

Many of the men and women in my counseling groups witnessed violence between their parents and suffered abuse as children. Here are some typical excerpts from a discussion of childhood abuse:

- *Joe: "My father was no alcoholic, he was just an abusive man. We were always living on egg shells. We never knew what he might do, it just depended on his mood."*
- *Sharon: "I remember him ripping my mom's fingernails back."*
- *Mary: "I would hide under the covers with my brother when my father beat my mom. We just didn't know what to do."*
- *Don: "I told him to leave my mom alone, and he came after me. He beat me with a metal bar until I was bleeding. I took 30 aspirins because I thought that would end my life."*
- *Linda: "I wrote him a letter saying I can't have you in my life anymore."*
- *David: "I remember asking mom to divorce my dad because of the violence."*
- *Pamela: "He would kick me in my chest. He'd make me sit on the floor in front of him and he would kick me. The neighbors even knew but they never called the police."*
- *Phil: "I got used to it. I would try to escape it by staying away from home. Their divorce was a relief."*

What is Child Abuse?

The easiest way to define child abuse is to review the legal definitions of abuse. This is not a pleasant subject to talk about, but you need to have this information, especially if you're the parent of a child. First and foremost, parents need to understand that child abuse is serious *criminal conduct* which can be punishable by a fine, incarceration, or both. In addition to fines and imprisonment, and depending upon the severity and nature of the abuse, adults responsible for child abuse may also lose custody of their own children, be required to attend counseling, and even register as a sex offender. To help you understand what constitutes child abuse, I've listed some of the child abuse statutes below. Although these statutes are from the *California Penal Code*, they're fairly representative of child abuse laws across the country.

First of all, let's examine the legal definition of "a child." Article 11165 of the California Penal Code defines a child as a person who is less than 18 years of age. When people speak of child abuse, they are generally referring to acts committed against people *under the age of 18*. What constitutes abuse of a child? The following Penal Codes below summarize many of the behaviors toward children that are legally considered acts of child abuse:

- Sexual abuse: Sexual abuse includes sexual intercourse, sexual contact, intimate touching of intimate parts of a child's body for sexual gratification, masturbation in the presence of a child, and involving a child in an obscene act.
- Neglect and Endangerment: Neglect means treating or allowing a child to be treated in a way that harms or threatens to harm the child. The term neglect can apply to things that parents do, and to things that parents fail to do (these are called acts of omission). Examples of neglect include failure to give a child adequate food, clothing, shelter, medical care, or

supervision. Endangerment means placing the child in a situation that endangers the child's health, or failing to protect a child from such situations.

- <u>Willful cruelty, unjustifiable punishment, child endangerment</u>: This statute applies to parents who cause or permit their child to suffer, or inflict unjustifiable physical pain *or mental suffering*, or place or allow the child to be placed in a situation that endangers the child's health.

- <u>Unlawful corporal punishment</u>: This code prohibits parents from physically punishing a child in a manner that is cruel or causes a physical injury to the child.

Several points need to be made about the statutes above. First, child abuse laws apply to the person who abuses the child, *and to the parent who knowingly allows the abuse to happen*. That's what the statutes mean when they say *to cause or permit* and *failure to protect*. In plain language, if you know that your partner (or any other person) is abusing your child, you're legally obligated to take reasonable and necessary steps to prevent it. If you don't meet this legal obligation to your child, you may face criminal charges yourself. Secondly, most people think that child abuse only means sexual abuse or physically injuring a child. Those are certainly acts of child abuse, but there are other types of abuse that parents may not be so familiar with, such as neglect, endangerment, and mental suffering. These lesser understood forms of abuse may be as harmful to a child's well-being as the more familiar kinds of abuse.

As we talk about the various forms of abuse, keep in mind that the various types of abuse are not exclusive. In other words, a child that is physically abused may also be subjected to other forms of abuse.

Sexual Abuse

Let's make this simple. Child sexual abuse is *any* form of sexual behavior involving a child below the legal age of consent. Some examples are:

- Engaging a child in any sexual touching or sexual behavior.
- Forcing a child to watch sex between two adults.
- Forcing children to engage in sex acts with each other.
- Exposing a child to pornography, or taking sexually-explicit photos of a child.
- Sexualizing a relationship with a child through the use of sexually-oriented language, jokes, or comments.

I want to clarify what I mean by "sexualizing a relationship." When this topic is discussed, many of the men and women in my groups need to be reassured that it's alright for them to hug their own children and give their infant a bath, and no, they don't have to panic when their three-year-old asks, "Daddy, where do babies come from?" Expressions of love and affection towards your children are not only appropriate, they're indispensable. Never worry that you're showing too much love toward your children. If anything, worry that you're not showing enough.

Sexualizing a relationship refers to something very different from the natural esteem-building love that most parents feel for their children. Let me give you an example of a sexualized relationship. Several years ago a woman came to my office seeking help for her depression. As I worked with her, I began to suspect that she might have been sexually abused as a child. We talked about the possibility, but she couldn't recall ever having been abused. Several weeks later she visited her parents, who she hadn't seen for some time, to celebrate a major holiday. After she returned she told me the following story.

I felt uncomfortable as soon as I walked into my parents' house, but I didn't know why. My dad made some joke about the size of my breasts, and I just laughed it off. I remember making some kind of sexual comment back that he thought was funny. I don't know why I did that, it just seemed natural and what he expected. I realized that this is the way it's always been between my dad and me. That night he told me a lot of very graphic sexual jokes and made remarks about my sex life, like how often I had sex with my boyfriend and what we did. I felt very uncomfortable, but I didn't let it show. I just laughed the way I always had. My sisters were there, but I noticed that he didn't talk to them the way he talked to me. That night I slept in my old room. When I turned out the lights I felt nervous and a little scared, and I remembered feeling that way when I was a child and wishing there was a lock on the door. My dad didn't touch me in a sexual way, and I don't think he ever has. But I hated the way he made me feel! I don't think I'll ever go back there.

It's possible that her father never physically molested her. I'm not even sure that a district attorney would regard his behavior as criminal conduct. Yet I can assure you that he inflicted injury on his daughter by sexualizing their relationship. I witnessed her struggle to work through the pain and humiliation her father had caused her.

Sexual offenders sometimes suggest that their actions should not be considered criminal if the child participates willingly. This attempt to rationalize abusive behavior has no basis in fact. A child can *never* give consent for sexual behavior. Consenting sex requires that a person have enough experience in life to a) know the difference between right and wrong; b) understand the social, legal, and moral consequences of the behavior; c) understand how the behavior will affect their relationships with family and peers, and, d) be on an equal playing field with the other person in terms of power, experience, and knowledge. A child is easy prey for unscrupulous adults because a child is in a powerless position relative to an adult. A child does not have the maturity, knowledge, experience, or insight to make such far-reaching decisions about his or her life. For these reasons, a child can never give consent to sexual interaction with an adult. Child sexual abuse is *always* destructive to the child, and it is *always* a crime. In addition, sexual predators of children are not likely to stop on their own. If you know of a situation where a child is being abused, call one of the agencies listed at the end of this chapter.

<u>Physical Abuse</u>

Physical abuse is intentionally or recklessly causing bodily injury to a child. Perpetrators of this form of abuse often try to rationalize the abuse by saying they were trying to "discipline" the child. Many parents use some form of corporal punishment (spanking) to discipline their children. In a national survey of violence in American families, 90% of the parents of three-year-olds, and 34% of the parents of 15-17 year olds, reported that they had hit their child one or more times during the year (Straus & Gelles, 1990). In most of these instances the violence was relatively minor. However, the survey also found that at least *1.5 million children per year are subjected to severe physical abuse (such as punching, kicking, and burning) at the hands of their parents.* Among this unfortunate group of children, infants were physically assaulted an average of 19 times a year, three-year-olds were assaulted an average of 32 times a year, and 17-year-olds an average of about six times a year. Keep in mind that these are the rates of violence towards children in a national study of American homes. The problem of child abuse appears to be much more severe in homes where the mother is battered by the husband. In one study of the children of battered women, 90% of the children had also suffered physical abuse (Giles-Sims, 1985).

Parents who hit their children are teaching them that violence is an acceptable way of handling family problems. In the Straus (1990) survey, for example, teenagers were found to hit their parents about as often as the parents hit each other. Research also indicates that parents who engage in abusive violence towards their children or their spouses had themselves received more physical punishment as a child (Straus & Gelles, 1990). It is also the case that while most physical punishment does not turn into physical abuse, **most physical abuse begins as ordinary punishment** (Kadushin & Martin, 1981).

Spanking is also a model for the child's own acts of violence. As the saying goes, violence begets more violence. When spanked, a child can easily develop core beliefs that it is OK to control and coerce another person through physical violence, and that when you are angry it's all right to express the anger by hitting the person you're mad at. As you read earlier in this chapter, the more violence children experience in their home, the more inclined they are towards violence against other children and even their own parents. An article in *Newsday* (August 15, 1978) reported that one in five parents suffered objects being thrown at them, pushing, shoving, and furious verbal abuse at the hands of their own children. It is likely, observed *Newsday*, that this abuse was learned "at the knee of the parent."

Physical punishment is not the most effective way to teach a child to behave. To be effective, discipline must *educate* a child. Punishment alone is not education. Punishment usually does not elicit true remorse for misbehavior, nor does it foster true sorrow for the harm that a child's misbehavior may have caused others. Rather, physical punishment fills a child with fear, anger, and defiance, and while violence may make a child fear you, it does not effectively teach a child to respect you. More importantly, it doesn't teach a child how to behave more responsibly in the future. Having children take a time-out, withdrawal of privileges, rewarding positive choices, and taking time to communicate are more effective methods of discipline than corporal punishment.

Hitting or spanking are not forms of discipline. Hitting and spanking are forms of punishment, and punishment alone is woefully inadequate in raising a child. Parenting takes more than punishment. Discipline and setting limits are important, but effective discipline involves finding a way to communicate values and ethics to the child. When you are not there to watch over them, it is the values and ethics that you have taught your children that will guide them in making the right choices and doing the right thing. On the other hand, if you rely on spanking to get your children to behave they may do the right thing when you are watching because they want to avoid being punished. But when you are not there and they're not afraid of being caught, the fear of punishment loses its influence and they may not make the right choice.

I remember one study of moral development in children that compared delinquents in juvenile hall with school children of the same age from the same neighborhood. Both groups of children were asked questions like: "Why shouldn't a person steal?" The school children provided answers like: *"Because it is wrong to take something you haven't earned. No one will trust you if you steal. It hurts when people steal something from you."* The delinquents, on the other hand, provided answers such as: *"Because you might get caught, and you might end up in jail."* Do you see the difference in their answers? The school children had internalized important values and social ethics, while the delinquents had not. When the two groups were compared further, it was found that the delinquents had been subjected to far more physical punishment by their parents than the school children had. The lesson is this: ***spanking alone does not teach children how to live their lives responsibly, and it often makes the situation worse***. When children misbehave, they need to be taught:

- *What he or she did that was wrong.*
- *Why that behavior was wrong.*
- *The natural consequences of wrongful behavior.*
- *How misbehavior makes others feel.*
- *Better choices that the child can make in the future.*
- *Non-violent ways to handle problems they're faced with.*

Slapping and hitting can't teach children the things they need to be taught, no matter how often or how hard they're hit. I can tell you of children who were hit so often that they lost all fear of their parents. Some of these children spent many of their adult years in state prison for homicide. An effective parent takes time to *teach* their children right from wrong. Good parents control their own anger and use their heads rather than hands to solve discipline problems. They remember that children have legal and moral rights of their own, and that they have no right to injure or inflict unjustifiable suffering upon a child in the guise of "discipline."

<u>Mental Suffering</u>

Verbal abuse, psychological abuse, and neglect are ways in which parents can sometimes inflict mental pain and suffering on their children. Verbal abuse is the use of words to deliberately inflict fear, embarrass, degrade, humiliate, or otherwise inflict emotional pain on a child. Some examples of verbal abuse are:

- *You're so stupid! You're disgusting! You make me sick!*
- *One of these days you're going to wake up and I'll be gone.*
- *I could get married again if it weren't for you.*
- *You're the reason your father and I got divorced. He couldn't put up with you.*
- *I wish you had never been born.*

Psychological abuse and neglect refers to non-violent actions intended to cause fear, inflict emotional pain, or cause a child humiliation. Here are some examples:

- Locking a child in a dark closet or room.
- Withholding reasonable access to clothing (forcing them to go naked), food (starving them until they are below their natural body weight), or denying children other essentials of living.
- Embarrassing or humiliating a child in public or in front of their peers.
- Forcing a child to witness violence to another member of the family.
- Refusing to speak to a young child for long periods of time.
- Inflicting pain and suffering on a child's pet, or destroying a child's favorite toy.

It is important to understand the pain and suffering caused by abusive words and actions. No child, no matter what they have done, *ever* deserves to be abused in this manner. Verbal abuse, psychological abuse, and neglect are always destructive. If the abuse is repeated over a period of years, it results in life-long problems from which the child may never recover. There is an old saying that goes: *"Sticks and stones may break my bones, but words will never hurt me."* This is most definitely not true. Verbal abuse *is* destructive, and it has long-lasting negative effects on children. In terms of the emotional pain caused, it can be more traumatizing than broken bones.

When a Child Witnesses Violence

Research on children who see domestic violence in the home consistently shows that these children experience significant emotional trauma (see Jaffe et al., 1989). Children who must live in a home where one or both parents are abused are denied the security and nurturing that they deserve. Instead, they live in an environment of fear, anger, resentment, shame, and guilt. Speaking of the consequences of spouse abuse on the children in the home, psychologist Lenore Walker wrote:

Children who live in a battering relationship experience the most insidious form of child abuse. Whether or not they are physically abused by either parent is less important than the psychological scars they bear from watching their fathers beat their mothers. *(From <u>Battered Women</u>, 46, 1979)*

Research on children who witness abuse between parents suggests that these children experience short-term and long-term developmental problems that are similar to those of children who are themselves the target of abuse. Chief Justice Margaret Workman of the West Virginia Supreme Court, writing about the effect of family violence on children, wrote the following:

Spousal abuse has a tremendous impact on children. Children learn several lessons in witnessing the abuse of one of the parents. First, they learn that such behavior appears to be approved by their most important role models and that the violence toward a loved one is acceptable. Children also fail to grasp the full range of negative consequences for the violent behavior and observe, instead, the short-term reinforcements namely, compliance by the victim. Thus, they learn the use of coercive power and violence as a way to influence loved ones without being exposed to other more constructive alternatives. In addition to the effect of the destructive modeling, children who grow up in violent homes experience damaging psychological effects. (What Therapists See That Judges May Miss, 11-12, Spring, 1988).

Reporting Child Abuse

If you know or suspect that a child is being abused, my advice is to report it to your police or sheriff's department, a county welfare department, or to the child protective agency in your area. In most cases you can make a report anonymously. You don't have to give your name, and your call may save a child's life. You may be the only person who's in a position to help the child, and you'll rest easier at night knowing that someone will look into the situation. The national child abuse hotline (Childhelp USA) is (800) 422-4453. Childhelp counselors can answer your questions and assist you by providing options based on the situation you describe. Also, there's probably a child abuse reporting hotline in your county. You can usually find the number online or in the front of your local telephone directory. In Los Angeles County, for example, the number is (800) 540-4000. There are also domestic violence hotlines staffed with people who can help you. The National Domestic Violence Hotline is (800) 799-7233, and provides highly-trained counselors that can assist you with information and help you examine unhealthy aspects of your relationship.

HOMEWORK ASSIGNMENT
CHAPTER 19

Write a letter that starts with the words: *The Promises I Make to My Children*. Write down the promises that you are willing to make to your children as a parent. If you don't have children of your own, write down the promises that you're willing to make to your future children. Don't just address material things. Be sure to write about the kind of parental relationship and home environment you promise to provide to them. Put some thought into your promises. These aren't like New Year's resolutions that people make and then forget the next day. Write down things that you're really willing to make a commitment to. When you're finished, put the letter someplace handy. Every Sunday, bring out the letter and read the promises you've made. Ask yourself whether you've kept your promises during the past week. If you have, congratulate yourself. If you haven't, resolve to do better during the week to come.

To help you get started, I've listed some of the things that I believe all children have a right to expect from their parents, such as:

- *A home free of violence, neglect, sexual, psychological, and physical abuse*
- *A loving and supportive relationship with both their parents*
- *A home where they feel safe and protected, and where their parents show consideration for each other and treat each other with respect*
- *To be corrected and disciplined as appropriate, but in a manner that respects them as a person in their own right*
- *Parents who provide for their basic emotional, educational, and material needs*
- *To be taught the difference between "right" and "wrong" through their parents' words and example*

I've also included parts of the letters written by two prior clients, Laura and Steven, which follow.

Laura's Letter

Dear Danny:

Hey baby it's mommy. I want to start this letter by telling you that I'm sorry for putting you through the pain that you're going through. I know that I've made a lot of mistakes in my life and because of them you are suffering. I'm sorry that you would see your daddy and I fight, you should have never seen those things.

I want to make things better. That's why I'm taking these classes, so I can learn to be a better mommy. When I'm done I know that you're going to be coming home, and when you do no matter who I'm being with I promise that you won't see mommy getting hit or me hitting someone else. I promise that when I get frustrated I won't take it out on you. I'll take time for myself until I cool down. I know you love me. I'm learning a lot, and now I understand why you would start crying and screaming when you would hear me yelling. I know that I've made a lot of bad choices, but I'm going make things better and we're going to be happy again.

Love,

Mommy

Steven's Letter

Dear David and Christina,

I want to start by telling you that I'm the happiest father in the world. You guys make me very proud to be your father. I know that you are very young, and this is only the beginning of the long road ahead of us, but the day you guys were born I knew in my mind and my heart that I would do whatever it took to be with you forever. I want to be able to show you by example that no matter what the situation may be, I will always be there when you need me. I want you to be able to trust and respect me, the way I will show trust and respect for you. I will treat you as fair as I would want to be treated, with the love and respect that you deserve.

Through our years I will maintain a relationship in which you will never feel a doubt about my commitment to you. I think the most important thing growing up is feeling love and respect from your parents. If I am able to make this happen I feel our relationship will be everything I wanted from the start. We would be able to talk about anything with the confidence of knowing it will be treated with honor and respect, not ridicule. We have a long road ahead and I know it is my responsibility to keep us in the right direction, and that is my promise to you. Well, here we go on our way. I love you guys very much.

Love,

Your father xxoo

To the best of my knowledge at the time of this writing, both Laura and Steven have kept their promises.

Chapter 20
Skill Building

Key Concepts: Reaching your goal of an abuse-free lifestyle requires both knowledge and practice. This chapter will help you consolidate your understanding of the material in the last three chapters and apply the concepts and skills in your relationships. Remember, to build your skills you must commit to applying them in your daily life. It's what you do, not what you know, that gets results.

Skill Building: Complete the following test to review any gaps in your knowledge of key skills and concepts. Provide detailed examples of your efforts to apply them in your Skill Building Log.

Once again, it's time to test your mastery of the skills and concepts you've learned in the last three chapters, and to put them into practice. The concepts in the chapters on acceptance, leadership, and child abuse have consistently helped my clients develop renewed respect for their partners and their children – an important characteristic of abuse-free relationships.

As you've done in the past, review the concepts in the last few chapters by taking the quiz. Check for any gaps in your knowledge, then go back and review any items on the quiz that give you trouble. As always, there's a new *Skill Building Log* to help you apply the concepts and skills you've learned.

Quiz
Chapters 17-19

1) Is it reasonable to expect your partner to change without taking their personality traits into consideration? (Chapter 17)

2) Explain your answer to question 1. (Chapter 17)

3) Using the five-factor model, describe the major differences between you and your partner. (Chapter 17)

4) Are there some behaviors that you should not accept from your partner? If so, what are they? (Chapter 17)

5) Describe at least one way that partners can manage their personality differences. (Chapter 17)

6) Describe two ways that acceptance and encouragement can be demonstrated to your partner. (Chapter 17)

7) What are the major differences between a leader and a tyrant? (Chapter 18)

8) Can a person be feared and respected at the same time? (Chapter 18)

9) What are some of the tools used by a leader? (Chapter 18)

10) Give two examples of male privilege. (Chapter 18)

11) To the degree you act like a tyrant people will _____ you. To the degree you act like a leader, people will _____ you. (Chapter 18)

12) Is power and control the tool of a leader or a tyrant? (Chapter 18)

13) Two forms of child abuse are sexual abuse and physical abuse. List three other types of child abuse. (Chapter 19)

14) The person who commits an act of child abuse is guilty of a criminal act, but what about a person who knowingly permits it to happen? Is that person also guilty of a criminal act? (Chapter 19)

15) What evidence is there that witnessing violence between parents is harmful to children? (Chapter 19)

16) What are some of the harmful effects of child abuse? (Chapter 19)

17) What's the difference between punishment and parenting? (Chapter 19)

18) What are some of the things that punishment fails to teach a child who misbehaves? (Chapter 19)

19) List two agencies that you should call if you know of a child that is being abused (Chapter 19)

When you're finished, check your answers and move on to the Skill Building Log.

Skill Building Log

Step 1: Select one or more skills from the list below that you want to practice. Selecting the right skills to practice is easy. Just answer this sentence: *"It would help me and my family the most if I would _____."*

Step 2: On a separate sheet of paper, write a detailed example of how you put the skills to use. Describe (1) who you were with, (2) the problem you struggled with, (3) any of your warning signs that came up, (4) the skills you used to handle the problem, (5) how things turned out.

TOOLBOX FOR CHAPTER TWENTY

Tools from Chapters 1-3:
- Memorize The Box
- Use The Box to guide my decision making

- Stay focused on problem solving during an argument
- Learn my own Warning Signs
- Watch for my Warning Signs when I start to feel angry
- Take a Time Out whenever I see my warning signs
- Memorize the rules to Time Out and follow them
- Explain time out to my partner
- Never cross the "I don't care what I say line"
- Never cross the "I don't care what I do line"
- Stop using any form of Verbal Abuse (stay in The Box)
- Recognize and avoid using Denial, Blame, and Minimizing

Tools from Chapters 5-7:
- Whenever I feel angry toward my partner, stop and ask myself, *"Is my thinking rational and logical right now? Am I making a big deal out of a small problem?"*
- Whenever I feel angry (or frustrated, jealous, etc.) I'll remind myself that I can choose to think in ways that escalate these feelings, or I can choose to think in ways that reduce them.
- Accept responsibility for everything I say or do.
- Lower my comfort level with violence. Don't minimize, call abuse something other than what it really is, or tell myself that such behavior is OK.
- Don't try to be my partner's boss or force my will on him or her. See my partner as my equal.
- Allow my partner the right to express his or her thoughts and feelings openly and without intimidation.
- Always stop and think *before* I react.
- Never "Awfulize."
- Stay out of the *"YOU MODE."*
- Self-talk to prevent or reduce anger.
- Identify my core beliefs about anger and aggression and modify them.

Tools from Chapters 9-11:
- See tension as a signal to problem solve rather than the opening bell to a fight.
- Remove all controlling, blaming, and hurtful language from my problem solving.
- Ask my partner if I come across as bossy, blaming, or hurtful.
- Ask my partner to tell me whenever he or she feels controlled, hurt, or blamed.
- Use the six problem solving steps.
- Whenever I step on a land mine, find out which mine it was and avoid it the next time.
- Write a letter to my partner expressing all of the feelings described in the letter writing exercise.
- Invite my partner to write a letter back to me.

Tools from Chapters 13-15:
- Develop a Big Picture and keep it in mind when problems come up.
- Let go of the adolescent idea of what it means to be strong.

- Live by the no-hostility rule.

<u>New Tools from Chapters 17-19</u>:
- Find constructive ways to deal with personality differences.
- Be more accepting of others.
- Find ways to encourage.
- Develop your leadership skills.
- Avoid male or female privilege and attempts to control your partner.
- Provide a safe and abuse-free environment for your children.
- Use less punishment and more parenting.

PERSONAL PROGRESS AND SELF-EVALUATION

1. Evaluate the progress that you have made so far in your counseling. Are you satisfied with the progress you are making? Are you putting forth your best effort? Is there anything you need to do to make your counseling experience more successful?

2. Select a relationship that is important to you. What can you do to make the relationship better? Set a specific goal for improving the relationship. What do you want to accomplish over the next month?

3. Have you seen changes in your thinking or behavior since starting this program? If so, provide an example of how your thinking and behavior have changed.

4. Are there skills from your counseling that you use on a daily basis? If so, what are they? Give a recent example of using them. If you are not using the skills you have learned on a daily basis, why not?

5. Select a skill or concept from the book that is important for you to use and develop at this time of your life. What skill did you select? How can using that skill benefit you and the people who love you?

Chapter 21
Drugs and Alcohol

Key Concepts: Alcohol and drug abuse have been linked to higher rates of partner abuse. Research suggests that the greater the drug or alcohol problem, the greater the risk of a domestic violence incident. The risk of future incidents of spousal abuse can be reduced by seeking help for a drug or alcohol problem. However, drugs and alcohol don't cause the violence. In addition to drug and alcohol counseling, counseling aimed at changing key beliefs is needed to maintain a violence-free lifestyle.

Skill Building: Understand the relationship between substance abuse and partner violence. Openly evaluate the role of drugs and alcohol in your own life. Get appropriate help if needed.

It was one week before his daughter's birthday party, and Francisco was worried. "My wife wants a big party at the park, and so do I," he told the guys in his group. "We rented one of those inflatable things the kids like to jump in, and there will be clowns, and a barbecue, and the whole family's invited." When Francisco said "the whole family" he meant everyone even remotely related to his daughter: grandparents, aunts and uncles, nieces and nephews, second and third cousins, everyone on the block where they lived – and their children and friends of their children. Francisco liked to do things in a big way. One person said the birthday party sounded like fun, and asked Francisco what he was so worried about. "Well," Francisco said, "my wife invited her two cousins and there's always been bad blood between us. They're trouble makers. I just don't want any problems with them. I asked my wife not to invite them, but she did anyway."

None of us were too worried about Francisco. He took his counseling very seriously and he had made strong progress during his six months in the group. We all thought he could "stay in The Box" and handle any problems that came up. The following week, however, Francisco was missing from the group. Three weeks passed before we saw him again. We asked him where he had been. "In jail," he told us. "Everything was fine at the party at first," he explained. "We started about ten in the morning, and everyone was just having fun. I didn't allow any drinking at the party, and my wife's cousins weren't causing any trouble. Everything was going so good that about five o'clock I gave in and let someone go on a beer run. By six o'clock the police were there. A fight broke out and I was arrested along with the cousins." Was it just a coincidence that the fight started when the drinking started? According to Francisco, everything was peaceful for the first seven hours of the party, but one hour after the beer arrived things turned ugly. Was it a coincidence, or was there a lesson to be learned from Francisco's experience? Did alcohol cause the fight?

There is a long line of research linking alcohol and drug abuse to domestic violence. The National Violence against Women Survey reported that binge drinkers (people who consume excessive amounts of alcohol when they drink, but don't drink on a daily basis) are three to five times more likely to assault their partners than those who don't drink. A study in Memphis found that 92% of the victims of domestic violence said that the attacker used drugs or alcohol during the day of the assault. They also found that 67% of the aggressors had used a combination of cocaine and alcohol (Brookoff, 1997). A study of Indiana men arrested for domestic violence (Roberts, 1987) found that 60% of the men were under the influence of alcohol during the domestic violence incident for which they were arrested. Another study reported that 70% of the abusers studied were under the influence of drugs, alcohol, or both at the time of the attack (Roberts, 1988).

Yet another study reported that Latinas who were in a relationship with a binge drinker were ten times more likely to be assaulted than those with partners who drank less (Kaufman, Kantor, & Straus, 1990). In a study of marital violence among military personnel (Pan, Neidig, & O'Leary, 1994), researchers interviewed 11,870 randomly selected men on 38 different Army bases. They found that 5.6% of the men had engaged in severe spouse abuse (choked, beat up, threatened with a gun, etc.) at least once during the past year. They also found that compared to non-violent men, the presence of an alcohol problem elevated the risk of severe spousal violence by 128%. The existence of a drug problem increased the risk by 121%. Other studies have found that more than half of prison inmates serving time for violent crimes were drinking or using drugs at the time of the offense, and that 40% of people who killed their partners were drinking at the time of the murder (Greenfeld, 1998; Willson, 20000).

In a nationwide study of over 8,000 families (Straus & Gelles, 1990), researchers found a strong link between drinking and family violence, as shown by the chart below. The greater the drinking problem was, the higher the rate of violence in the home. Among the men who abstained from alcohol, 6.8% had one or more violent acts against their spouse during the year of the study. In contrast, binge drinkers had a violence rate that was three times higher (19.2%).

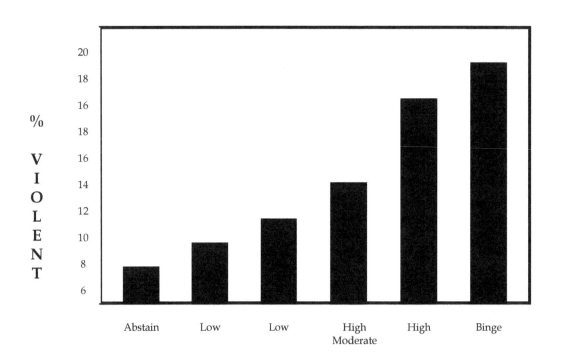

Most researchers agree that there is a strong relationship between drinking, drug use, and family violence – the greater the drug or alcohol problem, the greater the risk of violence. Binge drinking always increases the risk for victims of spousal abuse. In an effort to reduce the risk of further acts of violence, I strongly encourage clients with a substance abuse problem to attend alcohol or drug abuse counseling in addition to their domestic violence counseling. By maintaining their sobriety, they greatly reduce the risk of new episodes of violence. On the other hand, failing to maintain sobriety greatly increases the risk of new incidents of violence. Over the years, I've heard hundreds of stories like the one Francisco told at the start of this chapter. A man or woman will be making great progress in his or her domestic violence counseling when, full of confidence in their new skills and accomplishments, they get drunk or high. Under the influence of drugs or alcohol they seem to forget everything they've learned in their sessions and abuse again. In one intoxicated moment, they lose the trust that their partner and children have slowly given them. They lose the trust that they've worked for months to regain.

Increased Risk

How do drugs and alcohol increase the risk of violence? The following factors probably contribute to the increased risk of violence when under their influence:

- **Alcohol and drugs impair your judgment**. Whenever you use drugs or alcohol your judgment will be impaired. Let's face it, when you're under the influence you lose a whole bunch of IQ points (we all do) and it's easy to get stuck on "dumb." Also, the more frequently you drink or use drugs, the more likely it is that you will be under the influence when a crisis arises between you and your spouse. If a conflict arises between the two of you while you are under the influence, you're in trouble. You won't have the ability to think as clearly as you normally do or apply your skills as well as you ordinarily can. Many people in our program have said that they would never have done the things they did if they had been sober at the time. Because they were under the influence, they just didn't care about the consequences of their behavior. (They cared a lot when they sobered up, sometimes in jail, but they didn't care when they were drunk or high.) At the very time that they most needed their skills and the ability to think clearly, they were impaired by the drugs or alcohol.

Like an athlete who shows up for the game drunk, they weren't up to the challenge. That's how it is when you use drugs or alcohol when there's a lot of conflict and hostility in your relationship – you never know when the game is going to start. There's always the chance that the day you decide to have a snoot full will be "game day." To show you what I mean, let's use Larry and Bob as examples. Larry doesn't drink as often as Bob and he never uses drugs. Suppose Larry has a few beers on Friday at a barbeque, but he doesn't drink the rest of the week. Also, suppose that you know for sure that a major conflict between Larry and his partner is going to come up sometime during the week. What are the odds that Larry will be under the influence when the conflict starts? The calendar below shows the days of the week. The "B" indicates Larry's "Beer" day.

Larry's Week:

MON	TUE	WED	THUR	FRI	SAT	SUN
				B		

Larry is drinking one day out of seven, so the odds that he'll be drinking when a conflict comes up are: 1/7 = 0.14, or about 14%. There's a 14% chance that Larry will be under the influence then "the game" starts for him and his partner and he'll be called on to use all his skills. (Yes, I know this is an over simplification, but stick with me while I make my point.)

Bob is a different type of guy than Larry. In fact, some of the people who know him best will tell you that Bob's a drunk. During the week in question Bob drinks six days of the week. Suppose that Bob is also going to have a major problem come up between him and his partner during the week. His week looks like the calendar below, and the "B's" stand for Bob's "beer" days.

Bob's Week:

MON	TUE	WED	THUR	FRI	SAT	SUN
B		B	B	B	B	B

What are the odds that Bob will be intoxicated on the day that the conflict comes up? The answer is: 6/7 = 0.86, or 86%. The odds are 86% that Bob will be under the influence on "game day." There is an 86% chance that Bob will be under the influence when he needs his skills the most. Given what you've learned about the link between alcohol and violence, who do you think is more likely to have another incident of spousal abuse, Larry or Bob? The answer, of course, is Bob.

I used a sports analogy to make my point, but there's a difference between Bob and a professional athlete. If a baseball player shows up drunk to a game his next appearance may be in the minor leagues. But spousal abuse is a criminal act. If Bob shows up drunk at *his* game and abuses his partner again, his next appearance may be in criminal court, divorce court, the unemployment line, or in family court asking for supervised visitation with his children. If Bob is wise he'll put the beer (or dope) down and get in the best rehabilitation program he can find. His family will thank him for it, and he'll greatly reduce the likelihood of another incident of violence. There are other ways that substance abuse increases the risk of violence:

- **Alcohol and drug problems put severe stress on a relationship**. Many times the conflict between partners is caused by the drinking or drug use – that is the problem causing tension between them. Substance abuse problems frequently strain financial resources, give rise to alcohol or drug-related legal problems, cause problems at work, impair physical health, and place stress on a relationship in ways that are too numerous to count. The increased stress of a drug or alcohol problem results in more conflict between the partners, and increases the risk of the conflict turning violent.

To return to Bob, his alcohol abuse was the problem he and his partner were fighting about. His wife objected to his spending more on Budweiser than bills, and tried to take his car keys to avoid another DUI. She complained that Bob could more easily find his way to the liquor store than a job interview, and reminded him what his doctor said about his liver.

Drug and alcohol abuse creates its own stress on a relationship. As another example of the stress that alcohol and substance abuse can create, consider John's story. John didn't have a job and relied totally on his girlfriend for financial support. John wasn't much of a worker, but he was an all-star drinker. One Sunday, John asked his girlfriend for money to buy a "40 ouncer." She gave him the money and John took the short walk to the liquor store to buy his beer. John asked her for another "40 ouncer" a little later, and she gave John more money. When John asked for a third bottle a couple of hours later, his girlfriend refused to give him more money. She told John that he had had enough, and besides, she had better things to spend her money on than beer. By this time John was intoxicated, and his behavior showed it. He *demanded* more beer money and grabbed her purse. In the struggle over the purse John punched her. It's hard for me to see how domestic violence counseling alone would have been helpful to John – and to his credit, John agreed to get substance abuse counseling in addition to domestic violence counseling. By addressing *both* of these problems, John made good progress.

Does Substance Abuse *Cause* Partner Abuse?

Most researchers agree that there is a strong link between alcohol and substance abuse and spousal abuse. In other words, people with substance abuse problems have higher rates of partner violence than people who don't have substance abuse problems. But while the abuse of drugs and alcohol does make violence more likely, it does not **cause** the violence. If that were the case, everyone with a severe alcohol or drug problem would also batter their spouse, and that is clearly not the case.

Look again at the chart at the beginning of this chapter. Notice that binge drinkers engaged in more violence than moderate drinkers, and binge drinkers were three times more violent than non-drinkers. Nevertheless, only about 20% of the binge drinkers engaged in any form of domestic violence during the year of the study. This means that 80% of binge drinkers *did not* engage in any form of violence against their partner. If alcohol causes violence, why don't all binge drinkers assault their partners? The chart also shows that 6.8% of people who were violent toward their partners don't drink at all. Clearly, alcohol didn't cause the violence among couples who never use alcohol.

Substance abuse is an important contributing factor in many incidents of domestic violence, but the way people think is still the most important factor in abusive behavior. As you've learned throughout this book, people who think like an abuser act like one. The research described earlier suggests that people are more likely to think and act like an abuser when they're intoxicated than when they're sober. People who think like an abuser while they're sober *and* abuse alcohol or drugs are especially dangerous to their partners. This dangerous combination was shown in a 1990 study, which found that men who rarely drink but think it's OK to hit a spouse had higher rates of spousal abuse than heavy drinkers who think it's wrong to hit your partner (Kaufman, Kantor, & Straus, 1990). This finding suggests that thoughts and beliefs are even more important than substance abuse when it comes to partner violence. As would be expected, the highest rates of violence were reported among heavy drinkers who *also* believe it's OK to hit your partner.

You've learned throughout this book how important it is to understand the role that your thoughts play in anger and partner violence. It's equally as important to understand the role that your thoughts play in substance abuse. In chapter seven you learned the difference between childlike thinking (seen in core beliefs and automatic thoughts) and adult thinking (that is typical of self-talk). Childlike thinking wants immediate gratification, doesn't care about consequences, and makes selfish decisions rather than what's best for the family. Adult thinking considers long-term goals, cares about the consequences of their choices, and makes unselfish decisions based on what's best for everyone. It's vital that you think like an adult when alcohol and drugs are concerned, especially if you tend to abuse them. The illustration below shows the struggles that John (from the story above) went through in maintaining his sobriety. At first, he found himself constantly switching back and forth between his "child brain" and his "adult brain."

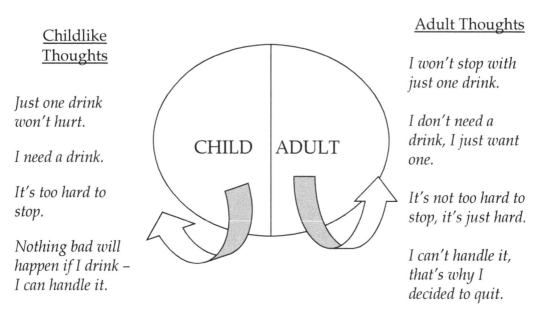

For a while it was like John had an angel and a devil on each shoulder. Both voices were talking to him at the same time, and John would have to decide which voice he would listen to. In time, John's adult voice became stronger and his child voice got weaker. His adult voice would talk to his child voice, almost as though his adult voice was a parent "raising a child." Of course, there was really only one John and both of the voices were thoughts coming from him.

But that's the way many people describe it – like having an angel and a devil on my shoulder – when their analytical adult side starts to battle with their childish core beliefs.

So, what conclusions can be made about drinking and violence? The research as of this writing suggests the following:

1. *The more one drinks, the greater the likelihood that he or she will be involved in a domestic violence incident against his or her partner.* Studies report that heavy or binge drinkers have a two-to-three times greater rate of assaulting their partners than people who don't drink. The same assumptions can be made about drug abuse.

2. *Drinking, in itself, is not enough to cause a person hit his or her partner.* Most heavy drinkers in the study shown at the beginning of this chapter (80%) did not hit their partners at all, despite their frequent drunkenness.

3. *Getting control of a drinking problem can do a lot to lower the risk of further violence, but it is no guarantee that the violence will stop.* Many people who stop drinking, or who have never had a drinking problem, abuse their partners. In the Straus and Gelles study, about 7% of the people who abstain from alcohol entirely had engaged in at least one episode of domestic violence against their spouse during the year of the study.

The conclusion to be made is this: if you have a drug or alcohol problem, get help. In so doing, you can greatly lower the odds that you will again assault your partner. However, more than substance abuse counseling is needed to get control over abusive behavior and violence. You must also change childish destructive attitudes, gain important skills, and accept full responsibility for your behavior towards your partner. Positive and meaningful changes in yourself and your relationships will come from getting control of your drinking or drug problem, *and* by applying the tools that you learn in this book.

If You Have an Alcohol or Drug Problem

How do you know if you have a drinking problem? First of all, if you are having a lot of marital problems, I recommend that you stop drinking until things are on a more stable footing at home. Drinking will only compound your problems and increase the risk of violence during an argument. Secondly, if you have engaged in *any* abusive or violent behavior in the past while under the influence, you should stop drinking altogether. If stopping your drinking seems like too hard a thing to ask, you need to re-examine your priorities. *Nothing should be more important to you than stopping the violence in your relationships.* You should be willing to make any changes in yourself that will help attain that goal. If you are unwilling to make those changes, it is time to look at your level of commitment to a violence-free lifestyle. If you are using street drugs, you have a drug problem, period. Now is the time to take whatever steps are necessary to get help for it. The chart below shows the drinking patterns of the adults who participated in the Straus and Gelles (1990) survey that we have used in this lesson. How do your drinking habits compare to other Americans?

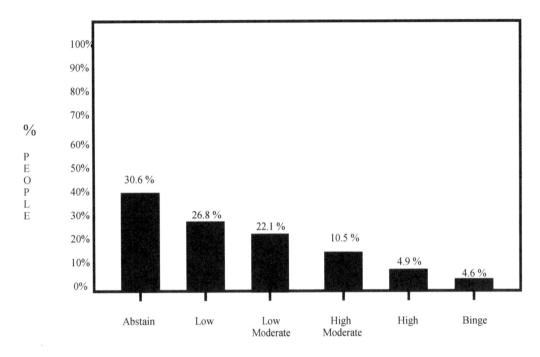

Severity of Drinking Problem

Abstain:	Never drinks alcohol.
Low:	Drinks from less than once a month up to 1 - 2 times a week, never more than 1 drink at a time.
Low Moderate:	Drinks 1-3 times a month up to daily, never more than 2 drinks.
High Moderate:	Drinks up to 2 times a week, 3-4 drinks a day.
High:	Drinks 3-4 times a week, 3 or more drinks a day.
Binge:	Drinks 1 to 2 times a week, 5 or more drinks a day.

While this chart doesn't provide answers to all the questions that can be asked about American drinking habits, it does suggest that over half of the people either abstain from drinking altogether, or drink infrequently. Please note, however, that even a person who drinks infrequently may have a drinking problem. A different test of whether or not a person has a drinking problem is to look at the consequences of his or her drinking. For example:

1) *Have you been arrested or had legal problems (DUI) due to alcohol or drug use?*

2) *Has drinking or drug use caused problems in your relationships?*

3) *Have you ever gotten into trouble at work due to your drug or alcohol use, or has substance abuse caused financial problems?*

4) *Has drug or alcohol use threatened your physical health or mental well-being?*

5) *Have you ever verbally, sexually, or physically abused your partner while under the influence of alcohol or drugs?*

If you answered "yes" to any of these questions, I recommend that you think about getting help, or at least talk to someone about a possible substance abuse problem. Being willing to acknowledge a problem and get help for it is a big first step in listening to your adult voice. The Alcohol Use Disorders Identification Test (AUDIT) is a widely used method of identifying alcohol problems. Answer the questions and add up your score.

The Alcohol Use Disorders Identification Test: Self-Report Version

PATIENT: Because alcohol use can affect your health and can interfere with certain medications and treatments, it is important that we ask some questions about your use of alcohol. Your answers will remain confidential so please be honest.

Place an X in one box that best describes your answer to each question.

Questions	0	1	2	3	4	
1. How often do you have a drink containing alcohol?	Never	Monthly or less	2-4 times a month	2-3 times a week	4 or more times a week	
2. How many drinks containing alcohol do you have on a typical day when you are drinking?	1 or 2	3 or 4	5 or 6	7 to 9	10 or more	
3. How often do you have six or more drinks on one occasion?	Never	Less than monthly	Monthly	Weekly	Daily or almost daily	
4. How often during the last year have you found that you were not able to stop drinking once you had started?	Never	Less than monthly	Monthly	Weekly	Daily or almost daily	
5. How often during the last year have you failed to do what was normally expected of you because of drinking?	Never	Less than monthly	Monthly	Weekly	Daily or almost daily	
6. How often during the last year have you needed a first drink in the morning to get yourself going after a heavy drinking session?	Never	Less than monthly	Monthly	Weekly	Daily or almost daily	
7. How often during the last year have you had a feeling of guilt or remorse after drinking?	Never	Less than monthly	Monthly	Weekly	Daily or almost daily	
8. How often during the last year have you been unable to remember what happened the night before because of your drinking?	Never	Less than monthly	Monthly	Weekly	Daily or almost daily	
9. Have you or someone else been injured because of your drinking?	No		Yes, but not in the last year		Yes, during the last year	
10. Has a relative, friend, doctor, or other health care worker been concerned about your drinking or suggested you cut down?	No		Yes, but not in the last year		Yes, during the last year	
					Total	

In a study of treatment matching with persons who had a wide range of alcohol problem severity, it was found that AUDIT scores in the range of 8-15 represented a medium level of alcohol problems whereas scores of 16 and above represented a high level of alcohol problems[33].

Don's Marijuana Time-Out

In closing, let me warn you about using alcohol or drugs to cope with conflict. Don, a member of my group several years ago, raised his hand during a session. "Dr. Adams," he said, "I agree with everything you say about alcohol and other drugs, but you're wrong about marijuana. Whenever my wife and I get into it I go to the garage and smoke a joint. My anger goes right away, and no more problem. I've done this for years and it works great!" Don was describing what might be described as a marijuana time-out, and he highly recommended it. Over the years, other clients have made similar comments about their drug (or drink) of choice. One client said cocaine reduced his anger, but alcohol increased it. Another claimed that wine was a good conflict-reducer, but tequila was deadly and should be avoided at all cost.

I asked Don, "If marijuana works so great, what are you doing in a domestic violence program? Did you score some bad weed or something?" Don blinked a couple of times, but didn't answer. I reminded Don of The Box (Chapter One), and how in reality his marijuana use increased tension between him and his wife, because they were not solving their problems and getting back to the real OK Zone. He was in a drug-induced OK Zone. Getting high made him *feel* like things were OK, but they were not. Getting high never solves the problems that cause tension between partners, and unsolved problems lead to lingering tension that grows and festers. Over time, the average tension level rises, and can eventually explode in an episode of physical violence. Drugs and alcohol can't get you back to the OK zone of The Box. You may not feel the tension when you're stoned or inebriated, but it's there, and it will be waiting for you when your sobriety returns. Running away only makes things worse. The only effective way to deal with conflict is to solve the problems that cause it, and that requires knowledge, skill, and character. You can't find that in a drug or a bottle.

HOMEWORK ASSIGNMENT
CHAPTER 21

Answer the following questions openly and honestly (without denial, blame, or minimizing):

1) *Do you think alcohol and drug abuse causes domestic violence? Why or why not?*

2) *How does alcohol or drug abuse increase the risk of domestic violence?*

3) *How can the risk of domestic violence be reduced by getting help for an alcohol or substance abuse problem?*

4) *Have you ever verbally or physically abused your partner or your children while under the influence of alcohol or drugs?*

5) *If so, what role did alcohol or drugs play in the abuse?*

6) *Answer the following questions fully. Keep denial and minimization out of your answers.*

   a. *Have you been arrested or had legal problems due to alcohol or drug use?*

   b. *Has drinking or drug use caused problems in your relationships?*

   c. *Have you ever gotten into trouble at work due to your drug or alcohol use, or has substance abuse caused financial problems?*

   d. *Has drug or alcohol use threatened your physical health or mental well-being?*

   e. *Have you ever verbally, sexually, or physically abused your partner while under the influence of alcohol or drugs?*

   f. *Do you have a score of 8 or higher on the AUDIT?*

7) *If you answered "yes" to any of these questions it's possible that you have a problem with alcohol or drugs. What do you plan to do about it?*

8) *Ask your partner (or someone who knows you well if you're not in a relationship) to answer questions "a" through "e" with you in mind. Are your partner's answers different from yours? If so, your partner may see some problems that you don't (or won't) acknowledge. If your answers are different, what are your thoughts about the differences between your answers?*

Chapter 22
Choices Chains

Key Concepts: Your success in life depends more on your choices than on the choices of others. If you want to change your life and improve your relationships, you have to change the choices you make. Choices chains can help you identify poor choices from the past, and find better choices for your future.

Skill Building: Develop an understanding of the true power of your own choices. Practice using choices chains to improve the choices you make in your relationships.

Throughout this book I've asked you to change the way you think about things. A lot of emphasis has been placed on taking personal responsibility for your choices. Specifically, you are asked to adopt the following beliefs:

- *Every day of your life you face situations in which you have to make choices. Your life today is, more than anything else, the result of the choices you have made.*

- *Do not blame others. Keep your focus on yourself, because only you can solve your problems.*

- *You are 100% responsible for how you choose to respond to every situation and person in your life. Everyone else is 0% responsible.*

- *Your choices are the most important factor in how you feel. Happiness occurs when you make wise and responsible choices, while unhappiness is the frequent companion of irresponsible choices. If you choose better for yourself and your family, you will experience the good feelings that accompany responsible choices.*

- *In the words of psychiatrist William Glasser, "Happiness occurs most often when we are willing to take responsibility for our behavior."*

- *Never make excuses, feel sorry for yourself, or blame others for your irresponsible choices. Irresponsible and childish behavior is never justified, no matter how much you may have suffered at the hands of others.*

- *To be successful as an adult, you must be willing to judge your own behavior and make changes when your behavior falls below your standards. If you fail to judge your own behavior you will not grow as a person and nothing will get better.*

- *If you get angry it is because you choose to anger yourself. If you remain calm, it is because you choose to stay calm and balanced. Your thoughts cause your anger. If you abuse, it is because you choose to abuse. If you do not abuse, it is because you choose to behave responsibly.*

- *You alone are responsible for your behavior. Right or wrong, you must accept full responsibility for your choices.*

- *Your choices are the single most important reason why your life (and your relationship) is what it is. In fact, your life at this moment is an accumulation of the thousands of choices you've made over the years. You chose your partner. You chose to stay in the relationship or leave it. When problems came up, as they always do, you chose to respond to them the way you did. You chose to say and do certain things, and you chose to not say and do other things. Every choice you made along the way had a positive or negative effect on your relationships and your life.*

- *Today and in the future, you have more choices to make. You will choose to apply the concepts and skills you have learned, or choose to ignore them. Either way, you will be the person you choose to be, and your relationship will be what you make it. You alone must decide whether you will take the responsible course.*

You may say, "Wait a minute, Dr. Adams, what about my partner's choices? What about all the hurtful things my partner has said and done to me? Why do I always have to focus on my choices?" Human nature being as it is, it's easier to identify your partner's poor choices than your own. But you can't change your partner – you can only change yourself, and by changing yourself you can often change your relationship. Change has to start somewhere, and with someone. You might as well step up to the plate and take a leadership role by starting the change process. It only takes *one* person to stop *your* abuse and *your* irresponsible choices – you. It's easier to ask your partner to change than for you to change. Like I said, it's easier to see your partner's shortcomings than your own. Most people I work with can go on and on about their partner's wicked behavior, but they find it harder to talk about the changes they need to make.

If you examine past incidents of abuse openly and honestly you will find that, regardless of the behavior of your partner, there were choices that you could have made that would have led to a more positive outcome. This lesson will help you understand the choices you made that resulted in abuse, and identify choices that, had you made them, would have led to a more positive outcome for everyone.

It is important to understand how your past choices led to abuse, and to identify better choices. With this understanding, it will be easier for you to make different choices the next time you are in a similar situation. Before going further, let me remind you of the pitfalls of blaming, minimizing, and denying. As you engage the exercises in this chapter, you will be tempted to see yourself as an unfortunate victim of circumstances. *You are neither powerless nor a victim, and you should not think of yourself that way*. You have the power to choose a violence-free relationship. You have the power to choose not to abuse again. You can choose to solve problems with your head rather than with your hands, to communicate rather than shout, to understand rather than demand. You can choose to remain calm, even when others aren't. You can choose better for yourself and your family, but only if you let go of your view of yourself as a helpless victim. If you are to take control of your future, there can be no room for blaming, minimizing, or denying.

Behavior Chains

The tool in this chapter – *the Choices Chain* – help you identify your poor choices, and find areas where you can make more responsible choices during times of conflict. Choices chains help you focus on yourself and your choices, rather than on your partner and your partner's choices. There's another way in which choices chains help you. If you're like most people, your first attempts to apply the concepts and skills in this book might not turn out as well as you hoped. If that happens, don't get discouraged. You just need more practice. It's easy to learn these concepts and skills, but it's more difficult to apply them in the heat of conflict. They're easier to talk about than to do. If you don't get the personal results you're looking for when you apply a concept or skill you've learned, make a choices chain. It will show you where the problem is and where things went wrong. By learning from your last attempt, you'll be more skillful next time.

When a problem comes up between you and you're partner, the goal is to get from *Point A* (a state of Tension) to *Point B* (back to the OK Zone of The Box), as shown in the illustration below. Suppose you try to use the concepts and skills listed in the Skill Building chapters such as warning signs, self-talk, problem solving, time-out, the Big Picture, avoid blame and control, and so forth, but instead of getting from Point A to Point B, you wind up at Point C (out of The Box). What happened? You might ask yourself, *"How did I get from Point A to Point C? I tried to follow the map (The Box) and use my skills, but everything went wrong. What happened?"* This is when choices chains help you out. They show each of the choices you made one by one. A thoughtfully prepared choices chain will tell you what went wrong – how you got from Point A to Point C, instead of Pont A to Point B – so that you can avoid making the same mistake next time.

A choices chain will help the fellow in the illustration understand what happened. Choices chains are like footprints in a field of snow. Each choice is a footprint. By following the footprints, you can easily see how you got from Point A to Point C, as shown in the next illustration. Yeah, I know there are a lot of illustrations, but my wife Deborah and I have a lot of fun doing them. (More importantly, sometimes it's easier to understand a concept when it's presented visually.)

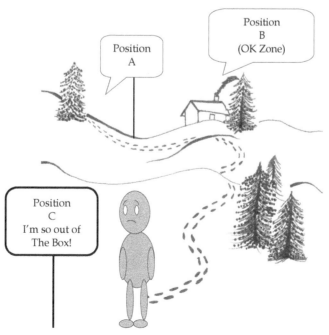

If he looks, the footprints in the snow will show the man in the illustration how he ended up so far from home. He didn't get there by accident – he got there one step at a time. That's also the way choices work. Every choice brings you closer to the goal (the OK zone of The Box), or takes you further from it. Choices chains are like looking at your footprints; they tell you the steps you took towards or away from the OK zone.

The examples that follow will show you how choices chains work. The first example was written by Louis. Louis is married, but he still likes to have fun with the guys, especially if the guys plan to go to a club. It isn't too surprising that Louis' wife has a problem with his club fun, especially when it gets out of hand. As I recall, Louis worked a swing shift at his job, so his hours were irregular. On the night described in Louis' choices chain, he got off work early one night and headed to a club with his cousin, where his fun lasted all night. As he was scheduled to work the morning shift at his job the following day, he didn't make it home that night and headed back to work from the club. To his surprise, his wife was waiting for him at work. The tension between them was high and there was some verbal abuse between them. The problem wasn't resolved that morning, so the tension followed Louis home after work, where the problem came up again. Louis made a series of choices which eventually led to his arrest. Let's look at his choices in the way he presented them to the group.

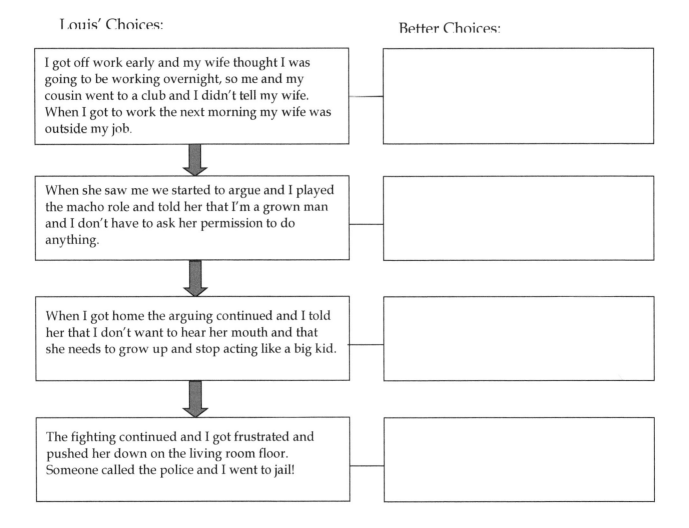

Any one of Louis' "Better Choices" would have prevented the violence that led to his arrest. When Louis started his counseling he blamed his wife for the whole incident. After doing a choices chain he understood the power of his own choices in the incident, and how he had several chances to make choices that would have led to a different outcome. Unfortunately, he didn't make those "Better" choices. He chose to abuse his wife, and by making that choice he chose to get arrested that night. He had the power to choose better for him and his partner, and he has only himself to blame that things turned out the way they did.

The second choices chain was written by Holly. Holly had been married for several years, and the first years of marriage were good. But recently, her husband had started drinking more and more. Her attempts to reason with him didn't help, and one night he came home in the wee hours of the morning reeking of alcohol and very intoxicated. Holly had been waiting up for him and met him at the door. Her choices chain tells the rest of the story.

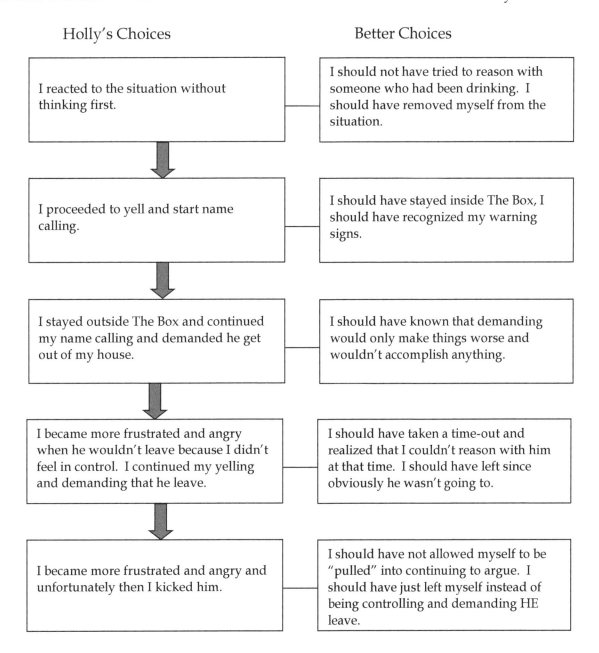

Holly's Choices	Better Choices
I reacted to the situation without thinking first.	I should not have tried to reason with someone who had been drinking. I should have removed myself from the situation.
I proceeded to yell and start name calling.	I should have stayed inside The Box, I should have recognized my warning signs.
I stayed outside The Box and continued my name calling and demanded he get out of my house.	I should have known that demanding would only make things worse and wouldn't accomplish anything.
I became more frustrated and angry when he wouldn't leave because I didn't feel in control. I continued my yelling and demanding that he leave.	I should have taken a time-out and realized that I couldn't reason with him at that time. I should have left since obviously he wasn't going to.
I became more frustrated and angry and unfortunately then I kicked him.	I should have not allowed myself to be "pulled" into continuing to argue. I should have just left myself instead of being controlling and demanding HE leave.

Like Louis, Holly blamed her partner for the incident at first. As she completed her choices chain, however, she came to understand that she had been in control of her own destiny all along. If she had made the "Better Choices" available to her, there would have been no violence and she wouldn't have gone to jail that night. Perhaps you sympathize with Holly. Certainly, everyone in her group understood the problem and understood Holly's anger, and everyone agreed that Holly had to do something about her husband's drinking problem. She couldn't be expected to just ignore it.

But Holly understood that her choice to deal with the problem by becoming verbally abusive and physically violent was a poor choice. In her own words, those choices didn't accomplish anything and it only made things worse. It was her responsibility to stay in The Box and express her anger in a non-violent manner. She chose not to. The only thing her choices got her was a night in jail. Like Louis, she chose abuse and violence for her partner and for herself. Any of her "Better Choices" would have led to a very different outcome. To her credit, she took responsibility for her poor choices that day, as did Louis. Holly didn't choose the situation she had to deal with, but she *did* choose the way she reacted to it. We all do. Even when faced with blatant wrongdoing from our partner, we have the choice to stay in The Box and act like a leader, or to leave The Box and behave like a tyrant.

The last example was provided by Richard, a divorcee who shared custody of his son Brandon with Linda, his ex-spouse. Because of Richard's past abusive behavior the court issued a protective order that required him to stay away from Linda at all times, but Richard sometimes ignored the order. Richard blamed Linda for their failed marriage, and objected to Linda having a new boyfriend. On the day in question, Richard picked up his son at school to take him to lunch. Richard knew that Linda worked at Brandon's school and that he might see her there. That's just what happened. As he was leaving the school building with Brandon he saw his ex, Linda. Richard's refusal to comply with the protective order – and his controlling behavior towards Linda – are about to cause new problems for him. Let's look at his choices one-by-one, as Richard later described them to his counseling group.

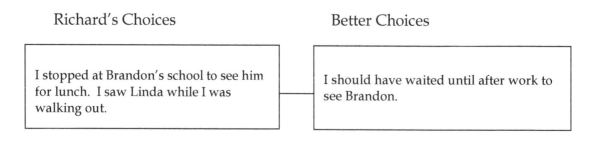

Richard's first choice was to ignore the court order by going to Linda's workplace. It was a poor choice. As Richard later acknowledged, he was angry with Linda and was looking for a chance to confront her. Picking up Brandon for lunch was an excuse to see Linda "by accident." Had he chosen to abide by the protective order the entire incident would have been avoided. Instead, he chose to ignore the order.

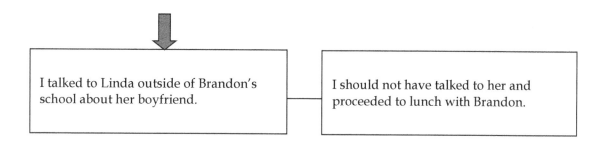

Richard still had time to turn things around. He could have chosen to avoid talking to Linda and simply gone to lunch with his son. Instead, he chose to violate the protective order by approaching Linda and bringing up an emotionally charged topic. Linda's relationship with her boyfriend was none of Richard's business, but he still wanted to control things.

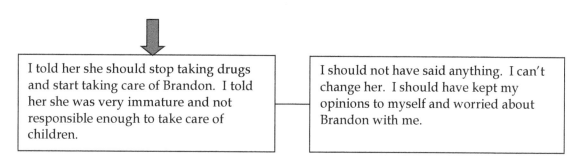

If Richard has reason to believe that Linda is endangering Brandon by abusing drugs with her boyfriend, there are appropriate ways to address the problem (raise his concerns in family court, report them to the Department of Children and Family Services, etc.). His choice to confront Linda in public on the steps of a school building, at Linda's workplace and in front of his son, and in a manner that violated a protective order was foolish and unhelpful. Richard's belligerent attitude and claim that Linda was unfit to care for Brandon was provocative and sent the tension level sky high. It was this type of behavior that led the court to issue a protective order requiring Richard to stay away from Linda.

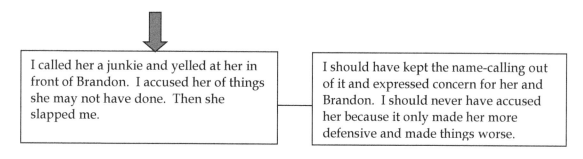

As you learned in Chapter One, nothing good happens out of The Box, and Richard was definitely out of The Box. He wanted to hurt Linda by verbally abusing her and he selfishly ignored the effect of his behavior on his son, who had to witness his father's humiliating tirade against his mother. Richard's concerns about Linda's behavior may or may not have been legitimate, but *even if his concerns about her were entirely valid they didn't justify his choice to abuse*

her. The police were called, and Richard was arrested (for violating a protective order) in front of Brandon and other people at the school. Any of Richard's "Better Choices" would have led to a different outcome for himself, his son, and Linda.

When Richard started counseling he was indignant that he was arrested. He saw himself as a victim and railed against the police and the court system. Richard created a victim role for himself by limiting his attention to his first choice *(I stopped at Brandon's school to see him for lunch)* and the end result *(she slapped me)*. As so many people do, he chose to narrow his attention to the last few seconds of the incident, and to ignore the choices that he made along the way. Like the man in the illustration, he refused to look at his own "footprints in the snow." He found himself at Point C (slapped and arrested), didn't like it there at all, and blamed others for it. He ignored his choice to use verbal hostility, and he paid no attention to "The Pull" that his choice generated in Linda (see Chapter 15 for a discussion about "the pull"). I'm not suggesting that Richard is responsible for Linda's behavior. She made her own choices, just like Richard did. I'm saying that Richard's assertion that he was an innocent victim in this situation was nonsense. He *chose* to go to Point C, step-by-step and choice-by-choice.

A choices chain forced Richard to stop thinking of himself as a helpless victim. As he worked on his choices chain, his footprints were unavoidable. They provided undeniable evidence that he had walked to Point C all by himself. He understood that, as far as his life went on that day, his own choices mattered more that Linda's choices. In fact, his own choices mattered more than the choices of the police, the district attorney, or the court because *any one of his Better Choices would have led to a very different outcome for him.* Had he chosen to use one of his Better Choices Linda wouldn't have hit him, the police wouldn't have been called, and he wouldn't have faced jail and the ire of the judge. *Richard acknowledged that his own choices were more powerful than any other person's choices in determining what happened to him on that day.* Choices chains are valuable because they show you the power of your choices. Remember Richard whenever you think of yourself as a victim. *When you see yourself as a victim you are pretending that your own choices aren't powerful. They are!* All you have to do to show yourself how powerful your choices are is to complete a choices chain. You'll quickly see your "footprints in the snow" – how you chose to go from Point A to Point C.

To their credit, Louis, Holly, and Richard were willing to look honestly at their choices and learn from their mistakes. Over the course of their counseling, each of them provided many examples of their ability to make better choices, and thereby choose a better life for themselves and the people who loved them. By following their example, you can do the same.

HOMEWORK ASSIGNMENT
CHAPTER 22

In this homework assignment you will gain experience in using choices chains to identify irresponsible choices and find better choices that you can make in the future. Think about an incident in which you became verbally or physically abusive (got out of The Box). In the boxes under *My Choices* describe everything you said and did. Be sure to go one choice at a time, and keep things in chronological order – like footprints in the snow. Only write down *your own choices*. Don't write down what your partner said or did, because you don't control those choices. In the boxes under "Better Choices," write down choices that you could have made that would have led to a more positive outcome. Use as many boxes as needed to cover all your important choices.

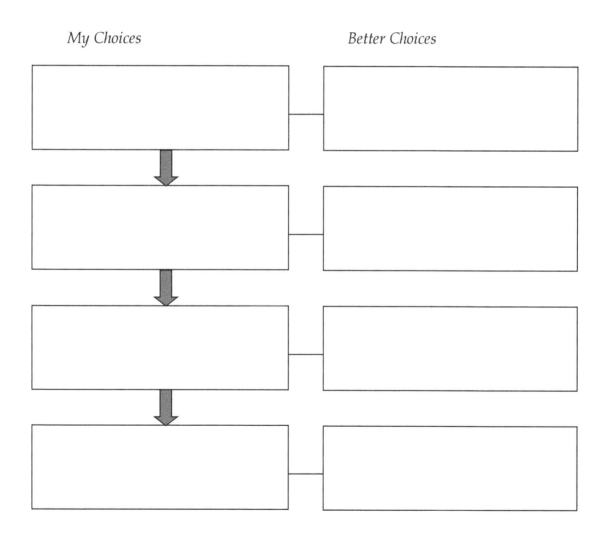

Chapter 23
Character and Trust

Key Concepts: Maintaining an abuse-free relationship requires character. Character is the strength to do the right thing when you want to do the wrong thing. Getting your partner's trust back takes time. Stay in The Box for the rest of your life, and let the clock run. Trust may come in time.

Skill Building: Understand the importance of character, and choose to live the life of an eagle rather than a chicken. Earn your family's trust by staying in The Box from now on.

Years ago, when I was a boy, someone told me a story about chickens and an eagle. It's an old story, and I've heard several versions of it over the years. The details changed depending upon who was telling the story, but the moral of the story was always the same. Here's the story as I remember it.

There was once a beautiful and majestic eagle who built a nest in the top of the tallest tree on the highest mountain in the land. In the nest she laid a single egg. A wise and noble mother, the eagle kept constant watch over her egg and protected it. She spread her wings by day to shade her egg from the heat of the sun, and she kept it close to her body at night to fend off the frosty air. She rarely slept or left the nest to hunt because she knew there were other creatures living on the mountain that would eat her egg if they got the chance.

One day a hunter saw her soaring high in the sky. He saw how beautiful she was and made up his mind to kill the eagle for her fine feathers, which were prized by the people in the valley below. When she flew back to her nest he followed her, and when he found her in the tree, he shot her. The next day the egg shook and cracked. A baby eagle was born. The young eagle called and called, but his mother didn't come. Struggling to the edge of the nest to call for her again, he fell from the nest to the ground below.

This would have surely been the last of the baby eagle were it not for a farmer who happened to walk by looking for a sheep who had wandered off. When he got near the tree, he heard the young eagle calling for his mother. Looking first at the nest above, and then at a few feathers on the ground that were left by the hunter, the farmer guessed what had happened. "You're alone now, young eagle. Your mother is no more," said the farmer. "I'll take you to my home where you'll be safe." The farmer put the infant eagle in his coat pocket and carried him to his farm in the valley below, where he put the baby eagle in a pen with his chickens.

A couple of summers passed. One day a man whom the people in the valley considered very wise happened to walk by the farmer's house, and there he saw something remarkable. Among the farmer's chickens was a beautiful eagle. The eagle pecked at the ground just like the chickens, and he walked and clucked just as the chickens did. Walking over to the eagle he asked, "Eagle, why are you here among the chickens?" "Sir, I don't know what you mean," replied the eagle." "This is my family." "No," said the wise man. "This is not your family. You are an eagle! You belong to the sky, not to the earth." The wise man tried to teach the eagle, but the eagle didn't understand. The eagle had never flown because no one had ever taught him to fly. He believed he was a chicken because he had always lived the life of a chicken.

The wise man thought for a long while. Then an idea came to him. He said, "Come with me and I'll show you who you really are." With that, the wise man picked up the eagle and put him on his shoulder. At first, it frightened the eagle greatly to be on the wise man's shoulder as he had never been so high above the ground, but at the same time he felt something familiar stir deep inside him. "Where are we going?" asked the eagle. "We're going to the top of that mountain where the sun is setting," answered the wise man. "Why?" asked the eagle. "You'll see in time," said the man. The eagle asked many more questions, but all the wise man said was, "You'll see in time."

The sun set as they reached the place where the mountain meets the valley, and all night they climbed toward the summit. The eagle couldn't remember ever being so far from the other chickens and the security of the farm. As they climbed, he heard the voices of other animals, both the howl of the hunters and the cries of the hunted, and it all seemed strange but somehow familiar to him. On they walked through the night. The sky was just starting to lighten when the wise man stopped. "This is where you belong," he said to the eagle.

The eagle was bewildered. The sky was getting lighter, but it was still too dark to see clearly. "I don't understand," said the eagle. "You will soon," said the wise man, as they stood facing the growing light in the east. Slowly, the sun rose, casting a golden light in the face of the eagle. The morning wind rustled his feathers. The sun rose higher revealing a valley far below, and the eagle felt his heart race in his chest. "You are an eagle!" shouted the wise man. "Fly!" With that, he threw the eagle off the mountaintop! Terrified, the eagle tumbled over and over as he fell towards the valley below. The air rushed through his wings and he fell faster and faster towards what seemed certain death on the valley floor. But then something rose up inside the eagle. He heard himself cry out, and the sound he made surprised him. It wasn't a cry of fear, but the screech of an eagle that was heard in the valley below. The eagle spread his wings and flew, soaring higher and higher in the morning sky. Now he understood. He was an eagle!

(I was about to write that the eagle swooped over the farm and ate a chicken, but that wouldn't be appropriate. Sorry, I just got carried away with the story. Give me a second to get refocused.)

Think of yourself as the eagle in the story. What sort of ending would you write for the eagle? You could write an ending that goes like this: *The eagle no longer lived the life of a chicken. He saw himself as an eagle and grew the heart of an eagle. He soared high over the valley and became the noble creature he was meant to be.*

Unfortunately, some people write this ending for themselves: *The eagle returned to the life of a chicken. Learning to fly was a lot of work, and his chicken friends thought all this flying and soaring was weird. They laughed at him and told him to knock it off and act more like the other chickens. He thought like a chicken and he had a chicken's heart. Soon the eagle was back to pecking the dirt and clucking with his chicken friends.*

Do you see yourself as an eagle or a chicken? I admit there's a lot more chickens than eagles, and in some ways a chicken's life is easier. Chickens don't take responsibility for their mistakes or try to figure out what's wrong. They just blame others for their problems. They don't take responsibility for their anger, and they're unwilling to learn or change. No one expects much from them. They just go on living their chicken lives.

There are relatively few eagles among us. Eagles have the courage to acknowledge their weaknesses and the wisdom to correct them. They have the strength to become a respected leader rather than a feared tyrant. They are responsible people who live their lives in a way that gives them a feeling of self-worth, and a feeling they are worthwhile to others. They maintain a satisfactory standard of behavior. They meet their needs in a responsible way that does not prevent others from meeting their needs. Eagles have no fear of chickens, and eagles' commitment to growth isn't shaken by the ridicule of the chickens around them. Courage, wisdom, strength, respect, responsibility, commitment – those words define an eagle. Most important of all, eagles have strength of character; chickens have none. The presence or absence of character is the easiest way to tell a chicken from an eagle. Eagles have it, chickens don't. Let me explain what I mean by character.

Character

Character means choosing to do the right thing long after the desire to do the right thing is gone. In other words, character is doing the right thing even when you're sorely tempted to do the wrong thing. It's easy to avoid violence when everything around you is the way you like it. Even chickens can do that. But when you're really angry and those around you are treating you unfairly or disrespectfully, it's harder to do the right thing (be a leader, use your skills, and stay in The Box). Sometimes people will deliberately try to provoke you. Now is when you find out whether you're a chicken or an eagle. Do you have the strength of character to do the right thing when others are not?

There have been people in my counseling program that talked like an eagle while in their group. When the going at home was easy, they acted like an eagle. But when things at home got tough and they were really challenged, they resorted to their old chicken behavior. They got out of The Box, forgot the skills and concepts they had learned over months of counseling, and abused their partners again. It's easy to talk like an eagle. It's a lot harder to live like one. Living the life of an eagle takes real character.

Let me tell you about Joe. Joe had as much character as any person I've ever met. Before I met Joe he had lived a chicken's life. In fact, Joe was the head chicken in his neighborhood. Active in a gang since childhood, violence was all he had ever known. He wasn't just violent – Joe was a killer, and even the other gang members feared him. His life was a revolving door of crime, violence, and prison terms. As one would expect, Joe was also abusive to his wife and children. Like I said, he was a chicken's chicken.

Joe came to my counseling group as a condition of his parole, after serving several years of a prison sentence. He wasn't a youngster any more. Joe was in his thirties and he was tired of chicken life. Joe talked about his wife and children in group discussions. He told us that he wanted to be part of their lives, and that he was determined to do whatever it took to be a good husband and a real father to his kids. Joe wanted to be an eagle, but I privately wondered if he had the character to live an eagle's life. Like the eagle in the story, all he knew was the life of a chicken, but Joe surprised me as the weeks and months went by. He participated constructively in the group and took his counseling very seriously. Joe took responsibility for his choices and set a positive example for others in the program. His homework assignments were crudely written, but beneath his almost illegible handwriting there was sound understanding and application of the concepts and skills that he was learning. I had to admit that Joe seemed to be transforming himself into an eagle, but the story he told in group one week astonished everyone, including me. Joe told us the following story, which I've written as best as I recall it.

Joe's Test of Character

I took my family to see a movie that my kids wanted to see. There were four or five teenage guys – want to be gangsters – sitting a few rows behind us, and they were talking loudly, swearing, and cracking jokes during the previews. I tried to ignore them, but I felt myself getting mad. My wife and kids were really looking forward to seeing the movie and I wanted them to have a good time. Besides, it cost a lot of money to see it. I used self-talk to calm down, but these guys kept talking. I felt my wife squeeze my hand. I think she knew I was getting mad and she was afraid what I might do. She didn't want me to get in any trouble.

The movie started and these guys just got louder. I knew my kids couldn't hear the movie. I think the other people there were afraid to say anything, so I stood up and told them to knock it off. I didn't yell at them, I just told them to be quiet so my kids could hear the movie. They quieted down after that, but then they started throwing popcorn and stuff and some of it hit my kids. I saw my warning signs. Mainly, I started to think about ways to hurt these guys, and I knew I had to get myself out of there or I was going to get out of The Box. I had to think about what to do. I got my family up and we went to the very back of the theatre where we could be alone. That seemed to solve the problem, and we watched the rest of the movie in peace.

When the movie was over I told my wife and kids to stay in their seat until everyone left. I didn't want any more trouble or to have another confrontation with those guys. But those guys didn't leave with the other people. They waited until everyone left and then came up the stairs to where we were sitting. I thought, "Well, here we go." Part of me said, "A real man doesn't take this shit! I've had enough. These punks asked for it and now I'm going to 'f' them up like I used to do." But another part of me said, "No, stay calm. Think of my wife and kids. They need me and I want to be with them. These guys aren't worth my time." (Joe meant the time he would have to do if he violated his parole by getting in a fight.) *The guys came up to me and stood in front of my chair, and one of them threatened me by flashing gang signs. They did this right in front of my wife and kids! I wanted to kill them!*

This was a true test of Joe's character. Part of him didn't *want* to do the right thing anymore. His prior life as a chicken told him to go one way; his recent life as an eagle told him to go another. He had to choose to continue living like an eagle, or to return to the life of a chicken. Conflicting thoughts ran through his head.

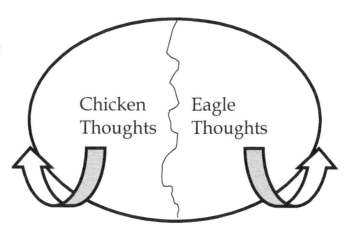

A real man gets angry and violent when people disrespect him.

People who don't get angry and violent are weak and punks.

What will other people think if I just sit here?

It's too hard to stay in The Box.

I have to make these guys respect me.

They think I'm afraid. This is awful and terrible and I can't stand it.

I have to prove that I'm a man.

Stop using your skills. Stop thinking and hit someone. I don't have a choice.

A real man makes wise choices for himself and his family.

Violence is easy, being a husband and father takes strength. My will has to be stronger than these kids.

It's what I think that matters. I'm a leader, not a follower.

I have the skills and strength I need to stay in The Box.

I could care less what these guys think, and I don't need their respect. They'll learn in time. I choose to go home with my wife and kids tonight.

I choose to stay out of jail, to give my wife a husband and my kids a father.

When the going got tough, Joe spread his wings and flew. He stayed in The Box and the guys walked away. He was an eagle, and he proved that he had the character to live an eagle's life. He thought about this as he walked to the car with his family. He really *had* changed. In the past, he would have been walking to a police car while his wife and kids looked on. Now things were different. He had the skills *and the character* to choose a better life, both for himself and for his family. Joe's group members were amazed that he had been able to keep his head in the face of such provocation, and they congratulated him. One of the less mature group members said, *"Hell, I wouldn't have taken that shit. I would have kicked their ass then tried to get away!"* Joe just looked him in the eye without saying a word. Some chickens will never understand why eagles want to fly.

Your Partner's Trust

"Dr. Adams, I haven't hit my wife in three months and she still doesn't trust me! How long is this going to take?" The man who asked this question was obviously frustrated. He had abused his wife for years, but seemed to think that after three months of semi-responsible behavior he should get a prize or something. That's not the way it works. It's easier to lose trust than to get it back. Once lost, trust returns slowly if it returns at all.

Trust is lost by getting out of The Box (see Chapter One for a discussion of The Box). Every "out of The Box" incident erodes the trust that your partner has in you. How do you get trust back? Well, sometimes you can't. If there have been a lot of "out of The Box" incidents, or if the incidents have been severe, your partner and children may never trust you again. Your partner may leave you. If that's what has happened to you, don't blame them. That's the price you pay for acting like a child. All you can do is take responsibility for your actions, and master the skills and concepts in this book so that you don't make the same mistakes in your next relationship. If you're still with your partner, getting back the trust you've lost should be foremost on your mind. *The only way to get trust back is to stay in The Box and let the clock run.*

IN THE BOX + TIME = TRUST

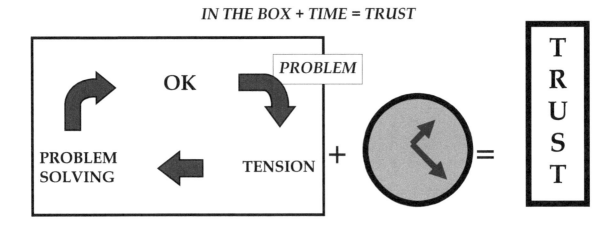

Words and promises aren't enough to win trust. Words are cheap, promises are easy to make and easy to break. Only by choosing to stay in The Box will you win your partner's trust. Someone once said, *"What you do speaks so loud I can't hear a word you're saying."* Expect that you will have to prove yourself trustworthy over and over again, and expect that winning trust back will be a gradual process that takes time. For those readers who want something more concrete, here's a two-step process that's almost guaranteed to get results:

Step One: Do something to show your partner that you are trustworthy.

Step Two: Now do it again one thousand times.

You didn't expect it to be easy, did you? If you start to doubt that getting back trust is worth the effort, pull out your Big Picture and read it. It should become clear that your efforts are worthwhile. Be warned, however, about the dangers of claiming to be an eagle and then returning to roost with the chickens. In other words, if you claim to have changed and then get out of The Box, trust will be harder than ever to win. *Getting out of The Box, even if it's only once every hundred times you get angry, will generate mistrust.* If you're going to win your family's trust and maintain an abuse-free relationship, you have to commit yourself to staying in The Box from now on. (To those readers who are asking: Yes, "from now on" means forever.)

OUT OF THE BOX = MISTRUST

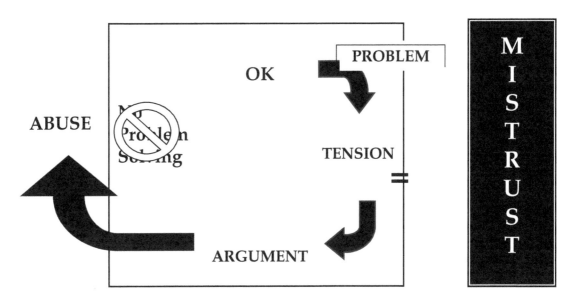

HOMEWORK ASSIGNMENT
CHAPTER 23

I have listed traits that define strong character below. Select five traits that are most important to you. Over the week to come, look for opportunities to apply the traits you selected. Describe the situation you were in, and tell us how you were able to apply the trait you selected.

Strong	Responsible	Dependable
Principled	Respectful	Dedicated
Trustworthy	Reliable	Mature
Loyal	Honest	Skillful
Honorable	Helpful	Courageous
Good	Decent	Competent

The five character traits most important to you:

1.

2.

3.

4.

5.

Give a recent example of using one or more of the traits you selected.

_____

_____

_____

_____

_____

_____

_____

_____

Chapter 24
Skill Building

> *Key Concepts: Reaching your goal of an abuse-free lifestyle requires both knowledge and practice. This chapter will help you consolidate your understanding of the concepts and skills in the last three chapters and apply them in your relationships. Remember, to build your skills you must commit to applying them in your daily life. It's what you do, not what you know, that gets results.*

> *Skill Building: Complete the following test to review any gaps in your knowledge of key skills and concepts. Provide detailed examples of your efforts to apply them in your Skill Building Log.*

It's time again to test your mastery of the skills and concepts you've learned in the last three chapters, and to put them into practice. The chapter on Drugs and Alcohol will help you understand the role of substance abuse in family violence. Choices chains help you identify poor choices from the past and identify better choices to use in the future. And the last chapter talks about the strength of character needed to maintain a violence-free lifestyle and regain your partner's trust.

As you've done in the past, review the concepts in the last few chapters by taking the quiz below. Check for any gaps in your knowledge, then go back and review any items on the quiz that give you trouble. As always, there's a new *Skill Building Log* to help you apply the new concepts and skills you've learned.

Quiz
Chapters 21-23

1. Researchers have found a strong _____ between substance abuse and domestic violence. (Chapter 21)

2. The greater the drug or alcohol problem a person has, the greater the _____ in the home. (Chapter 21)

3. Alcohol and drug use impair your _____. (Chapter 21)

4. Alcohol and drug use also put _____ on a relationship. (Chapter 21)

5. People with substance abuse problems have higher rates of _____ than people who don't have substance abuse problems. (Chapter 21)

6. However, substance abuse does not appear to _____ partner abuse. (Chapter 21)

7. Substance abuse is an important factor in partner abuse, but the way people _____ is still the most important factor in abusive behavior. (Chapter 21)

8. A person can greatly reduce the risk of a new domestic violence incident by getting control of _____. (Chapter 21)

9. If you abuse, it's because you _____. If you don't abuse, it's because you _____ behave responsibly. (Chapter 22)

10. You _____ are the single most important reason why your life (and relationship) is what it is. (Chapter 22)

11. How many people does it take to stop your abusive behavior? (Chapter 22)

12. You are not powerless or a _____ and you shouldn't think of yourself that way. (Chapter 22)

13. A _____ can help you identify poor choices and find better ones to use in the future. (Chapter 22)

14. Choices chains are like _____ in a field of snow. (Chapter 22)

15. Choices chains force you to stop thinking of yourself as _____, and they show you the _____ of your own choices. (Chapter 22)

16. When you think of yourself as a _____, you are pretending that your own choices aren't _____. (Chapter 22)

17. When you write a choices chain you should only write down _____ choices. (Chapter 22)

18. Character means _____ thing even when you're sorely tempted to _____. (Chapter 23)

19. It's easy to talk like an eagle. It's a lot harder to live like one. Living the life of an eagle takes real _____. (Chapter 23)

20. It's easier to lose trust than to get it back. Once lost, trust returns _____ if it returns at all. (Chapter 23)

21. The only way to get trust back is to _____ and let _____ run. (Chapter 23)

22. Getting out of The Box, even if it's only once every hundred times you get angry, will generate _____. (Chapter 23)

23. If you're going to win your family's trust and maintain an abuse-free relationship, you have to stay in The Box _____. (Chapter 23)

24. Partners who experience a high level of conflict in their relationship often have a problem with _____. (Chapter 23)

When you're finished, check your answers and move on to the Skill Building Log.

Skill Building Log

Step 1: Select one or more skills from the list below that you want to practice. Selecting the right skills to practice is easy. Just answer this sentence: *"It would help me and my family the most if I would _____."*

Step 2: On a separate sheet of paper, write a detailed example of how you put the skills to use. Describe (1) who you were with, (2) the problem you struggled with, (3) any of your warning signs that came up, (4) the skills you used to handle the problem, (5) how things turned out.

TOOLBOX FOR CHAPTER TWENTY-FOUR

Tools from Chapters 1-3:
- Memorize The Box
- Use The Box to guide my decision making
- Stay focused on problem solving during an argument
- Learn my own Warning Signs
- Watch for my Warning Signs when I start to feel angry
- Take a Time Out whenever I see my warning signs
- Memorize the rules to Time Out and follow them
- Explain time out to my partner
- Never cross the "I don't care what I say line"
- Never cross the "I don't care what I do line"
- Stop using any form of Verbal Abuse (stay in The Box)
- Recognize and avoid using Denial, Blame, and Minimizing

Tools from Chapters 5-7:
- Whenever I feel angry toward my partner, stop and ask myself, *"Is my thinking rational and logical right now? Am I making a big deal out of a small problem?"*
- Whenever I feel angry (or frustrated, jealous, etc.) I'll remind myself that I can choose to think in ways that escalate these feelings, or I can choose to think in ways that reduce them.
- Accept responsibility for everything I say or do.
- Lower my comfort level with violence. Don't minimize, call abuse something other than what it really is, or tell myself that such behavior is OK.
- Don't try to be my partner's boss or force my will on him or her. See my partner as my equal.
- Allow my partner the right to express his or her thoughts and feelings openly and without intimidation.
- Always stop and think *before* I react.
- Never "Awfulize."
- Stay out of the *"YOU MODE."*
- Self-talk to prevent or reduce anger.

- Identify my core beliefs about anger and aggression and modify them.

Tools from Chapters 9-11:
- See tension as a signal to problem solve rather than the opening bell to a fight.
- Remove all controlling, blaming, and hurtful language from my problem solving.
- Ask my partner if I come across as bossy, blaming, or hurtful.
- Ask my partner to tell me whenever he or she feels controlled, hurt, or blamed.
- Use the six problem solving steps.
- Whenever I step on a land mine, find out which mine it was and avoid it the next time.
- Write a letter to my partner expressing all of the feelings described in the letter writing exercise.
- Invite my partner to write a letter back to me.

Tools from Chapters 13-15:
- Develop a Big Picture and keep it in mind when problems come up.
- Let go of the adolescent idea of what it means to be strong.
- Live by the no-hostility rule.
- Recognize and resist "The Pull."

Tools from Chapters 17-19:
- Find constructive ways to deal with personality differences.
- Be more accepting of others.
- Find ways to encourage.
- Develop your leadership skills.
- Avoid male or female privilege and attempts to control your partner.
- Provide a safe and abuse-free environment for your children.
- Use less punishment and more parenting.

New Tools from Chapters 17-19:
- Evaluate your drug or alcohol use honestly and get help if needed.
- Make a choices chain to identify poor choices and find better ones.
- Continue to develop and maintain character.
- Continue engaging in behaviors that build trust.

PERSONAL PROGRESS AND SELF-EVALUATION

1. Evaluate the progress that you have made so far in your counseling. Are you satisfied with the progress you are making? Are you putting forth your best effort? Is there anything you need to do to make your counseling experience more successful?

2. Select a relationship that is important to you. What can you do to make the relationship better? Set a specific goal for improving the relationship. What do you want to accomplish over the next month?

3. Have you seen changes in your thinking or behavior since starting this program? If so, provide an example of how your thinking and behavior have changed.

4. Are there skills from your counseling that you use on a daily basis? If so, what are they? Give a recent example of using them. If you are not using the skills you have learned on a daily basis, why not?

5. Select a skill or concept from the book that is important for you to use and develop at this time of your life. What skill did you select? How can using that skill benefit you and the people who love you?

Appendix

Verbal Respect Contract

Understanding the importance of words in our relationship, we agree to speak to each other with words that convey respect. We agree to avoid language that is disrespectful, such as:

_____

_____

_____

Whenever we use language that is disrespectful, we agree to pay $ _____ .

After two weeks of keeping our contract, we will reward ourselves by:

_____

_____

_____

_____

Signature _____   *Signature* _____

Answers to Skill Building Quizzes

Chapter 4

1. Missing parts of The Box:
   1. Tension
   2. Argument
   3. Problem Solving
   4. Verbal Abuse
   5. Domestic Violence
2. They tell you you're getting out of The Box, and that you're about to express your anger in an abusive manner.
3. In an argument there is no verbal abuse (yelling, swearing, threatening, name-calling, etc.
4. Time-out rules:
   1. Use the words "time-out."
   2. No drugs or alcohol
   3. Spend time-out period alone
   4. Tell your partner when you'll be back
   5. Come back on time (15-30 minutes)
5. Terms:

   Denial: Flatly denying that you did anything wrong or that there's a problem to deal with.

   Minimizing: Make something that you did seem insignificant and less important than it was.

   Blaming: Avoiding responsibility for your actions, saying that someone or something else was responsible for what you said or did.
6. Warning Signs:

   Cognitive: Changes in the way you think when you get angry.

   Behavioral: Changes in the way you act when you get angry.

   Physiological: Changes in your body when you get angry.
7. Take a time-out, and then continue solving the problem with your partner.
8. Verbal abuse escalates anger.
9. Verbal abuse blocks problem solving. You can't attack a problem and your partner at the same time, and problem solving requires that you and your partner be on the same team.
10. The point where you're so angry that you don't care what you say to your partner.

11. The point where you're so angry that you don't care what you do to your partner.
12. Continue problem solving. Keep at it until you're back to the OK zone of The Box.
13. Denial, blame and minimizing keep you from seeing things as they really are.
14. Minimizing words include words like *only, just, sort of, kind of, a little bit, and argument.*
15. Blaming words include words like *he, she, and they.*

Chapter 8

1. Think about
2. False
3. Irrational
4. Reduce
5. Choice
6. Behave
7. Responsibility, comfort with violence, power and control
8. Responsibility
9. Control
10. Beliefs
11. Automatic thoughts
12. Reasoning
13. Think
14. Talk
15. Reasoning

Chapter 12

1. Blaming, Bossy, Hurtful
2. OK
3. Blaming, Bossy, Hurtful
4. Blame, blame
5. You
6. Bossy or controlling
7. Communication, negotiation, compromise

8. Hurtful
9. Reaction
10. Respect, responsibly, changes
11. Team, teamwork
12. Six problem solving steps:
    1. Real problem
    2. View the problem
    3. Point of view
    4. Solutions
    5. Mutually
    6. Progress
13. Letter writing
14. Anger
15. Abusive, stop the abuse

Chapter 16

1. Basically, the Big Picture is seeing past the day to day problems, keeping in mind how important your relationships are, and staying focused on what you want your relationships to grow into over the years.
2. Like other forms of self-talk, taking time to think about your Big Picture can reduce anger and keep you in The Box.
3. Time-out
4. Everything
5. Big Picture
6. Tuning out emotions because they make a person feel weak and vulnerable
7. Eight, one and a half
8. Violence, consequences
9. Is tough enough
10. A real man is tough and strong, violent, doesn't take crap off anyone, doesn't show feelings, always in control, etc.
11. Adults understand that success in the adult world requires qualities such as patience, listening skills, respect of others, understanding others, the ability to show love and affection, etc.
12. Hostility

13. Verbal

14. Pull

15. Participating, passively

16. Verbal, physical

Chapter 20

1. No

2. A person's basic personality is very stable. It usually stays very stable over a person's lifetime. However, people can compromise, negotiate, and find ways to minimize conflict in a relationship while accepting each other's differences.

3. Using the five-factor model discussed in Chapter 17, describe the most significant personality differences between you and your partner.

4. Examples of behaviors that should not be accepted are destructive behaviors such as verbal and physical abuse, infidelity, and substance abuse.

5. Accept your partner rather than trying to change him or her, learn to negotiate and compromise, encourage rather than discourage, etc.

6. For you to answer.

7. Lots of ways to answer this, but in general leaders respect and care about others, take time to listen and understand, express anger responsibly, etc. They stay in The Box and live by the no hostility rule. Tyrants are selfish and controlling, and rely on fear, intimidation, and violence to get their way.

8. No

9. Behaviors such as non-violent problem solving, compromise, respect, listening, setting a good example, self-control, etc.

10. Acting like "the boss," having the final say in family matters, and any other behavior or belief that stems from the idea that you should have most of the power in the relationship because of your gender.

11. Fear, respect

12. A tyrant

13. Neglect, endangerment, unjustifiable mental pain and suffering, etc.

14. Yes

15. Family violence has been linked to child suicide, core beliefs that accept violence as a legitimate problem solving strategy, violent behavior toward other children, increased likelihood that they will be abused by their parents, depression, school problems, etc.

16. Psychological and emotional distress, behavioral problems, school and learning difficulties, etc.

17. Punishment does not teach or educate a child, while parenting does.
18. Punishment does not help children understand why their behavior was wrong, the effect their behavior had on others, find better alternatives for the future, etc.
19. Police or sheriff's department, national hotlines, children's protective services, etc.

Chapter 24

1. Link, association, or correlation
2. Risk of violence
3. Judgment, ability to think rationally, ability to apply your skills, etc.
4. Stress
5. Domestic violence, spousal abuse
6. Cause
7. Think
8. A substance abuse problem
9. Choose to abuse, choose to
10. Choices
11. One (you)
12. Victim
13. Choices chain
14. Footprints
15. Victim, power
16. Victim; powerful or important
17. Your own
18. Choosing to do the right, do the wrong thing
19. Character
20. Slowly
21. Stay in The Box, the clock
22. Mistrust
23. Forever
24. Selective attention
25. Focus on yourself and your skills, notice

A Summary of the Concepts and Skills in *The Choices Program*

- Memorize The Box
- Use The Box to guide my decision making
- Stay focused on problem solving during an argument
- Learn my own Warning Signs
- Watch for my Warning Signs when I start to feel angry
- Take a Time Out whenever I see my warning signs
- Memorize the rules to Time Out and follow them
- Explain time out to my partner
- Never cross the "I don't care what I say line"
- Never cross the "I don't care what I do line"
- Stop using any form of Verbal Abuse (stay in The Box)
- Recognize and avoid using Denial, Blame, and Minimizing
- Whenever I feel angry toward my partner, stop and ask myself, *"Is my thinking rational and logical right now? Am I making a big deal out of a small problem?"*
- Whenever I feel angry (or frustrated, jealous, etc.) remind myself that I can choose to think in ways that escalate these feelings, or I can choose to think in ways that reduce them.
- Accept responsibility for everything I say or do.
- Lower my comfort level with violence. Don't minimize, call abuse something other than what it really is, or tell myself that such behavior is OK.
- Don't try to punish or force my will on my partner. See him/her as my equal.
- Accept my partner's right to express his or her thoughts and feelings openly and without intimidation.
- Always stop and think *before* I react.
- Never "Awfulize."
- Stay out of the *"YOU MODE."*
- Self-talk to prevent or reduce anger.
- Identify my core beliefs about anger and aggression and modify them.
- See tension as a signal to problem solve rather than the opening bell to a fight.
- Remove all controlling, blaming, and hurtful language from my problem solving.
- Ask my partner if I come across as bossy, blaming, or hurtful.
- Ask my partner to tell me whenever he or she feels controlled, hurt, or blamed.

- Use the six problem solving steps.
- Whenever I step on a land mine, find out which mine it was and avoid it the next time.
- Write a letter to my partner expressing all of the feelings described in the letter writing exercise.
- Invite my partner to write a letter back to me.
- Develop a Big Picture and keep it in mind when problems come up.
- Let go of the adolescent idea of what it means to be strong; maintain mature beliefs.
- Live by the no-hostility rule.
- Recognize and avoid "The Pull."
- Find constructive ways deal with personality differences.
- Be more accepting of my partner.
- Find ways to encourage rather than discourage.
- Develop leadership skills, and lead by example.
- Avoid male privilege and attempts to control your partner.
- Provide a safe and abuse-free environment for your children.
- Rely less on punishment and more on parenting.
- Evaluate your drug or alcohol use honestly and get help if needed.
- Make "choices chains" to identify poor choices and find better ones.
- Maintain the traits and attributes of strong character.
- Apply your knowledge and skills to rebuilding trust.

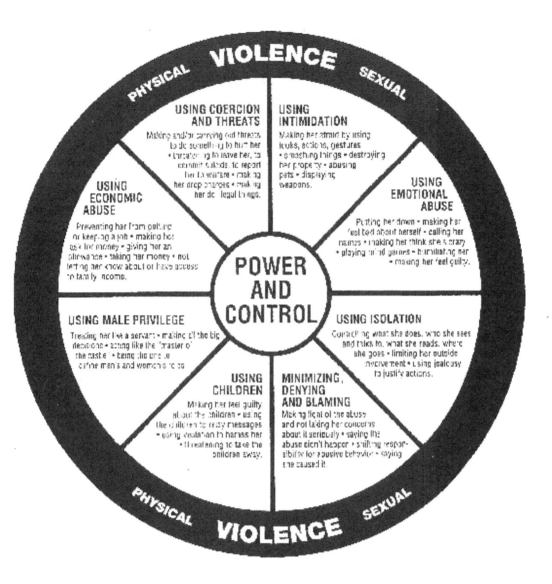

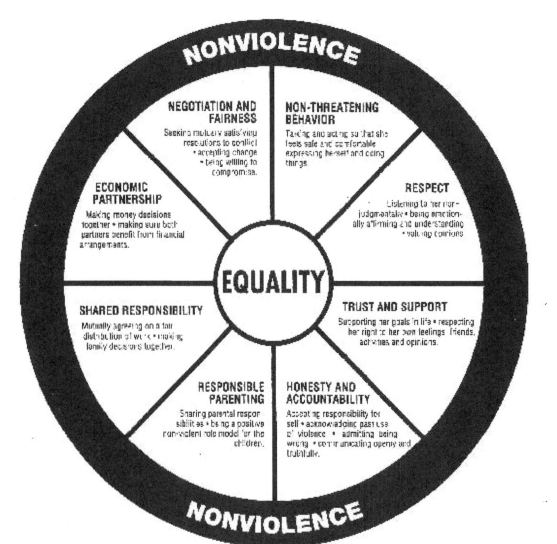